D1106522

GOD AND THE RICH SOCIETY

GOD AND THE RICH SOCIETY

A Study of Christians in a World of Abundance

D. L. MUNBY

Fellow of
Nuffield College, Oxford

London
OXFORD UNIVERSITY PRESS
NEW YORK TORONTO
1961

Oxford University Press, Amen House, London, E.C.4

GLASGOW NEW YORK TORONTO MELBOURNE WELLINGTON
BOMBAY CALCUTTA MADRAS KARACHI KUALA LUMPUR
CAPE TOWN IBADAN NAIROBI ACCRA

PRINTED IN GREAT BRITAIN BY THE WHITEFRIARS PRESS LTD.
LONDON AND TONBRIDGE

PREFACE

THIS book is the revised text of the Edward Cadbury Lectures, given in Birmingham University in the spring of 1960. I am grateful to the Trustees of Edward Cadbury for having encouraged me to write down some ideas on some important topics of our times.

I have benefited from comments on earlier drafts which were read by Mr. I. M. Crombie and the Rev. Daniel Jenkins. They helped me to improve what I had written, though I doubt if I have fully satisfied them.

I have taken the opportunity to reprint two articles previously published in *The Student World* and *The Journal of Religion* on kindred topics, and to add a paper given at a World Council of Churches Conference in 1959. I am grateful to the editors of the two journals, and to the Chicago University Press, publishers of the latter journal, for permission to reprint, as also to the editors of *The Christian Century* for permission to include in the text some passages which first appeared in articles in that journal; these are copyright 1959 by the Christian Century Foundation. The passages on pages 93 and 94–5 from George F. Kennan's Reith Lectures, first printed in *The Listener*, are here reprinted from his book *Russia, the Atom and the West*, by permission of the Oxford University Press.

Nuffield College, Oxford D. L. M.
December 1960

CONTENTS

Chapter 1

GOD IN THE ECONOMIC ORDER

'Things have been as they have been. There is no point in guessing what they might have been, if other things had not been what, in fact, they were. If this seems too dreary and unadventurous an attitude towards the course of history, one can make the more hopeful and adventurous assumption that the finger of God enters into human affairs.'—G. FABER.

'If we believe in a scheme of providence, all actions alike work for good.'
'Men have no right to complain of Providence for evils which they themselves are competent to remedy by mere common sense, joined with mere common humanity.'—S. T. COLERIDGE.

'For I saw truly that God doeth all-thing, be it never so little. And I saw truly that nothing is done by hap nor by adventure, but all things by the foreseeing wisdom of God: if it be hap or adventure in the sight of man, our blindness and our unforesight is the cause.'
'For like as the blissful Trinity made all things of naught, right so the same blessed Trinity shall make well all that is not well.'—JULIAN OF NORWICH.

IN the middle of the twentieth century, one may be pardoned for thinking that many Christians are retreating into their fastnesses, and abandoning the unequal struggle with the world. It appears to be abandonment and retreat, rather than the call of conviction to renewal in the desert. The call to the desert is a call to be respected; the call to a complacent pietism is more usually but the reverse of a worldly abandonment of the Gospel. It is perhaps not surprising that, whereas in America the boom in religion tends to be associated with the development of a homogeneous pattern of 'American' community living, in Britain the retreat to the purity of the Gospel takes the form of a personal pietism and a concentration and consolidation of the organizations of the churches. The dangerous tendency is the withdrawal within the churches' buildings and associations. In neither country is it more than a tendency; exceptions can be found to the trend, and there are many growing-points of constructive action. But it can hardly be denied that the characteristic temptation of our day is to give up the struggle with the world; or, if we do really live out our lives in the world, we do not struggle with it.[1]

There are good reasons for this as well as bad. If we think that the tendency is fundamentally the work of the devil, it is the more necessary to look at the good reasons that have led people to this retreat. First comes the revival of theological seriousness and the revival with this of the theology of the Church. It is no longer possible in Britain to confuse the Christian faith with any kind of social gospel, to identify the Kingdom of God with the coming glories of a new social order or the present reality of a comfortable civilization. It is not possible to tie up the Gospel with current philosophies and cultural realities. But in being aware of the uniqueness and separateness of Gospel truth, we are in danger of making it irrelevant to the modern world. We are not in danger of confusing Biblical language with the language of the philosophers or the market-place; but are we not in danger of making it meaningless? We are not in danger of confusing the Church with the State or with any voluntary body; but are we not in danger of making it a ghetto?

With this sound theology and deeper sense of the true mission of the Church has gone a more widely based acceptance of the true basis for the Church's concern with the world—at least in general outline. The gospel is not merely concerned with the improvement of the world and its arrangements; the Church is not merely an institution for civilizing men. We know that our concern is with God, and that God rules over the whole world. He rules, and he rules *over* the whole world, so that he is not to be confused with any part of its concerns. In asserting these truths, we have, however, been tempted to forget that God rules over the *whole* world. In attempting to express the reality of the distinction between God and the world we have been tempted to equate it with the distinction between religious and non-religious activities, so that in

[1] It is interesting to note two historians of ancient Rome talking of the first four centuries of our era (a period in several ways similar to our own) as 'an age in which materialism, a race for wealth, position, and the maximum of creature-comfort, were curiously combined with an intense preoccupation with the unseen world stretching beyond the frontiers of mundane existence and knowledge'. They relate the growth of a more optimistic view of the after-life to 'the increasingly individualistic outlook of the age'. (*The Shrine of St. Peter*, by Jocelyn Toynbee and John Ward Perkins, 1956; p. 109.)

the end we have almost come to the view that God is only active in the world when we say our prayers, or do things in religious buildings. We make a few perfunctory remarks about God's overruling providence, and then are tempted to forget the world and its concerns. Is not a Christian's concern with God? Is not this quite different from the average man's concern with the daily routine of the world's work and business?

The retreat has, however, been due not merely to the rediscovery of the distinctiveness of the Gospel reality from the realities of the world. It has also been due to a frustration that has arisen in Christian social thinking itself, at least in Britain. If we start with a demand for a Christian view of the social scene—and after all, if the Christian faith involves a unique view of the world, it would seem that there must be a unique Christian contribution—we soon find that we are looking for specifically Christian answers to social problems. But this is a blind alley. The allegedly Christian answers turn out either to be the pompous platitudes which so often satisfy ecclesiastical assemblies, but which are useless as a guide to action of any sort, or, alternatively, we find that our 'Christian solutions' are merely the nostrums of the latest quack, which do not have the merit of being either intelligible or practical.[2] The platitudes may satisfy for a brief space, and the nostrums may inspire a few cliques, but their worthlessness soon makes itself manifest. It would seem that something like this has happened in Britain in recent years. Many, who admit that the Church cannot abandon its concern for the world without giving up its proper mission in the world, have in practice abandoned this concern because they have been unable to find any Christian answers to the world's problem's. But is it not possible that Christian concern for the world, when it is a proper concern, manifests itself, not in looking for Christian answers, but in some other form of activity? What then is this activity?

Before turning to answer this question, we must look at another blind alley that seems attractive at first sight. The Christian Gospel

[2] The Report of the *Lambeth Conference, 1958*, falls into the first category in its section on 'The Reconciling of Conflicts between and within Nations' (for which see later Chapter 6). For the latter kind of error, see my *Christianity and Economic Problems* (Macmillan, 1956), Appendix, also 'The Disordered Economic Thinking of the National Church' (*Theology*, March, 1957), and 'The Importance of Technical Competence' in *Essays in Anglican Self-Criticism* (S.C.M. Press, 1958).

provides a kind of map of the world, in which we can find a schema of the world's history, its beginning, centre and end, its functions and its destiny. The Bible provides us with a perspective; it lays out before us the pattern of the world, and it gives us guidance about the roads on which we are travelling. We are told today that the Church is a pilgrim church, and that we are a pilgrim people;[3] which, no doubt, includes a profound theological truth. Pilgrimage has always had a fascination for Christians whether in the Middle Ages, or in the Protestant setting of *Pilgrim's Progress*. We may conceive of a pilgrim going on a set journey to a set destination; however bad the roads or dangerous the surroundings, some sort of map is available, or some sort of guidance about the route. Then what more natural than to ask for more information? What more simple than to expect that those who are knowledgeable about the ultimate truths should also provide us with a detailed map of our journey? Thus arises the demand for some sort of synthesis of knowledge, some sort of unitary clue to our way about the world.[4]

If the demand for a synthesis arises naturally from the desire to understand our way about the world, the attempt to supply such a synthesis arises naturally also from the way in which the intellect does its work. Any intellectual understanding always proceeds from the particular to the general, from the example to the rule, from the actual to the mathematical, so that it may work downwards again from the general to the particular. Intellectual activity as such is concerned with the general, and it is therefore natural for the intellectual to try to comprehend ever larger assemblages of fact under general rules, so that at the end all facts may be understood as a unity. But just at this point where the intellectual tries to embrace all facts in unity, there arise the sinful delusions and pretensions of human reasoning. There is no unity to be found but in God, and God is a person, not a law or

[3] See e.g. *The Evanston Report* (S.C.M. Press, 1955), pp. 84 f., and 'The Pilgrim People of God' by Edmund Schlink (*Ecumenical Review*, October, 1952).

[4] 'The attractiveness of the synthesist type of answer to the Christ-and-culture problem is doubtless felt by all Christians. . . . Man's search for unity is unconquerable, and the Christian has a special reason for seeking integrity because of his fundamental faith in the God who is One.' . . . 'There are many yearnings after such an answer; one hears demands that it be furnished. But none is in sight, either as the product of a great thinker or, what is more important, as an active, social life, a climate of opinion, and a living, all-permeating faith.' (H. Richard Niebuhr, *Christ and Culture* (Harper Torchbooks, 1956), p. 141.) Much in what follows is owed to this book.

generalization to be comprehended by the human intellect. But the pretensions of the human intellect are not curbed by the mere recognition of this truth. This we can see from the fact that theologians are as liable to these delusions as others, and perhaps more so. It is the theologian who has tried to meet the demands of the ordinary man for a complete map of the world, and theologians have often claimed to be able to provide the synthesis of divine and social truth for which we are looking.

It is, however, not possible to have a synthesis of Christian social thought that will be universally valid, or even valid for any given period. The facts are too diverse, society is too complex, and the human mind is too limited to comprehend but a small part of the whole reality. This is not merely true of the complicated and large-size world of the twentieth century, it has probably always been true. But formerly this truth was obscured because people in simpler societies took so much for granted which we cannot take for granted today. It was possible to have a synthesis, because the substructure was unexamined and because the provincialism of static societies assumed that what happened to be so was always and universally so. (Today we know better, though it does not make us any wiser or more capable of coping with our problems.) And this impossibility of any synthesis would be equally true even for those who avoid the error of thinking that a Christian social pattern could be deduced from Christian theology in some sort of Platonic way. I have dealt elsewhere with the way in which this 'Platonic' misuse of natural law has occurred in Anglican social thought of recent years.[5] But, even without this misuse, it seems unlikely that any synthesis would prove possible. It is not in a grand intellectual schema that Christian social concern should manifest itself.

To say that there is no grand intellectual framework for Christian social thinking which it is possible for us to construct, and to suggest that to attempt to create one would be a fruitless and useless task, which perhaps the devil would like us to undertake, is not to say that there are no Christian principles of social action and social order. There certainly are Christian principles which are applicable, some to most periods of history, others to limited periods. There is a great

[5] See *Essays in Anglican Self-Criticism*, op. cit.

tradition of Christian social thinking that has a long history and finds recent expression in Papal Encyclicals, on the one hand, and, on the other hand, in the reports of the ecumenical conferences of this century, and in the writings of many theologians, such as J. H. Oldham, William Temple, Reinhold Niebuhr, Emil Brunner, Karl Barth and so on. And also in the resolutions of church synods and the official or semi-official reports of ecclesiastical bodies, many of these principles are to be found clearly stated or discussed. One can refer to the famous series of wartime reports from the General Assembly of the Church of Scotland, or the various Lambeth Conference reports. Across the Atlantic, the National Council of Churches in the United States not only produced the series of books on Ethics and Economic Life, which is the only major contribution to discussion in this field that I know of, but has also sponsored a series of conferences on this subject which have produced notable reports.[6] One does not need a very extended knowledge of this literature to know that there is a very wide consensus of opinion about the Christian principles applicable to social situations in the twentieth century. There *are* Christian principles; they are widely accepted; and, if they are not better known in this country, it is not because they are not fairly readily available.

These Christian principles do not provide a synthesis; they result not from close theological reasoning based on impeccable theological axioms, but are rather the judgments that naturally arise when

[6] E.g. William Temple, *Christianity and Social Order* (1942); R. Niebuhr, *An Interpretation of Christian Ethics* (1936); id., *The Nature and Destiny of Man.* (2 vols., 1941, 1943); E. Brunner, *Man in Revolt* (1939); K. Barth, *Against the Stream* (1954); C. C. West, *Communism and the Theologians* (1958); *God's Will for Church and Nation* (reprinted from the reports . . . presented to the General Assembly of the Church of Scotland during the war years) (S.C.M. Press, 1946); *Lambeth Conferences (1867–1930)* (S.P.C.K., 1948); *Lambeth Conference, 1948* (S.P.C.K., 1948); *The Lambeth Conference, 1958* (S.P.C.K., and Seabury Press, 1958); *The Churches Survey Their Task* (Report of Oxford Conference, 1937, on Church, Community, and State) (Allen & Unwin, 1937); *The First Assembly of the World Council of Churches* (Amsterdam, 1948), ed. by W. A. Visser 't Hooft, (S.C.M. Press, 1949); *The Evanston Report: The Second Assembly of the World Council of Churches, 1954* (S.C.M. Press, 1955); Edward Duff, *The Social Thought of the World Council of Churches* (Longmans, 1956); *Ecumenical Documents on Church and Society (1925–1953)*, (World Council of Churches, Geneva, 1954).

Also Series on Ethics and Economic Life (Harper & Bros., New York): A. Dudley Ward (ed.), *Goals of Economic Life* (1953); K. E. Boulding, *The Organizational Revolution* (1953); H. R. Bowen, *Social Responsibilities of the Businessman* (1953); E. E. Hoyt, M. G. Reid, etc., *American Income and its Use*; J. C. Bennett, H. R. Bowen, etc., *Christian Values and Economic Life* (1954); A. Dudley Ward, S. Leavy, etc., *The American Economy—Attitudes and Opinions* (1954).

Christians (of very varied backgrounds) look at the twentieth century world. They do not form a system, nor do they enable us to act in any particular situation with any sort of certainty of general Christian approval. They are maps on a very small scale, which are of little or no use in deciding which turning to take at the crossroads. An actual society is, however, made by these daily decisions and by the concrete institutions of which it is composed.

Because what Christian principles we have do not enable us to make clear and certain decisions at the point where they have to be made, it does not follow that one form of society is as Christian as another. These Christian principles are not merely principles to guide us in action, they are principles that suggest the patterning of a Christian social order. There is nothing improper in the idea of a Christian social order, so long as it is not misused. The idea is indeed misused when it is suggested that there is one pattern of a Christian social order, valid for all time, or for all parts of the world. It is misused when it is suggested that there is necessarily something uniquely Christian about such an order, so that we have to look for a special 'Christian' solution for our problems. A Christian social order will be a society where men can live as God created them to live, and Christians are not a special sort of men. It will therefore be compounded of the ordinary tissue of social life, the ordinary ideas and institutions of the so-called secular world. It may surprise the 'humanist' to find such an order called 'Christian' as much as it may surprise the pietist; but neither of them understands the true nature of the Christian Gospel. It goes without saying that it is a misuse of the idea of a Christian social order to think that it can be deduced from the reasonings of theologians, or indeed, of any sort of intellectual.

It is dangerous to over-intellectualize the contribution of Christian thinking about society. But it is equally a mistake to argue that there is no place for any principles and theories at all. There is a pragmatic approach which suggests that all that is required is the day-to-day decision of each man in the situation in which he finds himself. This is often combined with a Biblical religion which suggests that, out of a pondering on the Bible and on the concrete situation as it emerges, there comes a Christian judgment. For some kind of decisions this may be right, but it seems clearly inadequate when it comes to the major decisions about social questions. These decisions cannot be rightly taken merely by meeting the situation as it arises. The situation has to be understood, and the relation of this situation to the whole social framework and all the institutions of society. Some principles of social action will be involved, however crude, and some ethical principles (if only the ethical judgment that the choices are ethically neutral). None of these things will be better done by obscuring the principles involved, and refusing to think clearly about them. And this is as true, if we are thinking about the small-scale decisions we have to make in our everyday work or as voters, as it is obviously true for those statesmen and others who have to make the more decisive choices that affect all our lives. If there seems a decent humility about making decisions without principles, there is little to be said for a thesis about Christian social action which allows no place for Christian statesmen or for those whose business it is to lead society.

So far I have argued that there are no exclusively Christian answers to social problems, and no possible Christian synthesis, but that there are Christian principles and Christian standards, by which to judge the institutions and arrangements of a social and economic order, and which will guide us in action—up to a point. The purpose of this book is to see what light can be shed on our economic arrangements in the mid-twentieth-century from Christian sources by the judgment of one Christian. It might therefore be thought right to proceed to outline the principles that Christians should apply to present-day economic problems, as they appear to the author. But I do not propose to do that, partly because these principles have been adequately set out in many other places, such as those referred to above, and partly because I have to some extent already done that elsewhere.[7] What I propose to do is to ask another set of questions, which perhaps go to the root, both of the concern of the theologians, and particularly the Biblical theologians, and also of those who would stress the importance of the situation in contrast to principles.

My first question is 'What is happening in the middle of the twentieth century? Are there any trends of importance to which we can draw attention?' As my concern is with economic matters, it is with economic trends that I am concerned, but my concern is not with

[7] *Christianity and Economic Problems.*

these for their own sake, but in their bearing on human life in general. That is to say, important trends are to be judged by their human importance, and not by their importance to economists. In fact, there is not a great deal of difference between these two perspectives, in so far as economic matters have general human significance, though only a limited importance. Exaggeration of the importance of economic matters is more often found among theologians than among economists! *Omne ignotum pro magnifico!*

Why should we be concerned with trends? Why is it important to ask where other people are moving, before we can take our bearings as Christians? Why should we follow the fashions of the time, except in so far as we need for pastoral reasons to be sensitive to what people are thinking and doing? Is there any significance in trends at all? In terms of ideas, it may be that a negative answer must be given to these questions; but in terms of economic and social realities, the matter is different. There are clear trends here, which have an importance of their own.

It seems to me that Christians have spent a great deal of time in unnecessary discussions about the Christian view of history, and have often succeeded in making a mystification about history itself. Whether I am right or not in this, there are certain simple facts about the development of human societies as we find them in time, which are relevant here, and for the understanding of which we do not require any complicated theories. First, though the ultimate datum of our concern is the human person, and not societies, institutions, cultures, civilizations or historical processes, human persons do create these entities, and human beings are not found outside societies and without institutions, even if these are often of the most rudimentary kind. Secondly, if societies and institutions are ultimately merely persons in all their complex interrelations, together with all the physical paraphernalia that human beings collect around themselves (buildings, documents and so on), these complex interrelations themselves (and even the physical paraphernalia) in their turn mould the human beings, and may be almost completely decisive in moulding any particular human being. Thirdly, this process of social determination is not merely one that occurs at any given point of time; it occurs through time. Human beings die, but the institutions, the buildings, the documents, and the habits of thought which they have created, have a sort of independent life. In this way the present is chained to the past, and itself enchains the future. Fourthly, it follows that historical processes are irreversible, and additive. We cannot go back, and we are the inheritors of the riches of the past. We carry on our backs the lumber of past ages; the books pile up in our libraries, and the documents accumulate in our archives; the buildings, even when we pull them down, determine the layout of the new plan; and the institutions rarely die, whether they be companies, universities, charities or churches.

It is from these facts that historians are able to deduce 'trends' and to notice patterns and tendencies, and apparently inevitable sequences, all of which it is proper to describe in their place, so long as it is realized that all these are made up of the complex actions and interactions of human beings, and do not have any life of their own. It is also proper to notice that, human life being lived under conditions of choice which restrict the possibilities open to us, once developments take place in a certain direction, other developments in other directions are precluded. Revolutions can indeed break the course of development, but even revolutions, when the ferment has settled down, are found to settle into patterns, which show remarkable continuities with the past. And this is not surprising, in so far as human life is not lived in a vacuum. It is therefore quite appropriate to ask what are the trends which are to be found in ideas, societies and institutions at a given period, and to try to distil the major forces at work, and the major characteristics of human endeavour in one particular epoch. No doubt any such generalizations are perilous, and one is tempted to overlook much evidence that does not fit a particular theme; but others can be left to call attention to these neglected facets. In general, because to choose one thing prevents us choosing another, there are some limits to the variety possible in any given society.

All this is particularly true of the economic field. The most characteristic feature of economic life in the 'capitalist' or 'post-capitalist' world is that technical knowledge is embodied in complicated means of production which often last for many years. This technical knowledge and these machines enable us to explore further boundaries of knowledge and continually to improve our methods of production. They are a characteristic example of irreversible and additive social processes.

My purpose, then, in dealing with the first question, is to spotlight some of these significant economic processes, as they are working in the middle of the twentieth century. It is, unfortunately, often necessary to draw attention to fairly obvious features of our world, as the complexity of modern life makes even intelligent people unaware of what is happening around them, even when it is not difficult to find out what is happening.

My second question follows when we have looked at the trends; it is to ask what positive achievements we can see in them from a Christian perspective, and where men are being led astray into false paths. The human ideals and endeavours that have made, and continue to make, a certain pattern of society, are a compound of good and evil. As Christians, we cannot deny that in every positive action of men we can see something of the pattern of God's creation, even if always perverted by human sin and in some degree distorted. Men are always searching out the glories of God's creation, and discovering in their creative acts some new aspect of his magnificence. What appears to man as one of the highest flights of his creativity, whether in thought, art, invention, or the creation of human community, appears to God to be but the discovery of the reality of his world, and its incarnation in human life, ever more or less imperfectly. The cultural, social and economic achievements of men at any particular time are thus the discovery of new aspects of God, which he is making known to men in various ways, whether we are aware of it or not. He has made us, and all our actions take place within the framework he created. To 'read the signs of the times' is to see how the diverse activities of men fit into this framework, and where they are but negative denials of what God is revealing to us.

'Maurice had a principle, gained from J. S. Mill, that commends itself to us. He affirmed that men were generally right in what they affirmed and wrong in what they denied.'[8] In the last resort we know that there is nothing constructive in sin and its manifestations, though we need to be careful not to deny its powerful reality in the world as we see it around us. Even where the reality of man's sin is more obvious in the social disorders of a given time than the more positive achievements, we need still to be aware of what are the positive aims and

[8] H. R. Niebuhr, op. cit., p. 238.

ideals which are to be dimly seen in the perversions. It is in the positive aims and ideals that lie behind our fumblings that we can see the activity of God, leading, persuading, inspiring. In so far as these positive aims and ideals inspire the trends, we can find the hand of God in them. Thus God is at work in the middle of the twentieth century in so far as the positive aims and achievements of men bring to light new glories of his creation, which is not to deny that he may also be at work where our activities are purely negative.

If we are concerned with economic reality, we must be careful not to over-emphasize the things people say and purport to believe. Christians have enjoyed themselves too much in a sort of history of ideas which paid quite inadequate attention to the relationship between what people say and think, and what they do. Many great human achievements have been produced under the inspiration of terrifyingly false slogans, by people whose genuine ideals were very different from their verbal credos. The realities of men's lives and the institutions they create can be only partially explained in terms of the explanations they themselves give of them. Men often act, and explain afterwards; or they distort what they believe, when they put into operation what they think are their beliefs. It is the height of folly to judge men by what they write and say, and one is hardly likely to understand the positive values for which they stand, merely by reading the books that affirm their values in abstract generalizations. And yet this is what Christians have only too often done. We must, on the contrary, look as much at the institutional and economic realities if we are to understand the positive achievements of our epoch. It may be that these positive achievements are often the result of no careful plan, and no directed aim, but emerge as a by-product of other endeavours. The grace of God in a bounteous world is such as to bring these results to light as men work out their several plans in a seeming chaos. It requires further grace for men to see these results for what they are and make them their own. But again we often see this to happen in our societies, as men come to realize the full value of some development, which was almost an accident when it first began.

Following from this, I come to my third question, which raises the largest issues. This is the question that arises, as it seems to me, from the writings of that great nineteenth-century Anglican theologian, F. D.

Maurice. It is a question that naturally springs from the fundamental concern of the Christian with God's work, rather than with the works of men. It is the question 'What is God doing in the economic order of the middle of the twentieth century?' It is a question, which, if we can answer it at all adequately, should give us a basis for sounder action than any timeless principles we might otherwise think fit to apply. An answer should also illuminate these principles and set them in their proper place. For principles of themselves are not very helpful if we do not know where we are going. And how should a Christian know where he is going, if he does not know what God is doing? I do not claim to have any final answer to this question, much less any simple easy answer. But one can but point to things as one sees them, and, if one is misled, one can but hope that others with more insight will be ready and able to point to one's errors and the truths that one has missed.

A preliminary objection might be that the acts of God are to be found in the Bible, that his mighty work was in its essence completed in the life and death of his Son, Jesus Christ, and that in the Church is to be found the summing up and continuation of that work in so far as it proceeds and extends in time. That this thesis is a true statement of the fundamentals is undoubted; but to deduce from it that the Christian's only concern should be with church history would be to return to the pietist delusion. God is to be found in his Church, his Body, if we would seek for him; but it would be blasphemous to deny that he is at work outside his Church as well as within it. It is indeed difficult to draw close boundaries round his Church for this purpose, however necessary this may be for disciplinary or evangelical purposes. For the church historian, who is concerned, not with the history of ecclesiastical institutions, but with the operations of God in the world, there is no boundary, as Charles Williams found in his brilliant but necessarily fragmentary history of the Holy Ghost, *The Descent of the Dove*. It is the more difficult in the modern world, where so much that is patently anti-Christian is equally patently the inheritor of a long tradition of Christian culture. It is not surprising that God is to be found working sometimes more powerfully today among the anti-Christians than within the ranks of the faithful, who, in their proper attempts to disentangle themselves from the superficialities of a nominally Christian culture, are tempted to fall into a Pharisaical puritanism, which is the very antithesis of what the Puritans set out to do.

A theologian might like to probe deeper into the theological significance of the question 'What is God doing in the economic order of the mid-twentieth century?' The question is sometimes put in a form which suggests that, whereas the Son works in his Body, the Holy Spirit has a more wide-ranging sphere of operation in the wholly secular world. Others might reply that the Spirit proceeds from the Son as well as the Father, and that his operations are above all concerned to bring to light the work of the Son, whereas it is the Son who is the pattern of creation, in whom 'all things consist';[9] just as it is God's Word in the Old Testament, which is actively operative in events, and which the New Testament equates with the Son. Others again may want to distinguish between the work of the Father in the created order and the work of the Son in redemption. These are proper questions for theologians, but it may be that we do not need to probe them very deeply to answer the question as it appears to the economist or ordinary man seeking for guidance. To answer their questions we need to know something of the way in which God works in the world, and how his actions can be recognized, but not to which person of the Trinity they are to be attributed, if such attribution is indeed proper.

There was a time when every event and every happening was attributed to the Providence of God; if God was not to be blamed for the wicked actions of wicked men, at least he over-ruled them, so that they served for the sanctification of the saints, or the greater glory of his Church. If the hand of God did not reveal itself clearly in the day-to-day happenings of ordinary people, at least it was clear that he was operative in the world through the special events, whether earthquakes, famines, epidemics, miraculous cures, comets, or dreams, which seemed to the unscientific ages of faith such obvious manifestations of divine power (a concept which still survives in the insurance companies' 'Act of God').[10] As science progressed in its understanding, it became less fashionable to attribute to God's special activity events which could be fitted into the normal so-called 'explanations' of

[9] *Colossians* 1.17.

[10] *The Times* (25 November, 1959) tells us of an official Italian report on an air accident, which describes the immediate cause as '*fatalità* (act of God)'; this reads as 'a fortuitous and fatal conjunction of circumstances' in the English translation.

everyday science. God was then left with either the scientifically inexplicable—the weather (for which prayers have survived for much longer than for many other similar events), the mentally diseased, the extremer forms of human consciousness such as mysticism—or with the merely random and individual.[11] But as the social sciences have progressed and moved into fields which not so long ago could be left to the theologian, it has become more difficult to rescue any area of life which can be wholly reserved for God's Providence. As a result, to a twentieth century Christian it becomes more and more difficult to attach any real meaning to the Providence of God, with serious consequences for our spiritual lives and a resultant failure to communicate to others the realities of the Christian faith.

I might quote Bishop E. R. Wickham to this effect also:[12]

> Both the 'scientific attitude' and the implicit ideas in social revolution, can create and fortify the assumption that with knowledge and power men can make their own world—and that they alone must make it. And it is this assumption more than any other that appears to conflict with the traditional religious attitude, and in particular with the belief in God as Providence. . .
>
> It is a good question to consider whether this contradiction is essentially biblical, or whether it may not be in part due to the 'slum-world' in which the Christian statement has historically been formulated, and in periods of history in which men were ignorant of their possibilities in mastering the world. But if God is the Lord of history we are bound to look at the scientific and the social revolutions of our time in a providential and prophetic way. If the living God confronts men through the events of history, these two

[11] Thus Marianne Thornton in 1826 on the successful emergence of her brother Henry (a banker of the Clapham sect) from the bank crisis: 'I feel so convinced now that he is a *cork*, . . . or to speak more like a Christian, that gracious Providence which we know always watches over us, has in this instance made plain those ways which are sometimes hid in darkness for years . . . I think the setting up Henry again one of the most providential events that ever fell to the lot of Man.' (E. M. Forster, *Marianne Thornton: 1797–1887*, pp. 119, 122). It is difficult in the middle of the twentieth century to know whether in reading this quotation we are more disturbed at our own lack of piety, or Marianne Thornton's lack of sensitivity to the universal claims of a God who can hardly be domesticated as the tribal deity of the prosperous inhabitants of Clapham.

The theological answer seems to have been given by Julian of Norwich many centuries before. 'And when God Almighty had shewed so plenteously and so fully of his Goodness, I desired to wit of a certain creature that I loved, if it should continue in good living, which I hoped by the grace of God was begun. And in this singular desire it seemed that I letted myself: for I was not taught in this time. And then was I answered in my reason . . . . ". . . It is more worship to God to behold him in all than in any special thing." ' (*Revelations of Divine Love*, ed. by Dom R. Hudleston, 1935, p. 86).

[12] 'The Encounter of the Christian Faith and Modern Technological Society,' *Ecumenical Review*, April, 1959, p. 265.

remarkable facts must take on profound religious significance, despite the confusion they seem to spell for traditional theological thinking. As yet the churches have in general failed to give prophetic articulation to these facts of our time.

He goes on to argue that, when God is 'understood to be providentially at work through and in the web of human relationships and human endeavour, of which industry is a supreme example', 'this is biblical; it is one illustration of the re-interpretation of Providence that might convey something of God's nature and purpose to modern men, at the point of their strength.'[13]

Whatever may be the proper approach at the personal level, it is with the more general aspects of Providence that I am concerned; with those issues which the prophets of the Old Testament dealt with, when they saw the hand of God in the actions of Cyrus, rather than with those issues with which the book of Job deals. How then do we see the hand of God at work in the world?

First, then, we see God at work in the new and positive achievements and aims of our society, in the trends and tendencies which underlie much of our day-to-day inconsequences. It requires, indeed, the insight of a prophet rightly to discern these trends and tendencies, but it is up to all of us to try to do so. To assert that there are any such trends and tendencies that can rightly be regarded as the working of God is indeed a matter that requires proof of some sort. Alternatively, it would be possible to regard the chaotic purposes of men and groups everywhere as so chaotic and disruptive as to form no pattern or trend at all, or to regard what trends there are as so neutral as to be insignificant in relation to God's Will and Purposes. Either alternative could be true, but it does not seem so. The proof of the pudding, as so often, is in the eating, and the only test of the thesis is whether in fact it produces, without gross distortion, a satisfactory image of the situation. That there are trends in the economic field could hardly be disputed, but it might be disputed whether these have any more than technical significance. However, it does not seem possible again to doubt seriously that they have great human significance, and are not merely like the changes which the fashions of dress have undergone throughout history (which are no doubt of interest, but hardly of great signifi-

[13] Ibid., p. 267.

cance). The real doubt that can be raised is whether these positive tendencies are of such importance to God as well as to men. Are we at all justified in seeing in them the hand of God? It is up to the reader at the end of this book to form a judgment whether this can be said or not. It is certainly not claimed that what I say is all that is to be said, but if it does provide some pointers to the truth, something will have been achieved.

We must indeed be careful not to argue that, because the effects of certain actions are good, they were right at the time when they were done. There is no jobbing backwards in morality, whether personal or social. It may be that the good effects were entirely unforeseen and even undesired, and that the action, when done, was morally evil. Equally, there may be times when the right action is right even when it is correctly predicted that it will have appalling consequences, and despite these consequences. Here again the reader will have to judge for himself whether what I say is true of the particular judgments I make.

But secondly, God works not merely in the strivings of the best, and in the achievements that are added to their strivings as a sort of bonus, but also in resistance to the worst. There are distortions enough in the world in which we live. Men's noblest aims and ideals are alloyed with equally impure motives and desires; their lives are strewn with failures and muddied with impurities of all sorts, and the best actions and institutions often seem to turn sour in sober reality. Many of our disasters can be seen as resulting from the resistance put up by the healthy to the unhealthy, the sound to the unsound. In them is thus to be seen something of the true nature of God's world, where judgment in some form or other, slowly, if not quickly, follows from failure to recognize the inherent laws of the world and of our nature.

We live in God's world, and in the last resort the Will of God triumphs. Today the devil has a brief space in which to put up a show of success; but even today he is on the losing side. Over and above the positive achievements of our society and the disasters we bring on ourselves, can we not see how God overrules both our successes and failures to serve his own ends? No doubt here we must be careful, but are there not times when we can see him at work in the world around us? Can we not sometimes catch glimpses of his work in the midst of our self-conscious, highly efficient civilization, so that even today (with all the doubts proper to our modern scepticism, which also has its place in God's order) we can cay 'The stars in their courses fought against Sisera' or 'This is the Lord's doing; it is marvellous in our eyes'?[14]

My fourth and last question follows directly from the preceding one. 'What then shall we do?' Our proper action is to do the Will of God, and if God is working towards certain ends, which can be seen, if dimly, in the positive and constructive achievements of our culture, it is for us to make them more in accordance with his Will. There is a sense in which it is the need to make decisions that drives us to formulate principles of social action. For better or worse we are remaking the structure of our society as we make our day-to-day decisions; it is our task so to remake our society that it may be more fashioned in accordance with God's Will, that it may be in some sense a Christian society, a Christendom. It is not at all an improper ideal to look towards a Christendom, so long as we recognize that we start from here and not from somewhere else, and that what we fashion we fashion from the historical reality of our times, and not from that of some other irrelevant period.

My theme is that there are positive achievements in our world. However much sin may have eroded our aims and may turn our achievements to dust and ashes, there are some achievements on which we can build, and in which we can see God at work. God is, indeed, at work in our failures, as much as our successes. I do not exclude this, but my theme does exclude the thesis that the achievements of our world are so negative and so unconstructive that no good can come from them, and that there is no way in which they can be redeemed into some sort of Christian pattern. There may be societies of which this is true; it may be true of societies in Eastern Europe (though probably much less true of Russia or China, at least in a very long run); it may be true of societies such as that of South Africa. For these societies there may be no possible constructive refashioning without destruction and disaster. It is not with situations such as these that I am concerned. It is therefore natural that I should stress the positive rather than the negative, the achievements rather than the failures, so that we can see

[14] *Judges* 5.20; *Psalm* 118.23.

our way forwards. This is perhaps rather an unfashionable approach for Christians, who prefer only too often the unconstructive prophecy from the sidelines, which echoes 'I told you so' whenever anything goes wrong, and prefers to ignore the challenge of success. But, if we are looking to the future rather than the past, it is the growing points that need attention, and not past failures. I must admit that I am more interested in 'Where do we go next?' than in 'Where have we gone wrong?' And so, if what is said sometimes seems unduly optimistic, one must not therefore conclude that this is all that is to be said in a total appraisal of the situation.

My aim, then, in the following chapters is to take up a number of themes, and in relation to them to try to see if we can answer the four questions. In the case of each theme, I want to try to see, firstly, what is the trend; secondly, what is the positive achievement or aim; thirdly, where God is at work in it; and fourthly, what we are to do to make that Will more manifest. The world does not fit into neat patterns, and it will not always be possible to deal neatly with these questions, but it is hoped that they will be in our minds as we go along, to guide us in our understanding of what is happening in the economic and social order in the middle of the twentieth century.

Chapter 2
GOD AND PROGRESS

'Profound researches, scientific inventions: to what end? To contract the sum of human wants? to teach the art of living on a little? to disseminate independence, liberty, and health? No; to multiply factitious desires, to stimulate depraved appetites, to invent unnatural wants, to heap up incense on the shrine of luxury, and accumulate expedients of selfish and ruinous profusion. . . . Every new want you invent for civilised man is a new instrument of torture for him who cannot indulge it.'—Mr. Escot (Shelley) in *Headlong Hall.* (T. L. PEACOCK.)

'It is the traveller journeying onward, full of heart and hope, with an ever-varying horizon, on the boundless plain, who is liable to mistake clouds for mountains, and the *mirage* of drouth for an expanse of refreshing waters.'—S. T. COLERIDGE.

'Unless Christians are to stage a sort of Nazarite revolt against modern means of movement, communication, production, and exchange, it seems necessary to accept the fact that we live in a world which is more and more organized in terms of the whole globe. This ought not to surprise Christians who are supposed to live under the commission "Go ye into all the world"; they ought to be more ready for it than anyone else.'—BISHOP LESSLIE NEWBIGIN.

ECONOMIC growth, as we have known it, to speak roughly, in the last two hundred years, is something quite novel in the life of man on earth. A very brief, and, no doubt, inaccurate, summary of human history suggests that man, who emerged perhaps 500,000 years ago, has spent most of the years of his life on earth in a state of food-gathering, such as the Australian aborigines practise today.[1] Some time before 7000 B.C. in the west, men began to cultivate plants, breed domestic animals, and live in townships.[2] Some time

[1] Gordon Childe, *What Happened in History* (Penguin, 1954), p. 23. Stuart Piggott, *Prehistoric India* (Penguin, 1950), p. 22, puts it at *c.* 600,000 years ago.

[2] Childe, op. cit., pp. 24, 48-9, 56-8. (Cultivation of plants and breeding of domestic animals 'perhaps not more than 8,000 years ago', i.e. *c.* 6000 B.C.). Piggott, op. cit., p. 47. (Natufian agriculturalists in Palestine 'well before 5000 B.C.'). Jericho, with its stone-built

before 3000 B.C. there was a great burst of invention, perhaps the nearest parallel to the industrial revolution of the eighteenth century. Men then began to make copper into useful materials; they began to write, and to employ animals for draught and for transport; and they started to use metal for measuring transactions. To this period belongs the use of the plough, the invention of the wheel both for making pottery and for transport, and the use of the sail for shipping.[3] Later technical inventions were rather sparse and less revolutionary. Perhaps about 1200 B.C. iron began to come into general use, and an alphabetical script emerged.[4] Coinage perhaps first came into use about 700 B.C. in Lydia; the water-wheel was invented towards the end of the first millennium B.C.[5] For 2000-odd years men exploited these advances, more or less efficiently; and then suddenly towards the end of the eighteenth century, there occurred a great burst of new inventions;[6] population, which had ebbed and flowed in slow movements of centuries, leapt forward dramatically in decades. Since then the world in the West has never ceased to be in a process of change, which is to be measured in decades rather than centuries; within the lifetime of each of us more changes in economic environment occur than occurred previously in thousands or tens of thousands of years. It is this accelerated rate of economic growth with which we are concerned.[7]

wall and settled agriculture 'began not later than 7000 B.C.' (Childe, *The Prehistory of European Society* (Penguin, 1958), p. 36).

See K. M. Kenyon, *Digging up Jericho* (1957), pp. 73-6, and Sonia Cole, *The Neolithic Revolution* (British Museum (Natural History), 1959).

[3] Childe, *What Happened in History*, pp. 24, 51, 69, 75 f., 80-5, 93, 110-1. 'The thousand or so years immediately preceding 3000 B.C. were perhaps more fertile in fruitful inventions and discoveries than any period in human history prior to the sixteenth century A.D.' (p. 69). Piggott, op. cit., pp. 51-65. R. Ghirshman, *Iran* (Penguin, 1954), pp. 32-50.

[4] Childe, op. cit., pp. 25, 181-3, 191-2. Ghirshman, op. cit., pp. 86-7. ('Although known to the Hittites and rulers of Mitanni in the fifteenth century B.C. and in Egypt in the fourteenth century B.C. [iron] did not become widespread until the ninth to seventh centuries B.C.') Iron weapons were found in the Alaja tombs in Turkey, dating from the third millenium B.C.; but iron was then a precious metal. (Seton Lloyd, *Early Anatolia* (Penguin, 1956), pp. 37, 96-101, 118).

[5] Childe, op. cit., pp. 192-3, 235, 246-7, 251, 271, 277.

[6] Strictly, it was the application of inventions that occurred then, but the two cannot be separated.

[7] Compare, for example, the late middle ages: 'The late middle ages . . . far from remaining static, were characterized by constant change—developments not as rapid as those of our own time, but swift enough to produce in three centuries a new culture. . . . Change was slow, and hard to see, since men still venerated the past, and still looked back,

Two hundred years is a very short span of human history, and it is not to be wondered at that men have not easily adapted themselves to the new conditions. (What is perhaps remarkable is that they have adapted themselves so successfully). Out of the quarter or half a million years of human life on this planet, the Christian Church has been in existence for some nineteen hundred years. God became man when, in the course of time—a very long time in relation to the time that has since passed, the high civilizations of the Mediterranean had already grown to a certain maturity. The course of human material history went on much as before, with many slow economic changes, and many political upheavals, until some two hundred years ago, when the Christian Church was already ancient in terms of the memories of human culture. Then began the startling march of economic progress.

Institutions find greater success in surviving than in adapting themselves creatively. It is perhaps not surprising that an institution as long-lived as the Christian Church should not have been remarkably successful in adapting itself to the new world. Its very nature (living in the life of Jesus Christ, God and man, whose environment on earth was in a very different world from our own) imparts a backward-looking frame to Christian theology, even when this has not been aggravated by addiction to the philosophical thought-forms of the ancient world or the Middle Ages, or a placid assumption that the social categories appropriate to the world before the industrial revolution are equally appropriate to our modern world. Together with the essential truths of the Gospel, which can hardly be disentangled from the images and words of Hebraic thought, the Church has carried into the twentieth century many preconceptions of what is natural to man which belong only to previous static societies, where changes were few within the lifetime of a man. It is perhaps fortunate that no institutions survive from the Old Stone Age, in which man has lived most of his years on this planet, and that the highly artificial conditions of settled agriculture, domesticated animals, and life in villages and small urban communities, which had spread over the Mediterranean world by the

not forward, to an ideal. It was still presumed that innovation and experiment were bad, and were to be tested, not by empirical methods, but by their degree of correspondence with traditional beliefs and authorities. In a changing world this meant an increasing discrepancy between theories and facts.' (A. R. Myers, *England in the Late Middle Ages* (Penguin), p. xiii).

time of the birth of Christ, after a very rapid expansion from their near-Asian centres in the course of a few thousand years, have been accepted as a reasonable norm by even the most conservative supporters of a static society. It might be difficult to disprove the thesis that the Old Stone Age with its food-gathering and hunting economy is more 'natural' to man than settled agriculture.

It is thus not surprising that there is little in the Bible, and the traditions of our theologians, that directly helps us to appraise these processes of economic growth; not surprisingly, as they are processes unknown to the writers of the Bible or the theologians of the past. Thus we find Canon Demant, who has himself been accused of unduly stressing the static elements in culture, writing:[8]

> It is necessary, however, to make clear here that when we speak of a Christian social order which Christians can use as a standard of judgment we are not speaking of a set and fixed type of social structure which Christians would wish to endure, even if it could, for all time. It is in the nature of God and the human soul to engender continual change in the social structure, and the future of human society on earth is unknown to man. Because of this, Christian teachers have had often to point out that very little specific guidance for describing the right social order can be found in the New Testament.

What then is this phenomenon of economic progress, which is so new in human history? The essential truth is to be found in the simple-minded answer that it means a growing volume of goods and services available for people to use, in technical terms a growing national income per head of population. But this definition requires three qualifications.

Firstly, growing national income per head is an average figure, and its distribution may vary greatly without affecting the average. I shall deal with this whole problem later, but it is important to note that national income per head can grow, while certain groups can be worse off, and, if we are concerned with the welfare of these particular groups, we might think the situation had deteriorated while the average figure had improved. Secondly, the increase is in fact associated with a reduction of effort in work. One would not call it economic progress, if national income increased with a corresponding or increasing effort in work, as, within limits, it always can. Thirdly, 'a growing volume

[8] V. A. Demant, *God, Man and Society* (1933), p. 47.

of goods and services' does not mean more of everything in proportion. Certain limits are reached in the consumption of some things before we are at all near the limit in other directions, and, more importantly, new overall patterns of consumption arise. The problems that beset the national income statistician in measuring the 'volume' of goods and services are real problems; there is no really satisfactory comparison possible between the goods and services we have available today and those our ancestors enjoyed at the time of the Roman Empire, or between our wealth and that of South-East Asia. Nevertheless for many purposes some rough measure of 'volume' of goods and services is adequate.[9] We could state it simply by saying that we could have the average standard of living of the Roman Empire or the Middle Ages, if we wanted, and much more besides.

In the last resort the test is that consumers choose it so. That is to say, there is a greater volume of goods and services, as we measure it, because we find consumers preferring the one set of alternatives to the other. Observation suggests that, however much we grumble about many of our so-called technical advances, we still prefer to use them rather than not—or at any rate many of the more basic. We prefer electric light to candles or wicks spluttering in bowls of oil; we prefer frozen and refrigerated meat and fish to the salted and dried variety; we prefer to live in a stone or brick house rather than a wooden shack with a thatched roof, and we would rather that the smoke of our fire went up the chimney than into the roof. Glass enables us to keep warm, and dry, and also to have light;[10] water

[9] A fourth qualification should also be included in a fuller treatment, namely that the increased volume of goods and services should be available for people to use, and not employed by Governments to build up military power or public monuments of no human value. This is hardly of significance in relation to long-range comparisons, but obviously of importance in comparing the wealth of Russia and more or less similar societies within similar ranges of national income per head. One can take two extreme positions, either that resources used by governments are of no use to anyone, and must be excluded entirely, or that they are merely different ways in which people prefer to spend their money. The latter might be more true of the Health Service, the former of Defence expenditure.

[10] 'Even in the most luxurious Roman house, the lighting left much to be desired: though the vast bay windows were capable of flooding it at certain hours with the light and air we moderns prize, at other times either both had to be excluded or the inhabitants were blinded and chilled beyond endurance. . . . The dwellers in a Roman house must have protected themselves, very inadequately, with hanging cloths or skins blown by wind or drenched by rain; or overwell by folding shutters of one or two leaves which, while keeping cold and rain, midsummer heat or winter wind at bay, also excluded every

closets are healthy and convenient and save us from the appalling stinks of former ages. With anaesthetics we have eliminated much of the range of pain that was formerly inevitable. One could continue the list, but it is enough to notice how economic progress in small everyday things has given us possibilities not open to our ancestors, and possibilities that we choose in preference to those which were available to them.

Economic change does not come about by idly wishing it. It has a long history in Western Europe, which goes back far behind the crucial point of upsurge at the end of the eighteenth century. Its roots lie in the scientific movement of the seventeenth century, and no doubt this was inconceivable except as the inheritor of the Christian humanist traditions of the Middle Ages. It depended on established systems of government and relatively efficient forms of administration. But, proximately, economic change comes from the growth of capital (in buildings, roads, irrigation plants, factories, machinery, improved plants and livestock, increased land fertility, etc.). Capital is only created as a result of human enterprise, and enterprise of this kind is a human ability that has not been developed in every kind of society, and can fairly easily be thwarted or side-tracked, even if it is not as rare a quality as some people make out. Again, neither capital nor enterprise can function alone without labour, and labour only becomes skilled and adapted to cooperate with capital and enterprise as a result of the working of complicated social processes.

We come back to men, men ready to explore the world in scientific back-rooms, men ready to explore the field of action in experiments which will enrich humanity's livelihood, men ready to change the pattern of their daily work in order to make these explorations bear fruit. Economic change in fact presupposes social change, and itself creates it. It is this continuous chain-reaction of social processes that is new in human history. Once the process has been started (and in fact the whole world has been infected with the virus), there is no going back, even if we wanted to go back. In a static world, the processes of social adaptation have worked themselves out into a condition where

ray of light. In quarters armed with solid shutters of this sort the occupant, were he an ex-consul or as well known as the younger Pliny, was condemned either to freeze in daylight or to be sheltered in darkness.' (Jérôme Carcopino, *Daily Life in Ancient Rome* (Penguin ed., 1956), p. 44).

they occur more or less automatically; no one takes thought about them, but each man is only concerned with how he behaves himself in his small group according to the accepted pattern. It is otherwise in our modern world.

The analysis of economic growth is now one of the major pre-occupations of economists and economic historians. It is not surprising that, with so recent a development, we do not know a great deal about its pattern and causation. But we do know in rough outline a good deal about many of the factors involved in it, even if we are not clear about how these can best be mixed, or what brings about the reactions between them. It is, indeed, difficult to disentangle the more important from the less important, but enough can be said to highlight many of the forces which are somehow at work in these complex processes.

Every element of human life is involved, and we must make some sort of selection. I take what seem to be the most important:

1. *Ideological systems* of thought. Capitalism is at the very least not entirely unconnected with the development of the 'Protestant spirit'. But economists can perhaps best leave that battle to be fought out by economic historians.

2. *The social framework* and the sociological elements in human behaviour. The extended family system is, for example, one of the more obstructive factors in the growth of economic enterprise.

3. The *political and administrative structure* of a society. Fifty years ago economists would have stated dogmatically that economic growth was closely linked with the development of democracy and freedom of thought. The achievement of Stalin has demolished that theory. But the failure of some countries to develop economically because of gross political and administrative mismanagement is too obvious to require comment. Perhaps Argentina under Peron and Iran under Mossadiq are examples.

4. The state of *economic organization*. This involves a complex of factors, of which we might take as typical taxation policies, the organization of business enterprise, and property laws, particularly as they affect land. Economists have amassed a great deal of knowledge on these matters, which cannot be built into theories. But it is clear that bad tax policies can frustrate economic growth, that inadequate property laws can prevent rational exploitation of natural resources,

and that modern economic units require the protection of limited liability, if capital remains in private hands.

5. Economic growth requires adequate *resources*, as does the maintenance of a given level of economic output. We can roughly classify resources under the traditional heads of land, labour and capital, with the addition of enterprise.

(*a*) *Land*. The land resources of a country may perhaps be the most important single determining factor in economic growth. This may sound paradoxical, in a world where we have long ceased to believe that land is a fixed factor. We *make* land today—the Dutch have long known how to do it; the rest of the world does it in various similar ways by means of drainage, irrigation, fertilizers, and all the paraphernalia of modern agricultural science. It may well be the original land inheritance that plays the most important part in determining growth. America is the classic case.

(*b*) *Labour*. The growth of population is clearly related to economic growth in various subtle ways. But it is not merely the rate of growth of population, which determines the age structure of the population, but also the quality of the population that matters. The skill of labour, its adaptability and adjustment to modern methods of production are vital. To explain these we have to go back to a discussion of education and political and social structures, which are responsible for the existing level of skill.

If new goods are being produced, and old goods made in new ways, the units of economic organization will be continually altering, and methods of work will not remain the same. These changes mean that people do not continue to do the same kind of work, that they do not work in the same firm or industry, for the same kind of employer, or in the same locality. If population is growing rapidly in relation to the rate of change, changes can occur by the mere rapid expansion of the new, without actual decline of the old. But even with rapid growth of the labour force this may not be so, and it will certainly not be so in the case of the slow-growing populations of Western Europe and America today. There are tendencies that slow down the rate of economic change to the rate of growth of the labour force; but, even in those countries in the West, which are alleged to stagnate the most, economic growth still involves movements of this sort. *Some* people *some* of the time have to change their jobs (even if not in name), their employer, their industry, and the place in which they live. These changes become more possible with the growth of education, and can be speeded up by means of training. In general, the more intelligent people are, and the more highly they are trained, the more adaptable they are.

(*c*) *Capital.* The importance of the capital stock and its increase has perhaps been too exclusively considered by economists, but it is clearly of very great importance. It is however worth noting that, though it is the existence of great accumulations of capital, and the use of capital-intensive methods of production, that characterize the modern period of vastly accelerated economic growth, the capital/output ratio in highly developed countries such as Britain and America is not very high. In fact the accumulated capital of Britain and America represents about two years' national output—rather a surprisingly low figure.

The changes involved in economic progress do not necessarily require more capital; they may be merely changes in skill and organization. But they usually require embodiment in new machines, new tools, new factories, new buildings of some sort. The faster the rate of change the more rapidly are old types of capital replaced by new ones (long before their physical life is exhausted); the exception is to be found in the case of countries, such as Russia, which expand by the more or less wholesale introduction into primitive conditions of new methods from advanced economies so that new investment is much more important than replacement. Whatever the form of capital investment, it requires the setting aside of resources from current use, in order to provide the future services that capital makes possible. In other words, saving is required. The higher the proportion of its resources that a community is ready to save and invest, the faster, other things being equal, is its rate of growth.

(*d*) *Enterprise.* It is not enough to be ready to devote resources to the future; they must be well-used, and not squandered. The test of success lies in the future, and cannot be measured in advance. The flair for achieving this success, and the readiness to take the necessary risks, are the marks of the entrepreneur. It is this I call enterprise, without assuming thereby that it is a simple quality, only to be found in a readily identifiable number of people, or that it is only to be associated with certain forms of organization, or only to be encouraged by certain inducements. The identification of those who have enterprise, the encouragement of its use, and the maximum exploitation of these human gifts, are precisely some of the major questions to be answered. Traditional economic theories, with their mechanical bias, took enterprise for granted, and subsumed it under capital. But we cannot take it for granted. Under enterprise we have to include the flow of inventions, their application to production, and all the activities that make for successful use of economic resources. Here is an enormous field about which we do not know a great deal.

(*e*) *The combination of resources.* Economic development occurs through the combined use of resources. Perhaps the most important single piece of wisdom that economists have to offer the world in this field is the platitude, that no one resource by itself is sufficient, and that it is in the successful combination of resources that economic growth comes about. The platitude of the interrelationship of variables does not seem a great deal to emerge from years of highly technical study, but its significance has again and again to be demonstrated and repeated. In practice, it is a platitude that is more often denied than accepted. The classical economists isolated population and land, and effectively ignored the importance of capital as a substitute for land (in terms of acreage). Enthusiasts today still make the same mistake, isolating the land/population ratio and producing horrific stories of man's economic future, again ignoring that enterprise can replace land, as can capital. A country can only be called over-populated in relation to its stock of land, capital, and enterprise, all taken together. On the other hand, modern enthusiasts of productivity often tell us that it all depends on labour and enterprise, and exhort us to follow America; but America is rich and expanding fast, not primarily because of the industry of her labour-force, or the enterprise of her business-men, but perhaps above all because of her favourable capital/labour ratio (which in itself is the product of a past favourable land/labour ratio).[11] Perhaps these examples are sufficient to show that the platitude of the inter-dependence of variables is a significant platitude, which produces

[11] The argument can perhaps roughly be put as follows: In America, land was plentiful and afforded a rich living to those who occupied it. Industry had therefore to attract people to work in factories with high wages, in contrast with the overpopulation on the land which drove people to the towns in Europe.

a rich harvest of results for the economist, and can be useful to practical men, if they wish to avoid folly.

6. *Access to resources and use of resources.* Here we come to the market, and all the factors that make markets larger and smaller, more or less perfect, and more or less effective. Are hindrances put in the way of the development of resources, land, labour, capital or enterprise? How efficient is economic organization in making economic resources available? Does monopoly, either traditional or deliberate, hinder progress? What importance are we to attach to the size of markets and their standardization? Here again economists have had a great deal to say, even if they have not developed much in the way of a coherent theory.

My list of important factors perhaps provides a sort of map of the territory. The man who, in my view, has produced the most valuable survey in this field is Arthur Lewis in his *Theory of Economic Growth.* He took over 400 pages to outline the territory; not surprisingly what I have said is grossly inadequate.

If these are some of the factors involved in economic progress, it is clearly a complicated process, involving manifold social changes. On the one hand, economic progress means 'transformation' of the whole economy, as new processes and products, new tastes and new wants emerge.[12] There is no stopping-place, and no going-back. Even if we lose the skill to make atomic energy or to produce contraceptives—more certainly, if we merely decide not to use them—human history can never be the same again as it was before these were known. New patterns of living are created in the development of new products, and not always apparently either consciously planned or desirable in themselves. I will deal in my next chapter with some of the problems arising from this.

On the other hand, not only is continuous adaptation required of all men in some degree, but the process involves the breakdown of the barriers between men that existed in the earlier static class structures of society. In the western world, we have seen a series of changes, which on the national level integrate society; integration of local groups into the national economy, integration of all classes into society, everyone

[12] The term 'transformation' is due to Professor Svennilson, *Growth and Stagnation in the European Economy* (U.N., 1954), p. 7.

tied together in the 'welfare state' in a way that never existed in our fragmented societies in the past.[13] In the chain-reaction of economic progress, the achievements of *élites*, whose fruits were formerly often largely appropriated by these small groups, seep down to all levels of society. With some of the things involved in this I will deal in Chapter 4.

In the case of such complex processes, about which we do not know a great deal, it would be rash to be dogmatic, and we must be careful not to be too certain about the inevitability of certain accompaniments of economic progress. Thus, as I have mentioned already, it was not so long ago that people would have dogmatically asserted that economic progress could only come about in a free, democratic society; today we are perhaps inclined to be too dogmatic in the opposite direction in fearing that India may find agricultural reform and industrialization more difficult than China. The real failure of Victorian England was not its confident belief in industrialization, but its brash dogmatism that industrialization ruled out many other things that we know today it does not, and did not. A free progressive society does not inevitably involve ugly insanitary cities, or a refusal to provide communally for those who fall by the wayside through illness, old age, or unemployment. Nor do economic arrangements, efficient in achieving one set of aims, necessarily achieve another set equally efficiently. Competition may produce textiles very efficiently, while creating chaos in the lay-out of a railway system.

It is to the dogmatisms of the present that we should pay attention when we have observed some of those of the past. We must be careful not to ascribe to economic progress evils that can be put right by some slight rearrangement of our affairs, which we are only precluded from doing by conservatism and prejudice. For example, it is sometimes assumed that we have to put up with all the evils that the motor-car has brought with it—I am referring to road deaths, danger and inconvenience in our cities, noise and traffic congestion, long journeys to work, and such matters—because they are inevitable, it is said, if we wish to enjoy the motor-car and the blessings it has brought. But this is of course not completely true. Mitigation, at least, could be produced for many of these evils, if we were ready to spend as much on

[13] See Gunner Myrdal, *An International Economy* (1956).

saving life on the roads as the railways are forced to do (as a result of the restrictive laws of the brash Victorians), or if we were ready to abandon our preconceived ideas about freedom to occupy the Queen's Highway at no cost to ourselves, or to use a most lethal instrument with only the most perfunctory test of our ability to do so. If we were not hidebound by our lawyers' ideas of the proper way to conduct trials, we might be able to make our arrangements for road offences more efficient, and more relevant to the circumstances of the twentieth century. And it might even be that we would be ready to be really tough with those who endanger others' lives, whether carelessly or otherwise, through incapacity, folly or drink. Whether these suggestions are right or wrong is not the important point. The point at issue is that, though we do not know how much of the evils attendant on the motor-car are inevitably linked with its tremendous advantages to human beings, we do know that at least some of them could be avoided if we really wanted to avoid them. Not all that happens as things change is the inevitable result of change.

It is necessary to say this, not only so that we may not take too seriously the technologists who are ready to ride roughshod over other interests in order to achieve their own limited aims, but also that we may be warned against the pessimists, to be found particularly perhaps among some littérateurs and Christians, who indiscriminately lump blessings and evils together as inevitable in a 'technological society', whatever that phrase may mean. The main, if not the only, really inescapable thing in our society is change. How far is this in itself a blessing or a curse?

Can human beings adapt themselves to change? How far should they be expected to do so? We cannot go back to a static society; should we want to, if we could? It does not seem that there is any Christian principle by which to decide the matter either way. Whether a society is static or dynamic is not of itself a matter that provokes judgment, though there are Christians in Britain who seem to regard stability as an essential characteristic of a Christian society, just as there are those in America who decry a static society *tout court*. It is the quality of the society itself that matters. The very bottom of Dante's Hell was frozen stiff, but it could equally have been a perpetually whirling nebula.

The crucial point is whether the rate of change, and the kinds of change that occur, are such that human beings can adapt themselves to them and live humane and human lives. An expanding economy does not make human life longer than some four score years and ten, though it enables significantly more people to live out their full span. The changes that occur in men's lifetimes are now so rapid that forecast is impossible, and in decades men see their environment altering in ways totally unexpected. It remains to be seen whether human beings can adapt themselves as rapidly as this. So far, they seem to have been remarkably successful, taking everything into account. But a serious question-mark needs to be put at this point.

The basic fact is that an expanding economy means an economy in which people are subject to changes in their work, their consumption patterns, their environment, and the whole fabric of their lives. But at the same time, our modern world provides more complex educational processes to aid adjustment, and affords more security against disease, hunger, and poverty in ill-health, unemployment and old age, than any economy before. Both security and change are necessary in our modern world, and to find the right balance is a continuous problem of adjustment (and also, rightly, a continuous matter of political dispute). The demand for security arises from simple and basic human needs. Even if it be granted that men require variety and change in their lives, there are limits beyond which the uncertainties of excessive change lead to breakdown. Only from within a certain stability is change possible.

A sane Christian critique is required at this point, as to which insecurities people should rightly bear, and against which they should be insured. But this requires a more careful discrimination as to the various kinds of security. In the economic field, the security that people demand can be analysed in terms of employment and job security, income security, security against having to change one's place of residence, and security against price changes. We need also to consider security in relation to changes in the pattern of consumption, and in relation to patterns of class behaviour.

(*a*) EMPLOYMENT AND JOB SECURITY

People require to be assured that they can, sooner or later, find a job more or less appropriate to their abilities. The immediate need may be for income; the ultimate need is for a place wherein they can contribute to society, and use their faculties constructively. With a proper full employment policy, there is no problem in meeting this need, though it may require special government measures to deal with pockets of unemployment in specially unfavoured areas, or where the sudden impact of change requires a degree of adaptation that is beyond the scope of normal economic forces.

A degree of job security is not incompatible with economic progress, rather the reverse; it is business-men, rather than workers, who complain in times of full employment at the excessive turn-over of labour with all its wasteful results. Nevertheless, economic progress demands that some firms must sometimes contract and release labour, and that some workers may have to change their occupations against their will. Work-spreading devices, except for dealing with short-term reductions in demand, are essentially wasteful. But it follows that more positive measures in the way of retraining and reordering a new distribution of labour are required than the mere release of workers from a number of firms. An expanding full employment world requires more careful study of ways by which a proper labour mobility may be promoted.

(*b*) INCOME SECURITY

One of the reasons for the demands for a full employment policy is to be found in the demand for income security. But this demand leads to other policies, some of which are much more dubious and dangerous. There can be little complaint about the kind of income security that is achieved by social security benefits for the unemployed, the sick and the aged, or the development of guaranteed weeks of pay in casual occupations such as the docks and buildings, or the more fully developed annual guarantee plans of certain large industries. Nor can there be any disadvantage in the mere fact of income guarantees to farmers, who are peculiarly subject to the uncertainties of harvests and the long planning periods required by agriculture. The problem arises when the methods used to guarantee a fair stability of income for particular groups in fact freeze the pattern of production. Instances of this come to mind immediately, in the case of the sort of price guarantees to farmers which lead to the piling up of surpluses at the expense of the community as a whole, or the restrictive practices associated with resale price maintenance which have led to a freezing of a certain pattern of distribution and the stifling of progress in, for example, self-service shops. (We are perhaps beginning to see some of the beneficial effects of the removal of some of the worst restrictions by the Restrictive Practices Act of 1956.) Where demands for income security are in fact demands on the part of entrepreneurs to be insured against the kind of risks that it is their function to perform, then to meet them is to encourage the development of new forms of feudalism. That these pleas are often framed in highly moral and persuasive language only makes them the more dangerous.

(*c*) SECURITY AGAINST HAVING TO CHANGE ONE'S HOME

Policies for 'moving work to the workers' can go a long way to iron out the inevitable problems of areas dependent on declining industries, though it has perhaps not been sufficiently realized, that these are not once-for-all programmes for rehabilitating 'depressed areas', but involve continuous study and action to prevent the emergence of new areas with like problems. Looked at from this point of view, it could be argued that such success as has been achieved has been due more to the high level of employment than to the particular brilliance of the policies that have been implemented.

But such policies will not always suffice. There will almost certainly be times when it is not reasonable to maintain communities in existence where the economic resources on which they depended have ceased to be of value. In such cases, what is required is a carefully planned migration of communities and their resettlement. The natural tendency is to leave the decision until too late, when the community has already disintegrated and survives only as an ageing, rigid and almost unemployable core, whose resettlement is likely to be unfruitful and economically wasteful.

(*d*) PRICE SECURITY

The maintenance of relative prices is neither possible nor desirable. As demands change, and methods of production alter, some prices will go up, some down; this is as it should be. Particular groups, however, are often tempted to offset and eliminate those movements which both reflect the underlying changes and help to bring them about. In so far as price stability may be a means to ensure income stability, and does not of itself damage the operation of the price system, as in the case of suitable stabilization schemes for commodity prices important in international trade, interference with market prices is justified. But this is never an end in itself, but only a means to achieve a more important end, which may often be achieved by other means. Particular care is needed here, because of the use of this means of control by monopolistic groups, who are concerned to maintain their position against the rest of the community.

The maintenance of general price stability is however another question of much greater importance. While there may be little to be said against slow price changes whether upwards or downwards, great changes in either direction lead to disintegration of the economic system, by undermining the contractual basis of a complicated economy. The avoidance of inflation in a fully employed world has become a major aim of policy in many countries, though the means for success are not at all agreed among experts. There is little disagreement that overall demand must be prevented from exceeding the possible resources available, by the same general means as are used for full employment policy. Many would add further that some general control of wages and incomes must also be undertaken to prevent the possibility of a wage-cost inflation, though this is not universally agreed, and the means to achieve it are uncertain, even if the policy were otherwise approved.

(*e*) SECURITY IN CONSUMPTION PATTERNS

There are important psychological values in a relatively static pattern of consumption. It is only against a background of more or less fixed wants, and ways of meeting wants, that a proper taste can be formed. The shifting pattern of habits produced by modern economic progress is not conducive to the development of fine taste, or an appreciation of style. Nor is it conducive to the kind of emotional stability and established pattern of conventions that human nature seems to require. But this side of man's life must not be over-stressed in comparison with the important need for change, variety and experimentation. No doubt, people vary in the preponderance of one or other of these needs; society must take account of both. It is not clear that the way in which a modern economic system develops new commodities, through the barrage of advertising and publicity, does adequately meet these needs. I shall have more to say about this in the next chapter.

(*f*) SECURITY AND CLASS STRUCTURE

What is good and permanently valuable in the different patterns of class behaviour that make up the life of a society is to be found in the considerations just mentioned. Class patterns of behaviour both stabilize conventions so as to afford a 'place' for the individual within the group, and at the same time provide different patterns for society as a whole, so as to allow some element of 'competition' and stimulus to change. But class patterns, as we know only too bitterly, produce barriers to that equality of opportunity, which is rightly owed to every man, and also necessary if society is to make the best use of the available talents; and, in various other ways, they hamper economic progress. It is well-known that some of the biggest barriers to the development of underdeveloped countries are firmly entrenched rigid class structures; but it is equally true that business in western Europe, though to a lesser degree in America, has suffered both from limited use of the potential talent available and from the snobbery which has syphoned off university-trained people into Government service and the 'professions'.

A proper balance of progress and security in all these various fields is clearly not an easy matter, nor is any particular mixture necessarily valid for all time. If we try to maximize the rate of economic progress, the cost in social and psychological terms may be too high. If, on the other hand, more security and less progress is desired, the economic cost must be met. A faster rate of economic progress allows for security needs to be met at a higher level, as incomes rise. The crudest example is to be found in the fact that only a high rate of agricultural output provides security against famine. But the price has to be paid in instabilities of other kinds. There is no simple principle which would enable us to achieve the right balance in the highly developed industrial countries of the west. We must not overlook the extent to which progress and security are mutually exclusive, but we must not ignore the extent to which they are complementary. The following story is revealing, if only as a warning:

> This fear of the average American business man of becoming prisoner of his past ideas is symptomatic of the whole nation. Some years ago, after studying one field of activity, it seemed to me that most people engaged in it were heading for disaster. 'They are like nothing so much,' I said to an American friend of mine, 'as a body of men aboard a juggernaut happily heading for a brick wall. They are all agreed they are going to hit it. The only thing they disagree about is who will be the sole survivor to be catapulted over.' 'That's our American philosophy of life,' said my friend. 'Security lies only in momentum.'[14]

In theory we could go back to a static world, if we decided to do so; in practice we cannot. Nor does it seem that a static society is really that to which men are called in the adventure of civilization. No doubt there is no virtue in mere movement, but the call to experiment and adventure is a permanent part of the human heritage. Those who are sometimes most critical of human desires for something new in fields of practical living and action are not infrequently those who, within the fields of the intellect or the imagination, are themselves the boldest innovators. Mr. T. S. Eliot, despite his notable, if not entirely convincing, attempts to persuade us of the necessity of a more or less static society, has always been a notorious innovator in his own field of poetry. Perhaps we would do better to follow Mr. Eliot's practice rather than his preaching.

Though men require a necessary security, and this involves many complex arrangements, the very changefulness of life breaks up the frozen attitudes into which sin drives us. An ever-changing society can no doubt always change into worse ways, but it has at least an opportunity of improving itself, though no guarantee that improvement once made will be sustained. And the fact that we cannot rely on any development which may have achieved a relative success may make us more aware of the contingent nature of human life, and our inescapable dependence on God.

God called Abraham out of the land of his fathers into a new country; so begins the story of God's covenant with men. It has no end on earth, and the Bible leaves us with an expanding Church spreading

[14] *The Times*, 15 November, 1956.

over the whole civilized world of the Mediterranean. The expansion has gone on ever since, and not merely geographically. Today we see that economic progress offers us continuously widening horizons, and ever expanding opportunities. There is no sin in making use of them, if we do not confuse them with their source in God. There is no final satisfaction for men except in the life of the Trinity, but it remains part of our destiny continuously to discover more of the glory of God in his Creation. Is it not at this point that God is at work in our world?

Christians have often pointed out that men have made a religion of progress. Our salvation lies neither in any future form of society, nor in any past state of bliss, but in the once-for-all Revelation of God in Jesus Christ. There is an undoubted repugnance between many ideas of progress and the Christian faith, as there is a necessary tension between a changing world and a faith that in its essentials is unchanging.

May I end with two quotations from theologians, whose fundamental orthodoxy can hardly be in dispute today, though one may perhaps suspect that they carry doctrine too far in their approval of progress? In any case, one can hardly accuse F. D. Maurice or Jacques Maritain either of Calvinist activism or of American dynamism.

F. D. Maurice wrote about the development of nations in the modern world:[15]

> Can we . . . not see something more than a permission of those national societies which the Church called into being, and with which, in the Western world, she became identified; must we not believe that this was a mighty step in the development of the Divine scheme, in the establishment of the Divine kingdom upon earth? . . . The establishment of outward law, the formation of national societies . . . [were] parts of God's great scheme for developing more fully the nature and character of Christ's kingdom. . . . This change [from the ancient world], I affirm to be not merely one in outward and material happiness, but one connected with the very ends for which the Church exists.

And Maritain, at various times, has written as follows:[16]

> Natural law essentially involves a dynamic development, and . . . moral conscience, or the knowledge of natural law, has progressed from the age of the cave-man. . . . And such knowledge is still progressing, it will progress as long as human history endures. (1951)

[15] F. D. Maurice, *Kingdom of Christ* (Everyman ed.), Vol. 2, pp. 234, 239–40.

[16] *The Social and Political Philosophy of Jacques Maritain*, Selected Readings by J. W. Evans and L. R. Ward (1956), pp. 55, 191, 193–4, 214.

Called upon by his nature, on the other hand, to unfold historically his internal potentialities by achieving little by little reason's domination over his own animality and the material universe, his progress on earth is not automatic or merely natural, but accomplished in step with freedom and together with the inner help of God, and constantly thwarted by the power of evil. . . . The horizontal movement of civilization, when directed towards its authentic temporal aims, helps the vertical movement of souls. . . . The progressive integration of humanity is also a progressive emancipation from human servitude and misery as well as from the constraints of material nature. (1942)

By virtue of the hidden work of Gospel inspiration lay consciousness has understood that human history does not go around in circles, but is set towards a goal and moves in a certain direction. . . . Progress does not lead to the recovery of Paradise by a revolution today or tomorrow, it tends to the elevating of the structures of consciousness and the structures of human life to better states, and this all through history up to the advent of the kingdom of God and the land of the resurrected, which is beyond history. (1943)

Chapter 3

GOD AND WEALTH

'Philosophical happiness is to want little, civil or vulgar happiness is to want much, and to enjoy much.'—EDMUND BURKE.

'Prosperity is the blessing of the Old Testament, adversity of the New. Still that Old Testament blessing would do a great deal of good to some of us.'—BENJAMIN JOWETT.

'I am a countryman, Lord, who comes from the country of the world. Teach me Thy City's ordered ways, the courtesies and gracious manners of Thy Court.'—WILLIAM OF ST. THIERRY.

HAVING discussed the general question of economic progress, I now turn to discuss its results. We have great wealth from the activities of our ancestors and as a result of our own skill and capacities. What does it mean to be thus better off? Are we really better off? Is it a good thing to be better off? Is there any Christian standard by which to judge whether we are really better off? What about the New Testament warnings about riches and the rich man? How ought we to use our riches? Are there any directions in which our society should clearly be moving? These are some of the questions we have to try to answer.

I. WHAT IT MEANS TO BE BETTER OFF

What is meant by being better off? What do our riches involve? The basic fact about an expanding economy is that it means an enlargement of choice, and an enlargement of choice in a variety of directions.

(*a*) A higher standard of living means more goods and services available for everybody, and the more goods and services there are available, the wider is the range of human choice. At low levels of income, people spend most of their time and energies keeping alive; their money is spent on food, shelter and clothes. Simple amusements and luxuries, such as cigarettes, drink and dancing, are possible even at these low levels. But it is only when standards rise to what are historically great heights that great opportunities of choice arise. A widening of choice does not preclude greater perversity of actual choices, but it also makes possible, and alone makes possible, the higher reaches of choice, and a greater breadth of interest. It is, in fact, one of the components of what is usually called civilization.

(*b*) A greater quantity of goods and services, as part of the widening of choice, makes possible more education, better health services, a greater devotion of resources to art and the dissemination of knowledge and beauty. Few with any knowledge of the facts in these spheres would dispute that more resources could usefully be employed in all of these ways, even in such a rich country as Britain.

(*c*) Greater productivity in the making of things and the provision of services releases human effort for making other things, or alternatively for quiet relaxation and leisure. Those who most stress the monotony of modern work—in my view, they exaggerate grossly, both in their view of what is, and their comparison with what might be—should welcome the greater possibilities of leisure. Others might indeed question whether leisure is indeed a good in itself (which does not prevent most of us taking it when it comes our way). More leisure allows us to extend our range of choice into the realm of activities in which we have hitherto been forced to engage in order to earn a living, as well as opening up other opportunities; we can now choose to spend our leisure growing food, whereas formerly we had no leisure because growing food occupied all our time.

In all these, and other, ways, economic progress involves an enlargement of choice. This enlargement of itself increases the insecurity of life, and it is not to be expected that everyone will want to bear the burden of decision. There is no greater security than is to be found in the womb or the prison, but both these environments are usually considered incompatible with the full development of personality. There is undoubtedly a price to be paid for the exercise of choice, but it is an inescapable corollary of something of greater value in itself.

It has sometimes appeared in the history of the Christian Church as if the Christian religion were ill-disposed towards the pretensions of men to exercise choice. The peculiar perversions of the Christian faith, to which both Catholicism and Calvinism have tended to succumb, have been to deduce, from the platitude that human choice provides both the opportunity for, and the sole occasion of, sin, the dangerous practical maxim that human choice is to be limited and restricted, whether by the Inquisition or the Kirk Session, so that the greater glory may be given to God by thus restricting the manifestations of sin. Unfortunately for our human ease, as Dostoievsky pointed out in classic form in the Legend of the Grand Inquisitor, God does not seek glory in circumscribing the actions of men, but his glory is rather to be seen in his patience with their follies. It is not merely a matter of the wickedness of coercion; this was not the fundamental end of the Inquisition or the Kirk Session, nor is this the main point of Dostoievsky's fable. The question is about the range of human choice. God made men to be the crown of creation, and his Son came that men might have life abundantly. The enlargement of human choice, whether through an expanding economy or through the discoveries of science or art or literature, is all part of God's design for men.[1]

Economic progress, however, does not merely enlarge human choices, nor does it always proceed by meeting more completely the needs and wants of consumers. It proceeds often rather by an alteration of the whole pattern of consumer behaviour. New products are created by entrepreneurs, and 'sold' to consumers by advertisement, so that the whole pattern of living and culture is altered before consumers have had an opportunity to judge the issue. It is true that there is a negative check in that consumers must at least be ready to buy, or the enterprise becomes unprofitable. But in so far as the producer creates the demand by cajoling people into buying so as to keep up with the Joneses, the check has limited force, the more limited in that it depends on an assumed pattern of choices among consumers, buttressed by some traditional social behaviour complex, which it is the purpose of the whole enterprise to break down and 'transform'.

It is better to regard economic progress as a creative process by

[1] Cf. V. A. Demant, *God, Man and Society* (1933), p. 49. 'A Christian social order will be one where the social conditions are such that the problems of men living together come as completely as possible within the sphere of free moral will. . . . The totality of these factors (i.e. of social structure, etc.) within which human beings have now to live, impose a measure of determinism upon the present aims of individuals and groups. . . . A society will approach the fulfilment of Christian conditions the more its social problems are moral, that is, within the sphere of the will, and the fewer structural, that is, imposing limits upon moral initiative.'

which human behaviour is altered and human choices refashioned in irreversible ways by small groups in the community. There is little difference in the *method*, by which social life has been revolutionized, between, on the one hand, the impact of artistic movements such as the 'Renaissance' or the 'Baroque' in altering our ideas of the Madonna, or the impact of the theologians of the Reformation or the philosophers of the Enlightenment on our attitude to work and nature, and, on the other hand, the impact of business-men in altering our social consumption patterns. There are obvious differences in the *speed* of impact, and the *aims*, and the *effects* of these actions. But all must be regarded as different aspects of the creative life of men, and judged accordingly. There is indeed a broad cultural problem here that needs considerable attention, and perhaps at a more detailed and concrete level than that at which it has often been discussed. About this I shall have something to say later.

But there is one particular problem about which we could undoubtedly do more than we do—the evils of advertisement and the deliberate creation of new (and unnecessary) wants. It is not an easy problem, as it is hard to distinguish necessary information from unnecessary creation of desires. It is difficult to see how new goods to meet new needs, or to meet old needs more satisfactorily, can be marketed under modern conditions without mass campaigns to persuade people to change their habits. (Old habits are not necessarily better, or worse, than new ones.) The obvious wastes of competitive advertisement for different brands may be a very small price to pay (in purely economic terms) for the rapid rate of economic progress that they accompany. But when all this has been said, the loss remains on the cultural and psychological plane.

No doubt the subtle dangers to the inner fastnesses of our souls by 'Hidden Persuaders' have been greatly exaggerated by sensational and emotional writers. It does us little harm if we have emotional fixations for one brand of toothpaste in preference to another which is (objectively) indistinguishable, but it may do us harm if we are led to believe that the choice of toothpaste is a matter of high emotional importance. It is in the field of taste that the greatest damage is done, and far more disturbing than the irrational choices that advertising may induce is the degradation of a civilization that might be judged, for example, by the advertisements to be seen in the London Underground. It is, however, unlikely that the subjects that preoccupy these advertisers preoccupy their onlookers to a like extent. Which is not to deny that they are a public nuisance, and that the whole scale of advertising, even if proper in itself, should be cut down on grounds of taste and aesthetics. And where we do, on sound moral and aesthetic grounds, judge wants to be unnecessary, and there do seem to be some clear cases in the modern world, then Christian criticism must be incurred by those who indulge them, and those who try to persuade others to indulge them further, though not by those who merely supply what others demand, where they have a right to exercise their freedom.

We must clearly distinguish the different categories of (*a*) those things that it should be illegal to produce and sell, however much some people may want to buy them, (*b*) those things whose sale it may be wrong to make illegal, but for which it may equally be right to refuse facilities for advertisement, and (*c*) those things which it is, in the Christian judgment, immoral or unaesthetic to make use of, though not fit subjects for legal action in a world where we properly allow great weight to a free man's responsibility. Much confusion arises because of the natural human tendency to want to forbid others to do things we think wrong ourselves, and because of a specifically Christian confusion about the distinction between moral condemnation and legal prohibition. The matter is the more bedevilled by the failure of Christians to work out any proper 'style of life' appropriate to Christian faith and the twentieth century.[2]

I conclude, then, that our wealth is fundamentally an enlargement of the choices we can make, even though these choices are often distorted by the purveyors of the goods which themselves enrich our choices.

[2] Compare the following, perhaps rather too aristocratic, remarks of Mr. Christopher Hollis: 'Once one has risen above subsistence standards, a large proportion of the articles that are commonly reckoned as constituting the higher material standard are little more than childish toys. Their very existence in society is tolerable only because they are comparatively few, and when everybody has them life for everybody becomes unendurable. . . . This ambition to make two television masts grow where one grew before and not to rest until every house has its telephone and every boy his motor-bicycle does seem as plainly dotty as any of the antics of the Emperor Heliogabalus. To demands for material progress we should surely reply with some discrimination, and say that some of the things demanded in the name of progress are sensible and some are idiotic.' (*Listener*, 19 September, 1957).

2. ARE WE REALLY BETTER OFF?

Before continuing, however, we must do something to still the doubts of those who question whether we are really better off than men used to be in the placid days before the industrial revolution, before we began our ceaseless economic changes. The main burden of the critique that many have offered of this world of lost innocence is that 'a technological society has dehumanized man'. It is not always easy to assess the significance of this generalized criticism. It is comparatively easy to make sweeping assertions in abstract phrases which sound convincing to those who have no obligation to try to give them a concrete reference. It is another matter to try to see what concrete actions, thoughts and emotions of actual men are meant by these phrases. Is it not perhaps a sign of the dehumanization of the theologians and philosophers who talk in these terms rather than about the actual men and women with whom a true humanism would be concerned? What we have to compare are the actual lives of men and women in different social situations, as they are and could be, and not what ideas they may have about themselves. In what sense can one say that in one situation men are dehumanized and not in another?

When we begin to compare the actual conditions of life of men in different periods (and it is by no means so easy as might be thought, because of our profound ignorance about the simplest matters of daily life in periods before complex statistics were collected), another difficulty faces us. In actual life we have to take the whole of our environment and not merely parts of it. Gothic cathedrals went with filth and beastly diseases, lawless knights and a brutal church; eighteenth-century culture and country houses went with ramshackle towns, brutalized mobs and little respect for human life; Victorian sanitation went with tasteless cities, contempt for the lower orders and a vulgar pushing society that was insensitive to finer shades of community feeling. Twentieth-century humanity, fraternity and equality go with a vulgarized press and entertainment industry, a ludicrous patience with the absurdities that the motor-car has brought upon us, and an easy-going complacency with life that is almost unparalleled in human history.

But none of these things are logically or necessarily connected with each other, as I argued in the last chapter in relation to the motor-car. It is a dangerous snare, into which culture-historians have fallen, to think that, because things have happened at the same time, they are necessarily bound together. No doubt, in a simple primitive society of great homogeneity, matters secular and religious are bound together in such a way that, if one changes one aspect of life, the whole social fabric undergoes change. Too much contemporary prophecy has tended to assume that this is as true of our world as of primitive societies. But this does not seem to be so. It is, in my view, a misunderstanding of the very nature of a complex society such as our own. In such a society there is not the tight and close fit, the network of relations binding each element of society together. The mere fact of complexity allows for many different patterns, and the fact that one particular pattern emerges is as often due to decisions by men exercising their free choice as it is the result of fundamental technical requirements. To an economist the decisive influence of these political or individual decisions is often more striking than the economic determination of a social and cultural pattern. One may therefore suspect the grand historians who weave their cultural designs out of the all-too-complex facts. To be fair in any comparisons of one society with another one needs therefore to compare not merely what actually happened but what men could have made of the opportunities before them. No doubt no final judgment is possible here, but at least one can recognize the absurdity of judging a man worse off because he had every opportunity before him, and chose to despise them all.

If we try to distil the essence of the complaints that seem to be involved in the accusations of dehumanization, we are led to look at three sets of problems:[3] urbanization and the agglomeration of masses of men together in megalopolis, industrialization and the specialization of work in huge factories, and cultural impoverishment in a world of mass media of communication and advertising.

Before turning to separate consideration of these three facets of modern society, it is important to note that the more serious conditions which provoke the criticism of dehumanization arise in the earlier stages of economic growth; then several things tend to happen at the same time, and ignorance aggravates an unwillingness to face the facts.

[3] See also Chapters 6 and 7.

People are uprooted from village life and herded in cities, in a novel environment to which they are ill-adapted and which creates tremendous social and psychological strains. The lessons of the early industrial revolution in this field have been at least partly learnt by our town-planners in the west, but the mistakes, which we now largely know how to avoid, have been repeated behind the Iron Curtain, and the growth of cities in the underdeveloped countries, at rates often faster than in the West, creates for them problems on a gargantuan scale. There is, however, a cure for some of these ills, partly in the concurrent development of the building industry at an adequate rate together with agricultural advance and industrialization, and partly in the devotion of far greater resources than is usual to social planning, and the provision of the means of social life.

At the same time as cities grow, a capitalist sector develops, that is to say the sector where enterprise grows, whether private or public. In both cases, the development of a pushing, resourceful entrepreneurial class is not a pleasant sight, whether its representatives are Arkwright, Carnegie, Mr. Khrushchev or their equivalent in West Africa, India or China. If the early entrepreneur is a crude unpleasant person who proclaims his devotion 'In the name of God and of profit', as did his early Italian prototype,[4] the benefits he brings to humanity must not be neglected.

With the entrepreneur tend to come inequalities of income and wealth, not necessarily as great as in static feudal societies, but perhaps more blatant and less acceptable. It may take many generations to eliminate these inequalities. With some of these problems I will deal in my next chapter.

It is at the point when change begins to take hold of a static society that the worst inhumanities tend to take place, some of which can be ironed out in time, though there is no necessary social process that produces this result. It is disturbing enough to be subject to change and not surprising that the first impact is the worst, before people have adapted themselves to it.

But how far *have* these inhumanities been in fact ironed out?

(1) First, let us look at the problems of city life. There is nothing of

[4] Inscription on ledgers of the fourteenth-century Tuscan merchant, Francesco di Marco Datini.

itself inhuman in life in cities. It could indeed be said that, as a fully human being, a man is essentially a city dweller, and that the city is the nursery of high civilization and great religions, even if the desert has been the actual birthplace of these religions. This, in spite of the fact that most men up to the present day have lived in the country and not in towns. But, whether man is more naturally a country or a city dweller, whatever may be meant by 'natural' in this context, today more and more men live in towns and cities, and will inevitably continue to do so, as long as our society continues on its present lines. And it cannot be disputed that men *can* live in cities in a civilized way. Equally it is not difficult for men to turn cities of any kind into a hell on earth, as they have often succeeded in doing in the past.

Cities are of many kinds. It is the mere size of modern cities that often appals; there seems no end to megalopolis and its extension. Fundamentally, the growth in size of cities is the result of improved transport and communications, making possible the advantages of economies of large-scale organization, whether of industry or services directly available to the public. At the human level without artificial aids the limit of human association is set by the span of human knowledge and control of other persons, and by the area men can journey over in a given time, as well as by the number of human beings that can be packed close together in the kind of houses permitted by known building techniques and accepted norms of crowding. With a given standard of crowding, the advantages of economies of scale can only be reaped up to a certain point until transport improves so as to enable more people from further away to journey to work. These advantages of large-scale operation may take the form of a large number of small businesses operating in close proximity to each other, as in the City of London, or the Birmingham industrial complex. Alternatively, they may take the form of large units of production. In the latter case, whose economies may depend on a particular form of technique, such as that of a modern integrated steel mill, or an automatized motor factory, there is a limit set by the span of human control, and it is here that artificial methods of communication may enable men to increase the area of direction and control.

There are thus three factors which in broad outline control the growth of modern cities, transport, communications and the advantages of large-scale organization. The last factor is not merely a technical one, enabling goods and services to be produced more cheaply; it is also a factor of human importance. A large city can provide amenities in the way of specialized services and entertainments that a small group of men cannot provide for themselves. The arts, music, specialized education and specialized medical services, a high-class football team, wide variety of choice in the shops—these are some of the obvious claims that a large city can put forward for being an essential nursery of civilization.

On the other hand, the evils of city life need little stress. The easy transport, which makes possible the growth of large cities and enables people to enjoy their amenities, itself becomes a curse, when traffic jams up city centres, and clutters up every inch of space so that all advantage of speed is lost. The long and crowded journey to work itself almost destroys any gain from greater choice of employment or shorter hours of work. And, while cities may provide specialized social services and health facilities, living conditions are often far worse. There is no law of nature that makes men live in crowded skyscrapers, or tenement blocks in cities; there is no technical factor that prevents housing conditions in large cities being the same as those in small towns or villages. But clearly there is a price to be paid for space, and, if men want to use it for other purposes, it is not available for individual family amenity around their houses. Thus men make for themselves a peculiar form of environment in cities, at least in the very largest, where they are surrounded by man-made objects and see little of the rhythm of natural seasons as it appears in the country.

Much of this is a necessary price that has to be paid for the advantages to be gained from large-scale organization. But many of the incidentals are not really necessary. Traffic congestion and many of the appalling journeys to work could be eliminated, if we were really ready to pay the price. The fact that we do not want to pay the price suggests that we value the choice that is open to us, at least to some extent, though it is not a simple one. This may seem too easy, but it would be perfectly possible to ban the use of private cars within cities and provide frequent and fast transport by public facilities. It would be equally possible to prohibit firms from employing people from beyond a given radius. These suggestions are not meant to be taken literally as serious contributions to a solution of our problems (though it may be that the prohibition of private cars in city centres has something to recommend it). But to state these suggestions is itself to reveal why the present situation continues—namely because we want it. It is true that as long as anybody is allowed to use a car in a city, it will be to my personal advantage to add to the confusion by using my own (at least up to a certain point), though it may be that on a clear vote on the issue I would prefer that nobody should be able to do so. But nevertheless the vote would hardly be a clear one, because of the sacrifice of other goods.

These questions need much more coherent consideration than we have been used to giving them. The whole network of problems tied up in city planning, housing, industrial location and urban transport are not simple, and cannot be dealt with separately, as they all too often are. Only with coherent planned thought and action about them are we likely to be able to construct the kind of urban environment we would really choose to have, and which would enable us to live a properly human life. Coherent planned action means action at some centre by a group of people looking at all the problems together; this is the kind of problem that cannot be left to any kind of market mechanism to work out (though there are many relevant economic problems that can), much less to the incoherent set of administrative bodies that we happen to have inherited from the past. Essentially it means co-ordinated regional planning that is not divorced from contact with the people whose lives are shaped by decisions in this sphere.

If we can see today, in spite of much nasty urban sprawl, that in New Towns and modern city centres, such as Coventry, there is an outline of a twentieth-century city life that is humane and urbane, we must be ready to look forward as well as backward. There are many Black Countries that still need clearing up, and perhaps will not be cleared up in this century. But there are some modern trends that suggest that the problems we have associated with megalopolis may not be permanently with us. To some extent the curse of modern city life is that transport has improved so much more rapidly than communications. People still like to be near each other for business and other purposes, and transport enables them to crowd together. But the development of modern techniques of communication (closed circuit television, computers, etc.) suggests that it may be possible in the future to have many of the advantages of closeness without actual physical proximity. It could be that the large city would then become a sort of dinosaur of uneconomic rigidity and unnecessary complexity. But today this is only a hope.

(2) When we turn to industrialization and modern working conditions, much the same conclusions emerge. There is nothing inherently inhuman in modern conditions of work, or at least no more inhumanity than technical conditions made necessary in other periods of history. Modern methods provide new opportunities, and set men new choices in which good and evil are mixed in new ways. Even if men can choose ways which have a minimum of evil in them, they do not always do so. Perhaps the most characteristic feature of modern industrial life is the great variety of possible kinds of work in contrast with the few choices open to men in the past. Further, our knowledge about human beings at work is limited, and what knowledge we have we do not always apply. It is therefore not surprising that it is possible to quote conditions where men are in fact dehumanized at work, as it is equally possible to quote conditions in modern factories which surpass those ever before available to men. Crucial problems again are those of the size and quality of the working group that fits human needs, and the span of practicable human control within an enterprise with the opportunities or necessities it sets before men. In all this field of problems, in which I am not competent to say anything of moment, there is a great deal of knowledge available, and a great deal of consideration has indeed been given to it by Christians.

(3) The third question arises about the cultural level of the modern world. Two points need to be clearly made at the outset. First, however much we may deplore the vulgarities of mass civilization, we have achieved a mass civilization, and this is to our credit. It is easy to compare the manner of life of an eighteenth-century country gentleman with that of a modern worker, much to the discredit of the latter's manner of life (but not necessarily to his discredit as a person). The comparison we require, however, is between the common man of past ages and the common man of today, and the sad fact is that we know so little of the common man of the past. He has never been a hero of the history books, and it is perhaps only as a result of the impact

of Karl Marx that historians have begun to take him seriously—perhaps too late for adequate documents or other knowledge about him to have survived. But if we try to do our best, and make what comparisons we can, it is not clear that the common man of today has a way of life less civilized than the common man of the past. If many of the physical surroundings of his daily life are badly made and tasteless, he is neither so degraded by dirt nor so brutalized by violence as our ancestors, whose streets were filled with dung, and whose amusements included bear-baiting and public executions.

Secondly, we need to look at what is possible as well as what occurs. It is the gap between achievement and possibility that should disturb us. And here again, perhaps the most notable fact is that we have chosen by due process to permit our own vulgarization, and that by the same due process we could unmake it.

To illustrate, let me first take the case of broadcasting. There are no doubt certain technical and economic requirements involved in any broadcasting system. But the pattern of development in Britain owes more to the initial decision to create a monopoly, the powerful influence of one man, Lord Reith, and the subsequent decision of recent years in favour of commercial advertising. This last decision was not entirely unconnected with the way in which the Reith system of monopoly developed, itself not the inevitable result of the initial decision to have a public monopoly. The present deplorable situation thus came about because of certain decisions by persons and political assemblies, which might well have been different. The contrasting situation of the press and the cinema industry has resulted not so much from definite decisions, as from failure to reconsider in altered circumstances the fundamental decisions in favour of a free press and uncontrolled entertainment, which were made before modern techniques and economic progress opened up mass markets and encouraged a concentration in a few irresponsible hands of power over people's opinions and emotions to a degree unparalleled in any previous society.

I shall return later to some suggestions about the directions in which we might be moving in these matters. There is no need to be uncritical about conditions of life in our modern cities and suburbs, about the inhumanities of some industrial establishments and the vulgarity of much that occupies people's leisure. There is no doubt that a complex large-scale society involves the abandonment of the face-to-face relationships that characterize all or most aspects of life in simple societies, but of itself this is a neutral matter; it does not prevent the development of a properly human life. But, having said this, we need not conclude that men are necessarily dehumanized in modern society. Some of the alleged dehumanization does not exist except in the minds of romantic naturalists, and some of it could be avoided without the abandonment of the most characteristic features of modern society. In other words, we are better off than our ancestors, and, in so far as we are worse off, it is because we have deliberately chosen the worse when we could have the better. Our failure is not in our circumstances but in ourselves.

3. THE DANGERS OF RICHES

We come now to one of the important and convincing areas of Christian critique. We live in a world of abundance and riches, and the New Testament has some severe things to say about the dangers that the rich incur. Before proceeding to comment, it is important to make a few distinctions:

(1) On the economic level, we must distinguish between relative and absolute wealth, and between our absolute wealth and the rate of its increase. No doubt, part of the sting of the riches which the New Testament condemns is due to their existence in the midst of poverty, and the insensitivity that results from this (an insensitivity that we would be well to beware of in the international context today). It is natural to be more conscious of those who are richer and luckier than of the many who are less well-off than we are. The euphemistic phrase, the 'middle classes,' reveals this common human psychological attitude, as it is usually used in a context where it means something like the richest 5 per cent. of the population, excluding the 0·05 per cent. at the very top.[5] But even the poorest he in Britain today is immeasurably rich by New Testament standards, and our riches go on increasing (which brings added dangers).

[5] Thus in 1959, there were 840,000 incomes of not less than £1,500 before tax out of a total of 26,350,000 incomes, or 3·2 per cent. of the total, 17,000 (or 0·06 per cent.) of not less than £10,000, and 3,000 (0·01 per cent.) of not less than £20,000.

(2) We do not do justice to modern economic progress if we talk, as we are wont, of the surfeit of 'gadgets' or physical goods that progress puts in front of us. Economic progress involves the field of services as much as of goods, if not more so. If anything, it involves rather less dependence on brute matter, at least in some important respects.

On the theological level, we must distinguish, as the Archbishop of York pointed out some years ago, between the contrast of nature and grace, on the one hand, and the non-Christian distinction between material and spiritual, on the other.[6] It is to be noted that, in the writings of many ascetics who have rightly won universal attention, the poverty that the Church properly proclaims seems often to be associated with a Platonic contempt of matter as such that is not in accordance with the gospel.[7] Too often the Biblical distinction between the world and God, or, more importantly, between the world as created, sustained, and redeemed by God, and the world as independent and separate from God, has been blurred into a distinction between matter and spirit. This may have been exaggerated by the monastic origin of much of the literature.

The issue remains: Can a rich man be saved? Can a rich society be saved? We must first notice that the Christian gospel has never said that material abundance was in itself evil. The Old Testament constantly reiterated that abundance was the fruit that came of following the ways of the Lord; the Son of Man ate and drank with sinners and publicans, though he had nowhere to lay his head; and the Church has constantly prayed for abundance and prosperity for its members and their societies.

The evils of riches, to the Christian, are the evils of distraction (the distraction that keeps men from thinking about God), the evils of a

[6] A. M. Ramsey, *Durham Essays and Addresses* (1957), p. 47.

[7] I refer to such rightly loved books as the *Imitatio Christi*, as in such passages as 'It is a great let that men abide in signs and sensible things and take little care of perfect mortification. I know not what it is nor what spirit we be led with nor what we mean, we that are called spiritual men, that we have so much labour and so much business about transitory things and vile things but of our inwards we think full seldom' (Everyman ed., p. 164); 'they that by despising of earthly things and mortification of the flesh follow thee be known verily to be wise men, for they are translate from vanity to verity and from the flesh to the spirit.' (pp. 169-70). It may well be that no Platonism is involved in this and other similar passages. It can hardly be doubted that they are often interpreted in a Platonist sense.

false dependence on the created order, and a would-be security that fails to take account of the inevitable fragility of human destiny on this earth. They are spiritual evils, not material evils, and it may be that they lead men to inadequate, not excessive, appreciation and enjoyment of the glories of the material universe; we tend to use, and abuse, material things, rather than to enjoy them. They are evils that arise at all levels of economic well-being, even if they are peculiarly the evils of a rich civilization.

Nor is it obvious that the distractions that riches afford are of their nature worse than the sins provoked by jealousy, envy, pride and ambition, all the sins that come from the love of power and position that have little to do with riches as such. It is the root failure of Marxist analysis that it does not adequately distinguish between riches and power, between avarice and ambition, the drive for profits and the drive for political dominion. There is little excuse for Christians to make the same mistake.

We need to be aware of the dangers of our riches; we need also to be ready to enjoy wholeheartedly the good things that God has given us to enjoy, and to be thankful for them. 'Riches and honour come of thee, and of thine own do we give unto thee,' repeats the Scottish Liturgy at the offertory; if we ponder on this text, we can hardly refuse to accept what blessings there may be in a world of economic progress, even if it may be the vocation of some people deliberately to eschew them.

We need to be sensitive to the way that material possessions divide man from man and break up human fellowship. We need to be ready to use our abundance in common rather than for personal and private enjoyment, as a canon on pilgrimage to Jerusalem in 1494 said of the Venetian gentlemen: 'They are frugal and very modest in their manner of living at home; outside the house they are very liberal.'[8]

Above all, we need to be aware of the mass of men living in poverty in the underdeveloped countries, whose condition we could do something to improve, if we were ready to make sacrifices ourselves on an adequate scale. The West stands under the shadow of the condemnation of Dives, and it makes much the same excuses as Dives did. (I shall return to this in my fifth chapter.)

[8] Canon Pietro Casola, *A Pilgrimage to Jerusalem in the year 1494* (tr. by M. M. Newett).

4. WHAT CAN WE MAKE OF OUR CULTURE?

The real questions only begin when all this is taken as read. Granted that we have tremendous opportunities that man has never had before, granted that our riches are to be used and enjoyed to the greater glory of God, what must we do? Where should we be making changes that will make our lives more creative and more nearly in accordance with the high standards set before us, and the opportunities that we have?

We must always try to be clear as to the persons or institutions on which we are making demands. Too much prophetic denunciation fails because it does not make this clear. At one moment it is asking individuals to change the pattern of their lives, at another denouncing particular institutions which may have been created by particular small groups of people, or may be the result of particular political decisions, which are the responsibility of the politically effective groups. And then again the prophets may be denouncing the overall aims and ambitions of a whole social order.

There is, first, the level of the life of the individual. Here is a rich field for specifically Christian endeavour, where the Church has naturally been strongest. And yet we cannot but be aware of the failure of Church groups to suggest new patterns of life, new styles of living, that are appropriate to our days. If Christians are to lead men to a deeper sensitivity to the ways in which we may learn how to use our riches to the glory of God, it will have to be seen in the style of our lives. We have failed dismally.

Then there are the specific fields where institutional changes are required, and where Christian leadership, both by laymen and through the organized institutions of the Church, could perhaps lead to changes. There are many such fields where we could more clearly reveal the possibilities of a rich world. An enormous amount remains to be done in the field of personal case-work with the various groups in the community who have special needs, which cannot be met by the ordinary machinery of administration. Within industry, and this means not so much by general political action, as by patient infiltration and education of the worst offenders up to the standards of the best, an enormous amount needs to be done in humanizing working conditions, giving people proper responsibility, and making the best use of available talents for managing men and things. There are all the problems of city life and city planning, on which I have touched, where activity is required at the political level, whether nationally, regionally or around the parish pump. And there are many other aspects of life on which I have not touched at all. I will, however, refer a little more to some cultural problems, which seem to me to be of importance for the whole tone of our society.

Freedom of choice is to me, as should be clear, a rather fundamental matter, which is bound up with the Christian view of man's place in the world. Many matters of culture are peculiar in that they are both intimate to individuals and yet matters of public concern in that they affect the enjoyment of others. In so far as this is the case, they are properly matters of legislation, and more properly so than many matters of morals that have been the subject of legislative activity. Thus my neighbours are offended if I build a monstrosity for a house; they cannot help seeing it. Similarly, the choice of films to be shown in a given town and the choice of newspapers available to the public are hardly merely individual matters, though I do not need to read papers that offend my taste, or see films that would bore me. They are not merely individual matters because their cultural influence may be widespread and pervasive. For societies which accept compulsory education in state establishments, it hardly seems wrong that there should be some legislative control of the activities of those who provide films and newspapers, in the same way as it is accepted in Britain that we must have some legislative restraint over broadcasting and television. The case seems far stronger than that for interference with the private sexual activities of consenting adults.

But what restraints, and for what purposes? It seems to me abundantly clear that, on the one hand, it is not the business of government to interfere with the absolute freedom of thought, speech, and propaganda that should be granted to those in universities and other similar places where creative and critical activities are carried on at the frontiers and in detachment from day-to-day concerns. But, on the other hand, it is equally clear that to leave cultural industries, such as the press and the cinema, entirely to the market produces a cultural degradation that no civilization could stand for long. This is partly due to the peculiar way in which these industries have developed, but perhaps chiefly because they are subject to great economies of scale. If there were no economic advantages in mass-circulation of newspapers, and no natural (or induced) tendencies for the production and distribution of films to be controlled by a small group of firms, it might not matter so much. It is possible that the better in such circumstances would more effectively compete with the bad. But it is at any rate clear that when enormous power is given by the market to a few more or less irresponsible money-makers to set the pattern of public taste, the result is intolerable. There is, to my mind, no moral, social, or political justification at all for the 'rights of the press' as we have it today in Britain. It is a scandal of a major order, and the pitiable reports of the Press Council merely show that in this field there are not, as yet, the professional standards that can effectively restrain those who have the power. It is equally clear that it would not be difficult to enforce higher standards on journalists, and perhaps more importantly on newspaper proprietors. A lay Press Council, with powers to prevent both journalists and editors, and also newspaper proprietors, from following their craft or business, could soon raise the tone of newspapers, as similar action has done in the field of medicine, dentistry, and the law.

This might not be enough. It would be perfectly possible for the state to provide opportunities for groups to express varied opinions, without itself backing any particular opinion. Once it is granted, as it has been for historical and accidental reasons, in the case of wireless, that the state has a right to interfere and provide opportunities, it is not all that difficult to frame conditions under which there is variety and controversy, within a continuing purpose of raising standards in every field, rather than that of appealing to the lowest common denominator. It is better that a few people should be bored, or even most people bored for some of the time, than that human beings should be generally deprived of opportunities to make the best use of the faculties they possess.

Another similar problem of an egalitarian society is the continuation of the provision of those cultural amenities for which the rich and privileged formerly paid. As I see it, that responsibility also has to be taken over by the state, in some form or another. The tragedy has been that, though the state has begun to undertake some of these responsibilities, it has lamentably failed of recent years to do it adequately. And the reason, I am afraid, is to be laid at the hands of our new demagogues. I am not very happy, when eminent men, such as Lord Radcliffe, denounce the vices of 'a society which combines a low level of thinking and feeling with a wide diffusion of general benevolence and good will', and attribute this to the fact that 'the majority of members of society will always beg not to be required to keep themselves in training'.[9] Many of the decisions have been taken by a comparatively small group of people, in that political party which one would least expect to be sensitive to the vulgarian impulses of the masses, if indeed the masses have vulgarian impulses.[10] But it is unfortunately true that it is these people who have debased our broadcasting and television, of which we once could be proud, refused to take any action about the abuses of the press, and limited or cut down government expenditure on creative and constructive items, because in this way they could satisfy the clamour for reduction of taxes and gain greatest public approval.[11]

We must be clear when we denounce the vulgarities of our age that the blame must often be laid at the doors of a few mean and short-

[9] *The Times*, 23 February, 1958.

[10] It may be the case that the Conservatives are peculiarly prone to be vulgarian because of their innate snobbery and the guilt it induces. But it would be better for all if they could honestly recant their snobbery and reassert the valid principles for which they stand.

[11] Let me take three examples:

(*a*) The National Marriage Guidance Council has received grants from the central government rising from £8,000 in 1956/7 to £10,000 in 1957/8 and £15,000 in 1959/60, but the cost of legal aid in divorce cases is well over £1 million. Nevertheless, in 1951/2, when grants were at the lower level, they were cut as part of an overall economy drive.

(*b*) A chronic crisis has overwhelmed the opera world for the last few years. As the Arts Council commented in its 1957/8 Report (p. 14): 'The lack of the means to sustain opera on the basis of ascertained and accepted need is due, year after year, to the fact that the Treasury grant to the Arts Council turns out to be substantially less than the careful and accurate estimate of requirements submitted'. Extra grants in 1959/60 put opera 'out of danger', but still left 'crises elsewhere' (see 1958/9 Report). Grants were still further increased in 1960/1.

(*c*) The National Gallery Report for July 1956-June 1958 reads: 'The stock of old masters or even of nineteenth-century masterpieces in the world is not a stock of commodities which in any legitimate way is capable of increase. . . . In a very few years the opportunities of further acquisition by even the richest of public collections will have narrowed to a small trickle. Only in the short period which remains, perhaps fifteen or twenty years at most, can we hope to remedy the omissions of the last fifty years. . . . If we do not act speedily a later generation will say: "In earlier days, though still comparatively poor, they laid the foundations of the best collection in the world; but when they grew rich

sighted statesmen, and other leaders who have often been richly endowed by society and prefer to win votes by offering *panem et circenses* to those they despise rather than trying to hand on the best traditions of the past to future generations. (Is it merely factious to suggest that those who act in this way are more usually found calling themselves 'conservatives'?) When the directors of the Bank of England have so little taste that they can dump down a huge block of masonry adjoining St. Paul's, and when the authorities of our universities, who might be supposed to be among the guardians of our cultural values, can spend public money on the tasteless fatuities of so-called 'traditional' architecture, it is not surprising that our cities give such little glory to God. Let us however not blame the common man for his 'low level of thinking and feeling', when the treason is to be found among the clerks and those who have been born to great privileges.

I would not want to end on this note of denunciation. There is enormous scope for constructive action in our society, at the individual and small group level, as well as at the level of large-scale industrial and political action. It is a measure of the Christians' failure that they have not made this impact. And, in particular, it is a measure of the failure of the *élites* in our society. One particular *élite* with special

they grew insensitive and allowed other nations and other collectors to take what was needed to realize to the full the splendid vision of its founders." . . . While the National Gallery grant has remained in the neighbourhood of, or even below, the grant of the early eighties, the grant to education in general has increased from £2,000,000 to £378,000,000. . . . Subsidies to food and agriculture, which in the eighties were £5,000, are now running at a level of well over £300,000,000. . . . Doubtless these increases are all reflections of policy. Are we to infer that the virtual stationariness of the National Gallery purchase grant, despite the shrinkage of its real value, as measured in cost of living units, to about a quarter and despite a vast appreciation in the prices of works of art, has been similarly willed by those in authority? . . . It is our contention that, even if central government expenditure *per annum* were two and a half billions instead of over five, £12,500 for the National Gallery purchase grant would still be Lilliputian. . . . The extra £137,500 that we suggest as appropriate making, for instance, the subsidy on eggs £43,362,500 instead of £43,500,00' (pp. 12-6).

In fact, the Government increased its grants to £100,000 in January, 1959, as part of a general increase in assistance to the Arts, but this still remains only two-thirds of the National Gallery's request.

Total central government expenditure on the arts was about £7 millions in 1958-9 (as compared with total government expenditure of about £6,000 millions). (See H.M. Treasury, *Government and the Arts in Britain*, 1958, and Lord Bridges, *The State and the Arts*, 1958 Romanes Lecture). The increases announced for 1959-60 involved less than £½ million.

responsibilities is that of university people, whether teachers or students. In the second half of the twentieth century in the highly industrialized and rich countries, the problem has largely ceased to be one of abolishing poverty, and become one of raising the quality of living. There is much we can all do in that direction.

Chapter 4

FAIR SHARES?

'Civil Equality is morally impossible, because no commonweal, little or great, can subsist without the poor. . . . But were all equally rich, there would be no subordination, none to command, nor none to serve.'—HICKS, DEAN OF WORCESTER, 1684.

'Envy in our time is confined to the contemplation of others of nearly equal income.'—J. K. GALBRAITH.

1. THE TREND TOWARDS EQUALITY

THE churches rightly stress the fact that the nineteenth-century missionary movement represented the first time in Christian history when the gospel had indeed been preached to the whole world. What is not perhaps always sufficiently stressed is that this was only possible because of the industrial revolution's mastery of the whole world, just as St. Paul depended for his missionary work on Roman roads and Roman order. It is surely not just accident that these happenings have occurred together. If we believe in a God who made one human race, in which each man has equal value, and which can neither be divided by any apparent differences in creation nor prevented from uniting in its Redeemer, Jesus Christ, it is not surprising that it should be part of the destiny of man physically to realize this unity in a world-wide civilization. This world-wide civilization we have today. The unity of mankind is a social, economic and political fact.

It is not surprising that this unity creates problems; there is no automatic assurance that 'The more we are together the happier we shall be'. The division of the world by the iron and bamboo curtains is however a much less significant fact than the unity which it reveals. There was a time when what happened in Muscovy or Cathay was as little important to the 'civilized' world as the obscure doings of Indians in the Midwest of America. Today what happens in Siberia or Tibet matters to the western world, and, perhaps more significantly, what is happening in these areas follows very closely the pattern of what happened in the Midwest in the middle or early part of the nineteenth century. What is happening in South America today is what happened in the Midwest about the turn of the twentieth century; as Chicago grew then, so now we see the growth of Sao Paolo. And in Africa and the Middle East the same ferment is at work as in Asia and Latin America.

The ferment has the same source. It is the spread of the Western Atlantic way of life with its age-long traditions of individualism and humanism, its scientific view of life and its applied techniques. In origin, it is a view of life moulded by Christian thought, though the stream has no one unique source. In practice, it is the nationalist democratic ideology that breaks up old social patterns, and the modern techniques that undermine old ways and give people visions of new possibilities; and the techniques are perhaps a force stronger than the ideologies. The ideology of the West is often learned superficially, and incompletely understood; being based itself on centuries-old religious traditions and embodied in well-established, but of their very nature fragile, institutions, it cannot easily be transplanted. But the techniques can. To build a judicial system takes generations; to build a dam takes years.

The result is that throughout the world there is spreading a uniform culture. Airports everywhere look much alike; luxury hotels serve business-men with the same food everywhere; 'cocacolonization' is not restricted to western Europe, nor American films to English-speaking markets. If the vulgarization of the world is the price that human sin has made us pay, at least it still bears witness to the dominant fact that we live in 'One World'. There are still innumerable barriers that divide men from each other, but the things that unite them are becoming clearer to those who have eyes to see. Have the churches the vision, or do they still tend to see the Church of God as the local temple of the tribal deity?

Uniformity and unity are also marks of what is happening within nations, as much as between them. Regional differences break down; different classes adopt the same pattern of life and buy the same goods; rich and poor are brought more closely together. It is no longer possible to have pools of human squalor within the wider community of the more or less well-off. Nor do we tolerate within the Western world the gross opulence of the multi-millionaires of the period before the First World War.

From the point of view of power, an advanced industrial society both redistributes responsibility and decision-making downwards among all groups in society, and also concentrates it in larger and larger units, as modern technical progress makes possible the control of larger organizations by small numbers of people. Firms grow larger, and governments more efficient and concentrated. The technical advantage of bigger units puts power into the hands of planners and managers, while they are now controlled not by small traditional *élites*, but by the representatives of the man in the street. It might almost be said that professionalism in business and vulgarization in politics are the mark of the new world. Inevitably there are tensions, especially as the pattern is still fluid and in process of change.

One of the characteristic achievements of modern industrial society is that it has brought the different classes nearer together in the national community. This may seem odd both to those brought up on the myth of the widening gap between workers and business-men that is supposed to be produced by the capitalist system (a myth that owes its origin to Karl Marx), and also to those who regard the trends towards a 'welfare state' and greater economic equality as entirely the result of direct political action. The truth of the matter is that the industrial system of itself produces the cohesion and equality that socialists wish to encourage and that business-men often try to discourage. The revolution is not merely the result of outside interference, but is also the work of the business-men themselves, the architects of the industrial system. The only real opposition to the trend can be found in old aristocratic feudal circles, where these still exist.

What is meant by saying that social cohesion and equality are the result of the capitalist business-man's activities? First, modern industrial systems unite geographically separated groups by breaking down barriers to communication. It is no longer possible for modern societies to have the variety of economies and cultures in different regions that was possible two hundred, or even fifty, years ago. First the railway, then the bus, now the aeroplane and the private car, have brought even distant regions near together. Differences between city and countryside, and between south and north, become less important, as labour and enterprise become more mobile and national systems of education and amusement spread a uniform culture via the mass media of the press, television and the school system.

Secondly, in terms of incomes, there is less difference between the richest and poorest in a developed industrial society than in the under-developed rural economies that preceded it. Income differences may perhaps increase in the early stages of industrialization, though even this can be doubted.[1] But whatever happened in the early stages, it is clear that in a developed industrial system the forces tending to equality are stronger. Some of these are internal to the economic system—for example the breaking down of positions of strength due to the dynamic element in modern industry, and the steady rise in the price of labour that is so characteristic of developed countries. These industrial trends cheapen the goods which the poor buy, while they make it uneconomic for any but the richest millionaires to enjoy the cheap labour services that the former middle classes took for granted. It is startling to realize that Karl Marx, living in London in the middle of the nineteenth century, under conditions that he (and his biographer Mehring, a left-wing German Social Democrat) could regard as penury (because he was never certain whether he could pay his meat bill or not), could yet enjoy the services of a full-time resident domestic servant. It may well be that the rising cost of domestic service has hit the bourgeois classes more severely than all the 'confiscatory' measures of left-wing governments. But the rising cost of domestic service is due to the high productivity that pioneers, such as Henry Ford, have made possible. The business-man has undermined the position of the bourgeoisie!

But, thirdly, the growth in modern society of equality, both of incomes and in other fields, follows from the indirect political effects of a modern industrial system. It is this system that has made possible and brought into being all that we mean by democracy and popular participation in government. Essentially, modern industry requires trained and educated people, and, though no doubt there are many other forces that led to the encouragement of education, this one has

[1] What happens characteristically is that the industrial system makes new men rich. These have different standards of living and different patterns of spending from the older rich, the landowning classes and traditional aristocracies; it is the new patterns of life that give offence, far more than the actual level of riches.

been fundamental. But education does not stop when factory workers have been trained to read instructions, and technical experts are available in adequate numbers. It sets other forces in motion. (Perhaps here lies the future hope for the Soviet Union. Stalin's forced pace of industrialization also involved a forced process of education to produce 'cadres', as they are called in the Marxist jargon. But it is doubtful if the process can be stopped once there are enough factory workers and foremen, and enough atomic physicists or rocket experts. Education is, fortunately, an essentially explosive force.)

Nor is it merely a matter of education. There is also the growth of trade unions and the other centres of popular power which make up a live democracy, and all of which result from the industrial process itself. With public education, the universal vote, and the growth of self-consciousness among representatives of the workers, a purely political process gives added force to the economic process of equalization. In the long run, the rich, whether the old feudal classes, or the new industrial business-men, cannot hope to move events against the trend of massive pressure from below. The political moves, which strengthen the position of trade unions, enforce the redistribution of income by taxation, and establish minimum standards for the poor, the unemployed, the old, the sick and the slum tenant, may move several stages ahead of the underlying economic process, but they are not moves in a different direction. This is the essence of capitalism in its broad historical context.

If this perspective is the correct one in which to view the present economic system in the Western world, it raises many questions about the validity of the internecine quarrels between groups that make the headlines of the political and industrial battlefield. How far are they disputes about the realities? How far are they merely battles about whether to move along the trend at greater or less speed? And in any case where is the trend leading?

In the first place, if the fundamental forces at work in a modern industrial system make for greater community and equality, Christians can recognize in this the hand of God. I do not say that they must recognize it as such because this is the tendency; what happens is not of itself the will of God, and to mark a tendency may merely be to mark the progress of the devil. But in this case, I believe that the will of

God is at work. The fundamental act of God in creation was to make mankind, not to make a set of different races and classes; whatever reality we give in the practical world to differences of race, class, social grouping, taste, culture, or intelligence, these are secondary differences within the unity of mankind. In redemption also, men are united in the one man-God, Jesus Christ, and all are equally made sons of his Father. That this unity and equality should be shown forth in greater community between men in particular ways and in greater equality in incomes, power and prestige, does not indeed necessarily follow from the Christian faith. But that somehow or other they should be set forth is necessary. It is not stretching the point too far to say that we are being called today to realize them in the particular forms of community and equality that a modern industrial system brings forth. That Christians are often called in this direction by secular groups and secular forces is not perhaps entirely surprising to those who are ready to acknowledge that the Lord God, the Creator, is perhaps rather greater than the parochial deity we often worship in our parishes. (And our parish here may not be merely a geographical unit, but also a too narrow set of ideas, or a whole ecclesiastical establishment.)

But to say this does not perhaps take us very far; it does however give us a sense of direction. The significant fact is not merely our freedom in a modern economy, but also the opportunity to live as men in community and equality. Whatever class divisions there are, and always will be, these are not laws of nature, whether static as in the old systems with the squire in his place and the peasant in another, or dynamic as in the belief that the world is the arena for a perpetual succession of struggles between different classes. The fundamental laws of God are calling us in the direction of community and equality. Some nations have progressed further in one way than others. In Britain we believe that, in matters of common welfare, support for the casualties of the modern world, respect for the trade union and the ordinary worker, and fair taxation of the rich, we have a lot to teach the rest of the world. The Americans and Scandinavians have a lot to teach us about real social equality and snob-free education, and also perhaps in the way of real opportunities to move upwards economically and socially. There is not necessarily one ideal pattern.

It is in terms of this background trend towards equalization of incomes and status that I want to look at some of the problems of income distribution within Britain and similar countries today. In the next chapter I turn to the international aspects of this problem.

2. INCOME, EFFORT AND WORTH

There is a deep-rooted prejudice which makes us want to find moral justifications in fields where such justification is inapplicable. We dislike the feeling that we live in a random world; we dislike being unable to give a rational or moral explanation for what happens; we expect to be able to justify our actions and our situation, and are uncomfortable when we cannot do so. It is a mark of some sensitivity of conscience to ask for justification, but it is not a mark of very great sensitivity to try to find justification where none is possible. The man who replies to a question how he is to explain and justify his income, by replying that what he has he holds and will continue to hold, betrays his insensitivity and denies all that makes a community more than a number of warring interests and classes. But this crudity is not far removed from the truth, and is indeed nearer to it than the reply of the man who justifies his income because he deserves it, either because of his own worth, or effort, or because of his contribution to society. The authorities to which he appeals may seem strong, even if he may find it difficult to apply them in his particular case, but examination will show that they are no more than broken reeds. In the last resort, we have what we have because we have it, and there is little rhyme or reason in it. There is indeed *some* rhyme and reason in it, but much less than we might think. The man of sensitive conscience, therefore, neither defends his income and wealth against all comers, nor tries to soothe his conscience by convincing himself that it is in any sense his due. He is grateful for it, and because he is grateful, he should be sympathetic to others who have less to be grateful for.

This requires some elaboration, and to examine the question it is simplest to look at some moral principles which might be thought to be applicable to income shares, and to see if any of them are practicable.

Let me start with the principle of payment for effort. In the real world, effort is an important factor involved in the determination of incomes. The laws of supply and demand do not cease to operate in the field of incomes, though some people regard them as unseemly, and others, by stressing the non-economic factors involved in the determination of the supply and demand curves, appear to think that they have thereby disposed of supply and demand. The fact that more effort is required in some jobs than others, that some people require to exert more effort to achieve a given result than others, and that extra work requires extra effort, all these considerations in some measure affect the income-structure by altering the supply of labour of different kinds and at different times. But they do not result in any clear relationship between income and effort.

It is not generally true that jobs universally accepted as unpleasant will be paid more because of their unpleasantness, unless it is also true that people can move easily into and out of jobs both in different places and in different industries, which is by no means always the case. Thus coalminers were paid badly in the inter-war years, not because the work was then held in higher esteem than it is today, when they are among the highest paid manual workers, but because of the existence of general unemployment, and because of special conditions of demand and supply in the industry. In so far as incomes are paid so that people may be persuaded to undertake certain jobs, their level will be determined by what it is necessary to pay to persuade the last man to undertake the job, that is to say the man who is least ready to undertake it, either because it requires more effort from him, or because he can do better for himself in some other occupation. Equally the extra amount that it will be necessary to pay for extra work will depend partly on people's willingness to work harder and the opportunities for attracting labour from elsewhere. But though what people will earn will be thus definitely settled, it will not be settled merely according to the effort put forth by the marginal man, or on the marginal job, and will indeed vary according to the circumstances of the time, and in particular according to the differing demands for the products of effort of different kinds.

When we turn to the morality of this, there would probably be general agreement that people should be paid extra for extra work. The principles of piece-work and overtime are generally, if not universally, accepted as both necessary from the point of view of incentives to work, and morally proper.[2] (The parable of the labourers in the vineyard offends our moral principles, as well as judging our practice, and its effectiveness lies precisely in that it does this.) But if we are ready to accept the principle of extra income for extra work, this principle neither helps us to fix the level of payment or the appropriate addition, nor does it avoid the difficulty that extra work and extra effort are not exactly comparable. It would be possible to rate occupations according to some general average criterion of difficulty and unpleasantness. But this would take no account of individual efforts. Effort cannot easily be measured, even if we have some rough idea as to whether a man is putting more or less effort into his work. For the fundamental difficulty is that effort cannot be measured by results. People vary enormously in their capacities, and what is easy for one man will be enormously hard for another; how then can we pay them according to the effort they put forth? At best, the most crude guesses would have to be made, and even then it would involve payments differing considerably for the same work, and would offend against another fairly deeply rooted principle, that of equal payment for equal work.

It can perhaps be seen from this that a rigid application of a principle of payment according to effort, whether in the form of a hierarchical grouping of occupations, or in the more extreme form of an attempt to pay individually according to the effort put forth by a particular person, would produce some rather odd results. It would not allow for differing demands, and would therefore remove one element of flexibility from the economic system. In the extreme form it would involve acute difficulties of estimation. Nor is it obvious that such a system would, on its own, commend itself on moral grounds.

If it is clear that people are not, and, in a real world of sinful men, could not, without great difficulty, be paid according to the effort they put forth, it is equally a will o' the wisp to try to find a justification for

[2] We do well, however, not to ignore the moral objections often felt to piece-work by trade unions. The argument is well put by a trade unionist in Disraeli's *Sybil* (1845). 'The man who does piece-work is guilty of less defensible conduct than a drunkard. The worst passions of our nature are enlisted in support of piece-work. Avarice, meanness, cunning, hypocrisy, all excite and feed upon the miserable votary who works by the task and not by the hour' (Penguin ed. 1954, p. 215). That most who write and teach about these matters are themselves usually paid by the piece might lead us to be more careful in what we say.

a man's income in his 'worth'. This is a concept that sometimes appears to be attractive to moralists, but it does not bear much examination. We can indeed see that one of the factors determining people's incomes is the amount that other people are prepared to pay for what they do. This is the demand side of the forces which produce the incomes that people actually receive. If the supply of labour of a particular kind depends on alternative opportunities and the inducements required to persuade people to undertake a job, the income finally paid depends also on what people are ready to pay for a given supply. Scarcity of a certain type of labour, whether natural or induced, can raise the incomes of those lucky enough to have the peculiar gifts in question, or those who just happen to be available in the right place or at the right time. It is not clear that because the conditions of demand and supply produce what appear to be fantastically high (if not always stable) incomes for film-stars, to take a notorious example, that this is what moralists mean when they talk about worth. It is not clear that, because people are prepared to pay large sums for the services of film-stars, they are therefore 'worth' this amount.

If this is not what is meant by 'worth', what meaning can be given to it? It would no doubt be possible to range occupations in some sort of order of merit, and to get some agreement about this. If we rule out the test of what people are ready to pay in the market, we are not left with any clear system by which to determine people's 'merit' or their 'contribution to society'. We have then to fall back on people's rough judgments of suitability, and land ourselves in the dilemma of the then Archbishop of Canterbury, who said, a year or so back, that an hour of a nurse's time was worth several years of a typist's—a judgment that seems to ignore the simple fact that hospitals cannot be run without typists, and that it is not difficult to imagine conditions under which typists might be scarcer than nurses. Nevertheless, there might be some scale of values for occupations on which it might be possible to achieve agreement, and which people might think to have some moral value. Its moral value would not, however, be obvious, at least to me; furthermore, it would run up against all the objections to a rigid system we mentioned above.

In fact, in societies of all sorts, people are ranked in terms of status, and varying symbols of status are attached to different jobs. By and large, in modern society, though there does not seem to be any necessity for it, status and income go together. People are not paid less for pleasant jobs with high status, but more. (*a*) The justification of this in terms of payment for responsibility assumes that people are unwilling to undertake responsibility, but it seems somewhat naïve to deny the existence of a rather general desire for power, which is, after all, merely the cruder expression of the same idea of 'responsibility' in this context. (*b*) Part of the reason why people are paid more for more pleasant jobs is that these jobs require abilities which are scarce, either because of the natural distribution of intelligence, or because of artificial barriers to equality of educational opportunity. (*c*) But there still remains what is perhaps a more fundamental reason for these inequalities, which is that people believe it right that money should be added to status, as indeed it almost always has been in history. But to join wealth and status is hardly to pay for 'worth' in any moral sense. It may be right that there should be status symbols in society, and indeed without them society may not cohere, but it can hardly be claimed as a moral principle that the additional status-symbol of money should always accompany the others. There is a good moral case for paying the less highly honoured the more in terms of money, and separating the distinctions of office from the opportunities of private enjoyment, though this might be regarded as so impractical as to be utopian.

If then a coherent system of payment according to effort or 'worth' is not plausible, is it possible to find any other principle? Payment according to need is possible, in a rough-and-ready sort of way; the objection to it is that it cuts across normal systems of payment for work done, fails to provide necessary incentive, and interferes with what is required to provide what the public wants according to the demand and supply conditions. Payment for need is better provided directly by means of insurance and social services, outside the normal pattern of income distribution.

Finally, there remains equality as an absolute standard, in principle quite unequivocal and simple, morally appealing, and, at least in some measure, universally accepted.

The fundamental objections to the criteria proposed on moral grounds from the economic point of view are that they do not allow for enough elasticity for supply and demand conditions to make themselves felt. To put it simply, they ignore the fact that differences in incomes act as incentives of various kinds and reflect the public's wants. It is always possible to create a desired income pattern by state fiat, but it will run into difficulties because of this. From the moral point of view, it is not obvious that any of the above criteria, except for equality, would be regarded as completely morally satisfactory by themselves, and they are of course contradictory if an amalgam is attempted. The claims of effort, 'worth' and need cannot be reconciled.

There is a further more fundamental moral consideration. It is doubtful if an unequal distribution of incomes based on some criterion of 'fairness' would be ultimately found to be satisfactory. Should merit be rewarded, however we assess merit? Is it not perhaps better that we should be forced to accept a certain incoherence in the pattern, so that no one can find in his income a source of pride, and society can be seen to have other criteria than money by which men are judged?

If we are ready to take account of the practical economic necessities of supply and demand, to allow for incentives and the judgment of the market as to what people want to buy, there is no reason why we should not try to smooth out those inequalities that are due to the deliberate rigging of the market by particular groups, and to work for a system of more equal distribution. Needs can be met by special payments by the state and by special provision of services for particular groups in society. The powerful force of the income-tax can be used to lower the higher incomes and create a more equal society, if we want it. If we can never achieve a perfectly rational system, there is no evidence that the existing inequalities cannot be considerably reduced without serious damage.

3. RENT, INTEREST AND PROFITS

Is there any justification for the incomes actually paid to people in the modern world? Let us look at those incomes which seem most indefensible, and have continually aroused criticism and denunciation —rent, interest and profits.

(*a*) *Rent*. To economists, where an income performs no function at all, it is called rent. (The peculiar scientific definition of rent by economists is not to be confused with normal use of the word for payments to owners of land or houses, which may include payment for managerial services, interest on capital, and the profits of business enterprise.) Pure rent to the economist is a pure surplus, that accrues to some people because of payments that have to be made to others. For example, if there are only two sources of raw material for cement-making, at one of which the costs of production are much lower than at the other, then the price to the public will be determined by the costs of the second source, if it is impossible to produce all that is required at the cheaper source. The owner of the cheap source of supply will then earn a rent over what it costs to produce from his property. This is a pure surplus in the sense that it would make no difference to the situation if it was subject to a 100 per cent. tax; the owner would still continue to produce as before.

The economic system in the normal way involves a large number of people receiving rents in this sense. Some of these are only rents in the short period, in that, if taxed away, the situation in the long-run would be altered. Let us suppose, for example, that the cheap source of supply of cement is cheap, not because of some natural feature, which cannot be altered, but because it is exploited by a much more efficient business-man. If we further assume that this efficient business-man, for some reason or other, is committed to working at this site, or cannot get a job of some other kind, then again his surplus is a rent. To tax it away would not prevent him from continuing to exploit this source of supply, and thus using his abilities to produce cheap cement. But, in the long-run, the situation might be different; if efficiency were always taxed in this way, it might be that people would not bother to acquire the requisite experience, or to use their abilities, if they could achieve no gain from doing so. Thus, though rents in the short period, such payments perform a function in the long-run, and the economic system would not be the same if they were taxed.

This discussion has revealed another point. Economic rent is not merely a payment for the use of the services of land, but can be made for services of any kind. Wages, salaries, interest, and profits all include an element of rent. The essential factor involved is that the services in question will be forthcoming whether or not the surplus is paid over to the provider of them; in technical terms, the supply is inelastic. Land is the most obvious case of this, but by no means the only case.

Supposing that film-stars are in great demand, and scarce, they will be paid very highly. If it happened to be the case that those with these rare gifts had no other abilities, so that, if there were no demand for film-stars, these people would only be able to earn a very low wage, then there is no need to pay them more than a very small margin above this low wage in order to attract them into the film industry. Any excess that they earn in fact over and above this small margin could be taxed away without there being any drying-up of the supply of talent to film-making. Is it not true that there is an element of this in payments to many people? Are there not many university professors whose alternative opportunities for earning money would be considerably less than their present salaries?

It should be clear by now that, though rents are to be found everywhere in the economic system, it is not easy to tax them away, though to do so would do no harm to anyone. Simple proposals for land-taxes fail to discriminate between rents in the economic sense and other payments to landowners. Nor is it possible, except perhaps in a few special cases, to discover classes of payment which are wholly rent. Even if all the members of a group receive rents, such as our film-stars above, it is not easy to discover the magnitude of the rent element involved. In practice, the rent element differs from individual to individual. Science and engineering professors have to be paid highly, so it is asserted, to attract them away from industry; clearly professors of Latin and Greek do not have the same opportunities of economic advancement. But even so, the marginal professor of Latin may perhaps be a man who could earn a high salary elsewhere, and who has to be persuaded to enter the academic rat-race, so that there is no element of rent in his salary, even if his colleagues earn far more than is necessary to keep them in the game. All that we can say is that rents are to be found throughout the economic system, and many, if not all, earnings involve a rent element. In principle, rents come by luck rather than good management; and their removal leaves the situation no different from what it was. But, in practice, we cannot disentangle them from other payments.

(*b*) *Interest*. Let us now turn to interest. Interest does perform a function in the economic system, in the sense that, if it were taxed away, the system would be different. To say that someone, or come activity, performs a function, merely asserts that the situation would be different if the activity were not carried out; it does not assert that any important or morally valid end is being achieved. Thus to say that interest payments serve a function does not necessarily assert that they serve a morally desirable end. This remains to be discussed. But before doing so we must clear away the confusion which has often resulted from Christian moralists who have condemned interest on moral grounds, but implicitly assumed that, because it serves no morally justifiable purpose, it also performs no function, and that therefore its removal would leave the economic situation unchanged. This is true of pure economic rent, but not of interest.

What function, then, does interest perform? Modern theories would assert that interest as a payment for a service performs two rather different functions. First, interest payments are inducements to save rather than spend our incomes. It is not, however, clear that anything very definite can be said about this inducement. Its necessity varies in different societies and from person to person. It is possible that in certain circumstances (such as when a person wants to save a definite income for retirement) high interest rates will lead to less savings than low rates. It is clear that savings are affected by many other things than interest rates, and probably many of these (e.g. incomes, social habits, social provisions for old age, etc.) are far more important. To some extent, however, in some circumstances, for some people or institutions, interest rates will affect savings, though one can be sceptical about the importance of this effect.

Secondly, whatever may be the case with savings, interest is a payment for not keeping wealth in the form of money. Once a man has some wealth, whether inherited, saved from his income, or borrowed, he has a choice between buying some kind of asset which will produce a stream of income, on the one hand, and keeping his wealth in the form of money, on the other. The other kinds of asset he can buy can vary from a savings certificate or a Treasury Bill to ordinary shares, land, or a house; but, whether they are physical assets or pieces of paper which represent debts of one kind or another, all these assets have one thing in common, that they cannot be changed into money immediately without inconvenience or risk of loss. Some can be sold immediately, but a capital loss may be incurred; others may involve no capital loss, but may only be saleable after delays of one kind or another. To the extent that there is no risk of money loss, and no delay in selling, the asset is more like money. But money is unique, and people are ready to pay a price to possess it, because only money can be used for ordinary payments (this is indeed what is meant by money). Interest is then paid in the last resort because the possession of money brings advantages that no other asset can provide.

It is perhaps clear, now, why moralists have fulminated against interest payments in the past. It is perhaps obvious to any sensitive moralist that there is little moral justification for large payments being made because people would not otherwise save, or in order to persuade them to part with money. This is the more clear when it is realized that most fortunes are not the result of saving, but the result of inheritance. Money breeds money, and not only because money marries money, but also because the possession of money enables a man to put himself in a position where he can earn a larger income than others. Inherited wealth therefore encourages the enlargement of fortunes, even if from the human point of view it encourages the dissipation of what the hard work of others has earned. The point remains, however, that the necessity to pay interest to encourage saving, if it exists, does not seem to have a great moral appeal, at least in rich industrialized countries. (In countries desperately short of savings, and struggling to develop their resources, high interest rates might, however, seem a very justifiable payment, if they did effectively encourage savings.)

Again, there does not seem strong moral justification for the payment of interest merely because of the inconvenience of parting with money.

So far we have dealt with interest as a payment for a service. An explanation of why interest has to be paid does not explain why anyone is ready to pay it. We cannot fully explain interest without looking at the demand side as well as the supply side. Firstly, corresponding to the payment for the inconvenience of parting with money is the convenience of having money for purposes such as paying creditors who threaten, spending more than one earns, or merely smoothing out the irregularities of receipts and payments that can be troublesome to all of us, as well as to the Exchequer at the national level. In practice, it is probable that it is not the rate of interest that checks such demands so much as the rationing that most credit institutions practice according to the good standing of the customer. It may therefore not be very important to have an interest rate to perform this function.

But the second function that an interest-rate performs on the demand side is more important, and it corresponds to the provision of savings on the supply side. People want to borrow money in order to invest in capital goods which will produce a future stream of income. The rate of interest here acts as sieve through which we filter the various schemes. It is to the public interest that the most productive schemes should be embarked upon before the less productive. The rate of interest can be regarded here as the price of time, reflecting our preference for present benefits rather than future enjoyments. There are times when the sacrifice of present benefits is small, and it is right then to embark upon schemes with a long horizon of advantage and small immediate enjoyment, such as will be stimulated by a low rate of interest. The most obvious examples of these are housing schemes (houses are built to last for at least sixty years), and public utilities such as power stations, docks, roads and bridges. On the other hand, if time is pressing, and there is great demand for present benefits, a high rate of interest will give preference to those investment schemes which will yield more immediate returns over those whose benefits only accrue after a long period.

Clearly, this method of rationing according to society's preferences for present over future enjoyments provides for a rational use of our resources, in so far as we can foresee the future at all. We do not yet live, in spite of some optimistic forecasts of some economists in a utopian mood, in a world where there is no gain to be achieved by employing capital instruments to provide for a larger stream of income in the future. Nor do we possess unlimited resources to devote to future benefits. We need some system of deciding priorities, and the rate of interest provides such a system.

Let us now ask how far it would be possible to perform these various functions of the rate of interest in some other way, so that we can then ask whether we want them to be performed at all.

There is no difficulty in reducing the rate of interest, at least to a certain point, though there may be a minimum below which it is normally difficult to go. Up to this point, the monetary authority can produce the required effect by increasing the supply of money. There being plenty of money about, the inconvenience of parting with it is reduced, and there is no need to provide for this function at a higher than the minimum rate. But the minimum may be more than seems justifiable on moral grounds.

As for the function of rationing investment schemes, it is certainly possible to achieve some of these aims by means of direct rationing of funds, and, in a centrally controlled economy, each investment scheme would be directly planned. But even so, if no criterion of return on capital is employed, irrational results will come about, as we can see from experience of the nationalized industries, whose investment schemes have only to a limited extent been subject to such a criterion. Even if no interest is paid, or if it is only paid to the government, a theoretical rate is still necessary for rational investment planning.

In an economy with a private sector, working under relative freedom, however necessary it may be to control overall investment programmes in other ways, it is difficult to see how it is possible to do without a rate of interest. In practice, the importance of monetary policy, which operates on the rate of interest and the supply of money, under the control of the Treasury and the Bank of England, may be overestimated, and it may be used where other means of control may be more effective—this is a matter of dispute among economists, and there is no need to go into it here.[3] But as long as there remains a private sector, some use should be made of monetary policy for control of investment and of the economy.

Furthermore, in so far as credit is freely available in the market, the liquidity function of interest will remain. This is not merely some freak of a private enterprise economy, or some wicked distortion of the natural order by money-lenders and avaricious merchants. It results from the simple fact that a complex economy requires money, that the possession of money provides convenience, and that there will always be some people ready to lend money temporarily to others in exchange for promises to pay, or debts of some sort or other. It is

[3] See the *Report of the Committee on the Working of the Monetary System* (Radcliffe Committee) (Cmnd. 827, 1959).

difficult to see how all these transactions can be prevented, even in a centrally controlled economy, though it might be possible under suitable circumstances. But it is fairly obvious that they cannot be prevented in any sort of economy with a free sector, where people run their own shops and farms, and borrow money to buy their own houses—without at all considering the question of large-scale industry.

I conclude therefore that the rate of interest performs a necessary function in the sort of economy we have today, both in making it possible for people to borrow and in giving some degree of rationality to investment decisions. If necessary, then moral, but not necessarily of a very high degree of morality. It is not surprising that moralists have waxed indignant about the alleged sacrifices involved in parting with savings, or other attempts to elevate a humble and necessary part of the economic system into a noble service. Indirectly no doubt humanity is benefited, which is what is meant by saying the function is necessary; but there is little of the benefactor in the man who lends his money at the going rate.

It is therefore natural that society has thought fit to make a distinction between earned and unearned income and to tax the latter more heavily. It is natural that we should try to reduce the rate of interest to the lowest possible level, and to prevent high incomes being earned from the mere power of lending money. Financial institutions of all sorts, from banks to building-societies, need to be closely watched, but we do not need to wax too indignant about them, as long as they perform their functions cheaply and efficiently.

We may perhaps even dream of a society where there will be no interest payments; some day it may be possible. Two points, however, require notice, before we embrace it enthusiastically. First, there is the old Whig argument that requires attention, that the possession of unearned income gives a man some security against his employers, the more important in a world where employers may be powerful government bodies. This is hardly a strong argument for a great concentration of wealth in a few hands, but might look different, if we could envisage a society where unearned income was really more or less equally divided.

Secondly, unearned income accrues to institutions of all sorts from charities and universities to churches. Without interest and similar payments, such institutions would depend entirely on current contributions either from individuals or from the State. It may be that this can be fairly easily achieved nowadays, without undue interference, as the University Grants Committee has shown. But for churches it is another matter, and the Church of England would not find life easy, as things are at the moment, if it had to depend on current contributions. Some may deplore the successful Stock Exchange activities of the Church Commissioners. If my line of argument is followed, there is no need to deplore it. Positively, the point may be made that churches, like universities, are institutions that have a long time horizon, and should rightly act as inheritors of the past as well as treasurers for the future generations whom we may be tempted to ignore in our short-sighted concern with the immediate present. If they are to perform this function, their income should be suitably adapted to it, and unearned income has the appropriate characteristic of linking past and future. To live on interest is perhaps as appropriate in its humble way as to live on the prayers of the saints of past ages. It is not obvious that to be footloose of the past is any more proper in the case of income for a church than it is in the case of more spiritual matters.

(*c*) *Profits*. In what we have said about rent and interest, a good deal has already been said implicitly about profits. In essence profits are a surplus of revenue over costs, accruing to those in a position to employ capital in productive undertakings. But this surplus varies enormously according to the type of enterprise and the method of its financing and control. At one extreme is the small farmer borrowing from the bank, with little capital of his own, whose profits represent a very meagre income, perhaps less than he could in fact earn in some capacity as an employee. At the other extreme there is the large public company, controlled by a small group of expert directors, obtaining their capital partly from their own undistributed profits, partly from loans, and partly from a mass of ordinary shareholders who have little effective say in the running of their business, except through the negative check of their operations on the stock exchange, which alter the price of the company's shares.

Speaking functionally, profits may and usually will include an element of management salary, an element of interest on capital, an element of economic rent (whether natural, or due to monopolistic positions of one kind or another), and an element of what may be called pure profit. To distil the element of pure profit from the total may however be a somewhat academic exercise. To speculate further as to whether pure profit is ever positive (and there is a strong case for saying that it is negative) is perhaps even more academic. Profits in effect include all these elements.

I have argued that simple moral justifications for incomes are not to be found, and that all incomes include an element of rent or surplus, which might from another point of view equally well be regarded as profits. The essential thing that makes profit incomes, normally so called, differ from other forms of income is that they accrue from some element of capital ownership associated with the taking of risky decisions.

I do not want to go into great length about the conditions of enterprise.[4] The function of risk-taking, the function that is of being an entrepreneur or a business-man, is a function that has to be carried out somehow or other in every modern economic system. Equally, profit-and-loss as an accounting system has to be used in any rational economic system to measure results; in particular, to measure whether consumers' wants are being met or not. It is the necessity to make such a surplus that keeps the particular units of our economy in tune with the needs of the whole, and this applies to the nationalized industries as much as to private enterprise. It may be that the spur of private profit, as it works, very differently, in different forms of enterprise—such as a small farm and a large company like Unilever—is necessary to keep the system moving forward with proper enterprise. It may be that this is not essentially so. But it is the way it works at the moment.

The questions that trouble moralists arise when these profits accrue to individuals. There are problems about motives, and problems about unfair distribution of the gains, and these two have often become confused.

As far as individual motives are concerned, profits enter into most men's considerations; they are a clear factor in any form of piece-work pay, and there are few men who do not work harder sometimes for more pay. It is fairly clear that a wise economic system allows for

[4] Partly because I have discussed some of these matters elsewhere in Chapter 10 of *Christianity and Economic Problems.*

appeal to motives both base and idealistic, without laying too much stress on either. We should not therefore be too sweeping in our condemnation of the profit-motive as such.

We can however ask whether industry's use of the profit motive does not so much distort the ethos and feeling of society as to lay an altogether excessive emphasis on money-making and profits. This has in fact been the burden of much Christian complaint about the capitalist system. It is a point that requires much attention. But a proper answer is not to be given by an assumption that the activities which are encouraged by profit-making are *ipso facto* against the public interest. Much if not all of the moral indignation aroused in the past was because it could be shown that profit-making led to anti-social activities; but equally many of these activities could have been stopped by deliberate action designed to limit abuses. Some of them have already been stopped, others may well be in the future. I would personally be prepared to argue that, in a suitably controlled private sector, profits will by and large serve as indicators of the public interest, and not conflict with them. This implies stern action against monopolists, and strict control in sectors where taste and public opinion are in question, as I have already argued. But for the rest, given the right amount of control, profits will generally be earned where people want to spend their money, and this freedom has itself much to commend it. This still leaves open, however, the question whether the system encourages too great concentration on profits and money, as contrasted for example with a proper concern for enterprise and a full awareness of consumer wants. But this case must not be made in such a way as to imply that most business-men are more profit-seekers than other men (which is hardly true), or that they are not also motivated by ambition, loyalty to the company or group, desire for prestige and power, and all the other motives that move most men. Business-men are in fact sometimes more dangerous to the public interest when they allow these more fair-seeming motives to dominate their actions, rather than a strict attention to the profit-and-loss account.[5]

The second set of problems about profits arises because of their unfair distribution. As the most important form of wealth in the modern world, their distribution is most important. By and large all forms of

[5] For all this, see Appendix C.

capital are less fairly distributed than are incomes; and, of the various forms of capital, ordinary shares are about the most unequally distributed. Ordinary shares are by and large owned by rich men, when they are not owned by institutions, and the large number of particular shareholdings in any large company is not in contradiction to this, as ordinary share-holders naturally do not hold large blocks of shares in one company, but spread their risks.

If we believe in equality, it is clear that we should try to spread ownership of capital as well as income, and, if we want to equalize ownership of capital, we should make serious attempts to widen the ownership of ordinary shares. If we really meant business about this, we could clearly go a long way. Nor should we regard it as sullying our hands with something unclean, as ordinary shares are all too often assumed to be. In essence, this is the only way in which the ordinary man can own the machines and factories which turn out the riches from which we all benefit. If there is to be a private sector, and there is a strong case for it to be flourishing and enterprising, however large we want it to be, it is reasonable that the ordinary man should have a share in it. He can indeed have this share indirectly in the form of a nationalized industry, or through state ownership of ordinary shares; but he can perhaps more obviously be made aware of what is involved by himself becoming directly an owner of shares, and partaker of the risks (and the profits and losses) involved. It would not however meet this demand for certain forms of property, such as houses, or government shares, to be left to small men, while a few rich men still obtained the dividends from ordinary shares. It requires a massive redistribution of capital from the few who are rich to the many. This is something we have never seen attempted on any scale at all, and which might prove more revolutionary than the redistribution of income we have achieved through income tax in the last fifty or so years.

4. CONCLUSIONS

I have argued that there is no moral criterion applicable to the distribution of incomes that is simple and universally valid. I have argued that we may get some of our income from the effort we put forth, even if one man's effort is another's leisure; that something comes to us because society has to arrange things that way in order to get the work done; and that a good deal also comes purely as a result of luck of one kind or another. To recognize that we are all profit receivers in this sense is not to justify every form of income, however apparently unjust and unnecessary it is. It should rather make us all sensitive to the rich bounty of God in giving to us so plentifully and so undeservedly. So with the parable of the labourers in the vineyard. The first lesson of this parable may well be that the Kingdom of Heaven is not like the economic arrangements that are necessary in this world where men are paid according to their contribution by the piece. But the second lesson may be to make us look again at the overwhelming bountifulness of God in showering on us the wealth of an abundant world.

In dealing with the distribution of income in practice, we have to balance possibilities with opportunities. Any pattern of income distribution has to meet certain practical facts. It has to allow for the economic claims of incentives; it has to allow for accepted differentials and traditional standards—up to a point. It has to be such as not to act perversely in relation to the flexibility required in any advanced economic system, but rather to encourage development where it is needed. It has to meet 'needs' (vague as these are) as well as purely economic requirements. It has, roughly, to satisfy what people think to be fair. But it will never be absolutely fair; there is no criterion of fairness that is unequivocal, except that of equality, which in its absolute form is almost certainly impractical. Personally, I would argue for a much greater degree of equality than exists even in the more egalitarian communities of western Europe, and I believe that this is a Christian standard we should use to measure our evasions in practice. But there will be such evasions, and to pay due recognition to accepted traditional standards of status and reward is not the same as to justify them. From the Christian point of view what is so obvious is how insubstantial is their foundation, not how unimportant they are in fact.

A prophetic witness that pointed out the impossibility of any absolutely fair distribution of income, and stressed the overwhelming element of 'luck' or sheer divine bounty, as well as recognizing the perversity in all of us (Christians and others equally) that requires some incentive in monetary terms (or other equally debased currency) to stir us to do our best—such a prophetic witness would help to undercut some of the bitterness that arises in disputes about these matters, and which runs through many political and social differences. In practice, each group not merely grabs what it can, but tries to justify itself. It has rights, it claims, to its income (inherited property), it is performing a vital social service (farming), it is a necessary payment to bring society the benefit of its special gifts (profits to enterprise, high incomes for professional people), it is paid less than other equivalent workers (any trade union)—and so the righteous claims mount. They are all unanswerable, and usually more or less equally unsound. Only the very rich and the very poor can afford to be honest and say that they want what they want and will keep what they have. In between, the richer a group the more sanctimonious it tends to be about its claims (trade unions are perhaps more forthright than business leaders and professional people). But once everyone stopped playing the sympathy game and settled down to bargain honestly without self-righteousness, it might be surprising how much we could agree. We are all crooks in the last resort, and not least those who write about the game.[6]

Of course there are times when relatively clear cases of justice arise for the Christian conscience in deciding between income claims, and, at any given time, some criteria can be used to help decide the issue. Economic forces decide at other times. There is always the claim of equality to be met.

May I repeat that nothing that I have said in any way mitigates to my mind the clear claim of equality. This claim arises both from the Christian stress on the uniqueness and equal worth of every man before God and also from the demands of community, which would lead us to break down any artificial barriers between men. If we take this claim seriously, we will be greatly concerned with what more can be done in our tax system about such matters as capital ownership, capital

[6] This is very relevant to the strictures often passed on gambling by church people. It makes nonsense of the kind of criticism illustrated by a speech of the Archbishop of Canterbury reported in *The Times* (20 November, 1959), in which he said: 'When the whole existence of the welfare state requires of its citizens that they should have a true understanding of the relationship between money on the one hand and the earning of money on the other by services rendered and honest work done and responsibilities fulfilled, it is a great disservice to public morals to encourage the belief that money is to be distributed by luck or pure chance or some kind of favour'. If the Archbishop is right, then his criteria imply a more devastating attack on the way in which in fact incomes are earned and distributed in Britain today than he has ever given evidence of wanting to make in contexts other than that of gambling.

gains, the possibility of an expenditure tax and other methods by which real incomes might be more equally distributed. But, above all, if we could take what we receive with gratitude for the divine bounty, we might be spared much heartsearching.

Chapter 5

SHARING THE WORLD'S WEALTH

'For God gave never a gift, but he sent occasion, at one time or another, to shew it to God's glory. As, if he sent riches, he sendeth poor men to be helped with it. But now must men occupy their goods otherwise. They will not look on the poor; they must help their children, and purchase them more land than ever their grandfathers had before them. But I shall tell you what Christ said: "He that loveth his child better than me, is not worthy to be my disciple." I cannot see how ye shall stand before God at the latter day, when this sentence shall be laid against you.'—BISHOP LATIMER, 1549.

'Even today . . . there remains a vast discrepancy between the monotony of peasant existence and the excitement of city life. A still greater gulf divided the peasant from the townsman of antiquity. So glaring was the inequality between them that, if we are to believe the learned historian Rostovtzeff, it pitted the one against the other in a fierce and silent struggle which pierced the dyke that protected the privileged classes from the barbarian flood. The peasant pariah abetted the invading barbarian.'—JÉRÔME CARCOPINO.

THE most important fact in the world today is the revolution that is taking place in the 'Areas of Rapid Social Change in Asia, Africa and Latin America', as they are entitled in the World Council of Churches' study programme.[1] A gigantic political,

[1] These countries are often called 'under-developed', which has become the official United Nations designation, generally used by economists and others. I shall continue to use it for this reason. Names do not matter, and any title is open to objection. In a very obvious sense, the U.S.A. is both the most under-developed country in the world and the area of most rapid social change, and after the United States would come many of the most highly-developed countries. To use the words 'poor' (or 'low-income'), or 'stagnant', which more nearly correspond to the realities, many find objectionable, as they do the word 'under-developed'. To call Indian or Arabic civilization 'under-developed' clearly shows a high degree of Western-centred bias. A Christian, who observes that most of the terrible evils of the modern world arise from 'Western' civilization, can hardly be happy about such an assumption. To add the adjectives 'technical' or 'economic' merely makes the phrase cumbersome. But in using the phrase 'under-developed' it should be realized that it is used in the economic sense, as far as possible without prejudice.

For more discussion of these questions see:

(I) Department on Church and Society, World Council of Churches, Geneva—(*a*) State-social, and economic revolution is taking place in many areas formerly stagnant in age-old poverty and bound by the traditions of ancient religions and of hierarchical social structures. (In other countries such revolutions are *not* taking place, but are badly needed, and will probably break out in the near future.) It is the West that has brought about this revolution, as a result of the impact of its progressive economy, its colonial infiltrations and, more important, its ideals and ideologies.

That these countries want poverty to be abolished, and quickly, without an appreciation of the difficulties, is due to the example of the West. That they want an end of 'colonialism' and 'imperialism', that they ask for 'self-determination' and the overthrow of traditional hierarchies and rulers, is due to the ideals of the West. That many of them react against the best the West has to offer them and prefer to turn back to primitive tribalisms and militant forms of age-old religions is due to the arrogance of the West and its failure to distinguish between the various gifts it had to offer. That social and economic disintegration has often followed the impact of the West's economy has been due to the fact that we rarely developed those countries for which we were responsible with a view to their needs as a whole, but allowed little enclaves to expand rapidly, where it suited the needs of the West and where Western entrepreneurs found it easiest to make their profits.[2] Only the poverty of these countries is not our responsibility, though

ments of the World Council of Churches on Social Questions (1956). (*b*) The Common Christian Responsibility towards Areas of Rapid Social Change (First Statement, September, 1955. Second Statement, October, 1956). (*c*) The Specific European Responsibilities in Relation to Africa and Asia: Report from a European Ecumenical Consultation, Odense, Denmark, 8-11 August, 1958. (*d*) Dilemmas and Opportunities; Christian Action in Rapid Social Change (Report of Conference at Thessalonica, 25 July to 2 August, 1959).

(2) An Open Letter to British Baptists, concerning their responsibility towards Areas of Rapid Social Change (May 1956, Carey Kingsgate Press Ltd., London).

(3) Scottish Churches' Ecumenical Association, 1957. John Sleeman, *Can we afford it?*

(4) *The Family in Contemporary Society: the report of a group convened at the behest of the Archbishop of Canterbury with appended reports from the U.S.A., Canada, and India* (S.P.C.K., 1958), especially Report, Chapters 3 and 6, and Appendix I, Chapters 8 (3)-(4), and 9.

(5) Sir Charles Snow, *The Two Cultures and the Scientific Revolution* (1959 Rede Lecture, C.U.P.).

[2] The first Colonial Development Act passed in 1929 was restricted to aid for agriculture and industry 'thereby promoting commerce with and industry in the United Kingdom'. The first aid given purely for development and welfare purposes was passed under stress of war in 1940. (See *Colonial Development and Welfare Acts*, Cmnd. 672, 1959, para. 5.)

it is that for which the West is often blamed. What has come from the West is the refusal to put up with poverty.

The claims of these countries are often laid before us in terms of charitable giving to the poor. This is a worthy appeal, but it is not enough, and by itself it is dangerous. It is dangerous because it is an appeal that stresses the relationship of giver and recipient, and tends to perpetuate it. It tends to keep the giver in the picture, whereas the best thing that could happen would be if the western countries could fade out of the picture—because they were no longer the sole repositories of wealth, wisdom and spiritual insight. It is only our arrogance that permits us to believe that this is so at the moment. But it is true that the West has, by and large, a monopoly of technical achievement, and immeasurably greater wealth. When the wealth is more evenly spread throughout the world, and the technical achievement generally diffused—if this situation ever comes about—then the other, and perhaps more fundamental, achievements of the different parts of mankind will appear more obviously in all their richness and variety. Only then will the West have accomplished its real mission, and if the wiser civilizations of the East, or of Africa, can then look back in amused contempt on the brash pushfulness of Europe, it should be a matter of pride for Europeans. Far more tragic would be the outcome if it were to result in pallid imitations of Western ways of life transplanted to alien cultures.

Giving to the poor is not enough, because the problem is not merely one of poverty, but of becoming partners in developing the resources of the world for the good of all, partners in the awakening of the masses of mankind to their full human heritage, partners in helping others to discover for themselves some of the lessons we think we have learnt in our history. The most dreadful thing that has happened in the last few years has been the revelation of the complete failure of our responsible Ministers to understand what is happening in the world today, and to be sensitive to the real growing-points of history. It is this insensitiveness that has revealed itself so painfully in our policies in Cyprus, the Middle East and Central Africa.

But cash is still needed, if cash alone is not enough. But, if the sympathy and understanding are not there, it is unlikely that the cash will be. Our first need is simply to make people aware of what is happening in the world. Perhaps above all the labour movement needs to be really sensitive to the simple fact that others in remote countries are demanding what they themselves fought for years ago; only today it is the workers in the rich countries that seem to be one of the main barriers to the growth of international sharing. This is a hard saying, and it is only partly true, but it is when we turn to the matter of hard cash that our sympathy is truly tested. It is not disputed that the labour movement is more aware of the needs of the underdeveloped countries than many other sections of the community, or that the Labour Party has formulated impressive schemes for aid to these countries. What is in doubt is whether the true cost in terms of the future standard of living of everybody in Britain has been counted and fairly put before the interested parties, the ordinary people who will have to foot the bill.

(*a*) But, first, we need to understand. There are two extremes to avoid, the 'realist' yearning for a past when Britain had a power and prestige in the world she no longer enjoys, and the 'idealist' assumption that self-interest can be ignored and that what we need is only to 'help' the poorer countries of the world. We live in a world where we are no longer able to impose our will, and this is as true of the Americans as of the British; but equally in a world where our 'help' is not all that is required. The welfare state involves the assumption that everybody has, as a right, a basic minimum standard of living, and the former dependence on 'help' from the rich is rejected as degrading. We are moving into a 'welfare world', where the people of Asia, Africa and Latin America are demanding, as a 'right', what we are beginning, very slowly, to recognize as a kind of 'help' we can graciously give.[3] It is not that the rich are not required to put their hands into their pockets, but they are required to pay in the form of taxation (i.e. help through the United Nations, the World Bank, the Colombo Plan), and not in 'charity' (i.e. surplus food donated by the United States). It is because we misunderstand the strength and persistence of the forces involved that we make this elementary mistake.

[3] The phrase 'welfare world' is used in Gunnar Myrdal's book, *An International Economy* (1956) (p. 324). This is an impassioned plea for a rational assessment of the problems of the under-developed countries, which summarizes many complex social, political and economic trends. It is pessimistic about the prospects of adequate understanding in the West. 'It is aid given by a single government I feel apprehensive about; . . . power must demoralize aid. The world cannot be run as a company town' (pp. 329-30).

It is certainly true that the revolutionary situation in the world involves many pretentious claims by the more unstable countries, and much foolish politics which the wisdom of the West has often, if not always, learnt to abandon. Because we sympathize with the desperate condition of the Egyptian fellahin, and understand something of the reaction of Arabs to the intrusions of the West that lead to exacerbated nationalisms, we are not required to agree with all the actions of Colonel Nasser, or to do other than regret the folly of the Arab world in refusing to come to terms with Israel. But it is not necessary to react from a simple sentimentality towards a political impatience and concentration on short-run interests that the political experience of the West has learnt to eschew in other fields.[4] It was not in this way that the transference of political and economic power to the people took place in the West, nor need it be so in the international field. The West should be mature enough to realize that the froth on the surface of a revolution is the least important part of it.

Professor George Kennan recently expounded a more subtle form of the 'realist' thesis that we should only consider our self-interest and refuse responsibility for the revolution taking place in the world. In so far as he is attacking the thesis that economic aid from the West will buy the friendship of the rest of the world, he is right to denounce what is perhaps a particularly American delusion. But he went further in his Reith Lecture when he asserted:[5]

I must also reject the suggestion that our generation in the West has some sort of a cosmic guilt or obligation vis-à-vis the under-developed parts of the world. The fact that certain portions of the globe were developed sooner than others is one for which I, as an American of this day, cannot accept the faintest moral responsibility; nor do I see that it was particularly the fault of my American ancestors. I cannot even see that the phenomenon of colonialism was one which could be regarded as having given rise to any such state of obligation. The establishment of the colonial relationship did not represent a moral action on somebody's part; it represented a natural and inevitable response to certain demands and stimuli of the age. It was simply a stage of history. It generally took place with the agreement and connivance of people at the colonial end as well as in the mother-country.

This argument is an interesting example of the historicist thesis that

[4] This is surely the lesson of the Suez débacle.

[5] G. Kennan, *Russia, the Atom, and the West* (London, 1958), pp. 76 ff.

Karl Popper has so rightly denounced, as both false to the facts and dangerous as a guide to action. No behaviour-patterns are 'simply a stage of history'; they are, perhaps unfortunately, always conceived as 'moral actions'. Just as the moral ideals that were enshrined in the American Constitution are not merely part of a stage of past history, but living forces affecting the behaviour of American politicians, so the moral ideals that were associated with colonialism both in the West and in other countries are active in the world today. But more serious than the denial of the existence of moral forces operative in men's minds is the placid assumption that we can ignore the links that bind us to other people because they do not involve any direct moral obligations. Kennan's remarks read strangely like the responses of the British aristocracy in the early nineteenth century to the extravagent claims of the industrial proletariat. As in their case too, it seems probable that the rich have the better of the argument. But this is to ignore the simple fact that, whatever the moral obligations of each, both do live in the same world, and that the rich cannot permanently be happy in a world of poverty. It was this fact of the solidarity of the human race that was the key message of the Christian Socialists, and the centre of the theology of F. D. Maurice. That we are one world is a theological fact, but one which has considerable sociological significance. Professor Kennan's attitude has its theological parallel in the concentration of the Evangelical movement on individual salvation, which, combined with a narrow doctrine of providence, satisfactorily salvaged the consciences of many upper-class Englishmen in the early nineteenth century. As then Maurice fought for the recognition of the fact of a cosmic redemption, so today we can see that the world is sociologically one.

In fact, Kennan would not deny much of this. He went on to say:

I can well understand that there are instances in which it will be desirable for us from time to time to support schemes of economic development which are soundly conceived and which give promise, over the long-run, of yielding greater stability and a new hopefulness for the countries concerned. I trust that we will not let such demands go unanswered when they arise. There is no fonder hope in the American breast, my own included, than that the experience we have had in developing a continent will prove relevant and helpful to others. . . . If there is a general impression in the recipient countries that this aid represents the paying of some sort of a debt from us to them, then the extension of it can only sow confusion. . . . Any form of benevolence, if prolonged for any length of time (even in personal life this is true), comes to be taken for granted as a right and its withdrawal resented as an injury.

Much of this is the highest wisdom. But it is not obvious why we should not look forward to a world in which the poorer countries should regard assistance from the rich as a right and a debt due to them, in the same way as the old and sick regard social insurance payments as a right, and a country such as Britain regards it as a natural part of national policy to give special aid to such relatively unfavoured regions as the Highlands of Scotland. Professor Kennan has to put on a hard face of realism, which he obviously finds embarrassing, precisely because he starts from the premise that any help from the West is a form of benevolence and that a rich country has a natural right to enjoy its riches, in the same way as the rich formerly used to regard what incomes they had inherited or earned as some natural gift to them personally by a beneficent providence, aided by their own (or their ancestors') hard work and merit. Nowadays we tend to regard the nation's wealth as a pool to which past and present members of society have contributed in shares which cannot be calculated, and from which people draw according to socially acceptable rules. This is a doctrine that accords more closely with the traditional Christian attitude to property, and it applies equally to the world as a whole. The riches of the world are the joint inheritance of mankind, and all men are involved together in the complex endeavour we call civilization.[6]

(*b*) If our first response to the world revolution must be a sympathetic attempt to understand what is happening, our second concern must be with the technical aid we can give in various ways to countries requiring it. The obligation of technical aid is well recognized, even if the challenge to the Christian conscience that is involved has not always met with an adequate response in the form of volunteers of the right sort.

(*c*) There is a third and more complex requirement. Britain depends on the import of food and raw materials for which we pay by means of exports of manufactured goods and services. The poorer countries of the world are among the main body of producers of the primary

[6] See Appendix B.

commodities, which we import, and they are among the major customers for our industrial products. The terms on which we trade with them (the relative prices of our exports and imports) are as vital to them, in so far as they may be dependent on the sales of a few commodities (whose prices may fluctuate much more seriously than even the general run of commodity prices, themselves more unstable than the prices of manufactured products), and also on sales to a limited number of markets, which may be subject to considerable changes. Traditionally, and in the main rightly, Britain has been concerned with cheap imports, in so far as the cost of imports is a major factor affecting the standard of living of the British people, and particularly the poorer classes in the community. But cheap imports can often be bought at the cost of ruining our customers and narrowing the markets for our exports, as happened in the thirties. It is a long-run British interest to ensure that the prices of primary products are relatively stable. If the cost of such a policy were to maintain the prices of our imports somewhat above what they otherwise might be, this would be a small price to pay for keeping our customers prosperous. It is a cheaper way of helping the under-developed countries than the kind of salvage operations required when markets have collapsed and development schemes are in ruins.

The dangers of a situation where the primary producing countries lose export income, as a result of stagnating production in the industrial countries, were highlighted by a letter to *The Times* of 29 October 1957 from a most distinguished collection of Oxford and Cambridge economists, of extremely varied political and social backgrounds.

An increasing supply of primary products, resulting from investment several years ago, is being confronted by a stagnant demand from the industrial nations; for manufacturing production has been virtually stationary in both the United States and the United Kingdom for nearly two years. There is now, moreover, a distinct danger that it will decline in the months ahead and that industrial production in many other countries will tend to level off as a result of the restrictive monetary policies being so widely pursued.

It is not always realized that a comparatively small fall in commodity prices is equivalent in its effects to a cut of billions of dollars in aid to under-developed countries. The western powers must not be surprised if, in the circumstances, such countries turn more and more to Russia as a potential trading partner; and the spectacle of industrial production stagnating in the West while it forges ahead in the East could create an unfortunate impression in those countries not firmly committed to either camp.[7]

Subsequent events may suggest that this letter was somewhat unduly pessimistic in the short-run, as recovery has taken place in the United States and elsewhere. But the question of principle remains, and the strains of 1957-8 may be repeated in later years.[8]

It is not suggested that schemes which may help to stabilize the prices of primary products are easy to formulate, without, for example, encouraging an excessive production of certain commodities. But, all too often, rich countries such as Britain have deliberately frustrated schemes of this kind, either because they hoped to be able to buy more cheaply outside them, or in order to bolster up the interests of their own farmers. Neither of these aims should be allowed to stand in the way of such schemes.[9] This is a principle which applies to a wide range of policy, where what we do has effects on other countries and cannot be treated merely as a British concern.

(*d*) When all has been said about the importance of these three ways of helping the under-developed countries, there still remains their glaring need for more capital for development. No doubt, they need to mobilize their own savings more effectively, and take steps to ensure that the rich devote their savings to productive investment and not merely to hoarding jewellery or to buying gold-plated Cadillacs or aircraft. But in most cases these sources of savings are quite inadequate; the exceptions are to be found in the rich oil areas of the Middle East. In most other areas, the countries are poor, and, if they are to be lifted significantly from stagnation, capital from outside is required. The original demand from the United Nations experts in 1951 for

[7] The letter was signed by Professor R. F. Kahn, Professor E. A. G. Robinson, Professor R. Stone, N. Kaldor, and W. B. Reddaway of Cambridge, and T. Balogh, F. A. Burchardt, Colin Clark, R. F. Harrod, E. F. Jackson, Sir Donald MacDougall, and G. D. N. Worswick of Oxford. On 30 October, Professor J. E. Meade of Cambridge wrote to *The Times* in support of this letter, and also of the proposal that 'the richer countries of the Atlantic community should make a grant of, say, 1 per cent. of their national incomes to an international fund for the economic development of the under-developed countries.'

[8] See *Colombo Plan: Seventh Annual Report of the Consultative Committee* (Cmnd. 610, December, 1958), Chapter 1, paras. 1-6, for the impact on South-East Asia; also *National Institute Economic Review*, September, 1959.

[9] Successful schemes actually in operation with consumer representation are the International Tin Council and the International Wheat Agreement, though the latter was long hampered by Britain's refusal of membership.

something like 2 per cent. of the national incomes of Western Europe, Australasia, the United States and Canada, or a total of about $7 billions a year (involving $3 billions, or 1 per cent. of national incomes, for inter-governmental grants) may have been incorrectly assessed.[10] A contribution of 1 per cent. means, in the case of Britain, something like £200 millions out of a total gross national product of some £20,000 millions. It is some such sum that we need to have in mind as a minimum in our thinking on the subject. It is indeed useless to throw capital away on ill-planned schemes of development in countries where there is no real political desire to improve the standard of living of the mass of people, or where the administration is incapable of coping with the problems. But the simple fact remains that there are plenty of countries, such as India, where there are, relatively speaking, well-planned development programmes, efficient administrations and the political desire to go ahead, which are held back by the lack of capital. It is the present refusal of the richer countries to consider these cases seriously enough that is one of the most tragic factors in the present stage of world history.

Suppose we decide to devote 1 per cent. of our national product for helping the under-developed countries; what does it mean? £200 millions is not a large sum; it is something rather more than 10 per cent. of our expenditure on defence, and about a third of what the health service costs. It is a very small sum in relation to the needs of the world, though it is considerably larger than our governmental contributions in the past few years.

There are, in simple terms, three problems for a country such as Britain:

(1) *Resources*. The resources are there, and the cuts in our standard of living would not be great, particularly when we remember that we should expect, with full use of our resources, to have an extra £500–£1,000 millions or more available every year as production rises. Nevertheless, £200–£300 millions is not a small sum, and it is often the last penny that hurts most. £200–£300 millions could do a great deal of slum clearance, road building, or improvement of our educa-

[10] *Measures for the Economic Development of Under-Developed Countries* (United Nations, 1951), pp. 79, 84. ('Billion' is here used in the American sense of 1,000 million, not the older British sense of 1,000,000 million.)

tional system, all things that need doing. It is not good enough to say that we can take it painlessly out of defence cuts. There may be a case for cutting defence, either on policy or strategic grounds, or because of waste; there is no case for linking discussion of foreign policy with help to aid these countries. As a socialist, I object most strongly to some of those Labour leaders who have been the strongest supporters of this kind of aid, but who have linked it with support of their brand of foreign and defence policy. Both may be true, but the case for foreign aid does not depend on being able to cut defence costs. This kind of complacency, which tries to sell good policies by pretending that they cost nothing, is not good enough for Christians.

(2) *Balance of Payments.* £200–£300 millions of aid means a surplus on our balance of payments to that extent. This has long been an aim of British economic policy, but it is not easy to achieve. If the aid we gave were always matched by purchases of British goods which would not otherwise be exported, there would be no special problem here, but this is hardly likely to be the case. We have then to face the need to sell even more exports, which is not likely to be easy. Over the last few years Britain has been running a surplus on her balance of payments. If we ignore the immediate post-war years 1946–7, when we were in a process of reconversion from war to peace, the only years in which we have run balance of payments deficits on current account have been 1951 and 1955. In the former, the deficit was £420 millions, and in the latter year £70 millions, but the 1951 deficit was offset by a surplus of £300 millions in 1950, and the 1955 deficit was less than half the surpluses in 1954 and 1956–8. From 1952 to 1958 the average annual surplus was about £210 millions, rising rapidly in the later years.[11] This figure is, of course, totally inadequate to Britain's needs. But it fell in 1959 to £140 millions, and to £35 millions in the first half of 1960.

[11] *United Kingdom Balance of Payments* 1946–1957 (H.M. Treasury, 1959), and half-yearly Balance of Payments White Papers (Cmnd. 700, April, 1959, and Cmnd. 1188, October, 1960). Later estimates have somewhat revised (downwards) some of the figures for the years up to 1958.

The above figures to some extent exaggerate the real surplus on current account, in so far as it is due to British effort, because of receipts of Defence Aid, etc., from the United States and Canada, offshore sales to U.S. Government, and U.S. and Canadian Forces' expenditure in the U.K. If these various items are deducted, the average annual surplus falls to about £60 millions, and the 1955 deficit rises to £235 millions; a deficit also appears in 1953 of £4 millions. What is a more reasonable figure to take is a matter of judgment, but it does not affect our general argument.

Our reserves are grossly insufficient even for our trading position, much more so in view of the fact that they represent the banking reserves of the whole sterling area. Britain has an urgent need to run a balance of payments surplus in order to build up adequate reserves, without which our whole position is likely to be endangered with every small swing in our day-to-day position, even though our basic situation may be sound. We are rather like a millionaire, who can never lay his hands on £50 to pay an unexpected bill, and who has given overdraft facilities to his relatives, which they can draw upon at any time, whereas he himself has no ready cash upon which he can draw.

If we are to help the under-developed countries adequately, it is obvious that this requires a continuous balance of payments surplus of something well over £300 millions a year. In theory, the mere cutting down of purchasing power at home to the required extent might free the resources, but it is not obvious that this will in practice be sufficient if we do not manage to sell enough exports. It may be that special measures to deal with our whole foreign position will be required. This is not the place to discuss them, but merely to point out the need for some such measures.

(3) *Taxation.* If aid is to be given by the British government in the form of grants, and probably also if it is to be a matter of inter-governmental loans, the sums must be matched by increases in taxation. The sums involved are not large, when we think of the £7,000-odd millions collected in taxes (including the national insurance contributions) in Britain in 1959. But to increase taxation is not easy, and must hurt someone. It is not good enough to say 'soak the rich', though personally, as I have suggested before, I believe that the rich could well be further taxed. Surtax only collected £180 millions in 1959/60, profits tax £260 millions, purchase tax about £500 millions. These figures give us an idea of the order of magnitude of the problem. Should the income-tax payer, who contributes about £2,300 millions, pay more? Or the motorist? Or should we increase purchase tax? Of course, the yield of these taxes rises with incomes, and, if government expenditure does not rise correspondingly, there is a margin to spare if tax rates are left at their existing level, and not reduced, as incomes rise. But the basic fact is that, in an inflationary world, where it is clear that personally and communally we have plenty of things we would

like to do with extra resources, if we want to help the rest of the world we must pay for it, and the payment must involve an extra burden on the man-in-the-street.

How much help has Britain actually given to the under-developed countries in recent years? To get the picture clear it is first necessary to distinguish the different forms of help. From the British point of view, and from the point of view of claims on our resources, which would otherwise be available for our own use, it does not matter whether the overseas country received aid in the form of loans or grants, repayment of debts due to them by us, or re-investment of profits earned by private companies abroad. All these involve resources being made available to others. One can distinguish between operations undertaken by private firms and individuals, and government activities.

(*a*) At the private level, resources are channelled abroad in various ways. Individuals can buy shares in businesses abroad, or they can invest in foreign government stock. Firms can use their resources to invest in their own companies abroad, or they can reinvest the profits they earn from these companies. In fact, these operations tend to be limited to particular industries and particular countries. Britain has invested in the oil areas, and otherwise mainly in the Commonwealth, the latter amounting to over £100 millions a year since 1952. A large part of this will have been in the highly developed countries of the Commonwealth, and much will have been rather particularly designed to meet the needs of the British consumer by developing rubber, copper, oil, etc. The contribution to economic development of the poorer countries will only be a part of the total.

(*b*) Secondly, there is the contribution that comes from the Government. This can take the form of grants or loans. We must also include the contribution that Britain has made in the post-war period by allowing countries such as India to use the debts we owed to them as a result of the war, the so-called 'sterling balances', to be spent on goods we could otherwise have used for ourselves. Britain came out of the war a debtor country in this sense on a large scale, and the mere fact of paying back our debts has been a considerable contribution to many poor countries, even though at the same time we have been borrowing from other poor countries.

Government loans and grants for economic development have been running at about £30 millions annually of recent years, if we exclude over £25 millions spent in areas suffering from economic disaster and 'threats to law and order', i.e. in fighting wars in Cyprus, Malaya, Kenya etc. Most of this went to the colonies, but it includes our contributions to the International Bank. On the other hand, if we look at the debt position over the whole post-war period, we have been net borrowers from abroad, loans coming, for example, from West Africa and Malaya and being spent by India and Pakistan. From 1945 to 1958 we borrowed £900 millions from the colonies, or about £70 millions per year.

If we add up the bill for the total claims on our resources, we find that we have in fact, in recent years, been contributing about 1¼ per cent. of our gross national product, or about £200 millions per year, to the Commonwealth in the form of investment and special help. But only £30 millions took the form of grants. Our conclusion is that the contribution that Britain has made to the development of the poorer areas of the Commonwealth has hardly been of an overwhelming nature in the post-war years, and, in so far as our contribution outside the Commonwealth has not been large, and has been deliberately kept low in view of our Commonwealth commitments, our overall performance has not been such as might have been expected from a country as rich as Britain. Though, in terms of resources, it more or less measures up to the 1 per cent. contribution, which has been frequently suggested, should not this be regarded as something of a minimum? It will also be seen that in terms of government contributions what has been done has been trifling.[12]

If we look as the problems of under-developed countries from their point of view, the division between the private and the public sector may not be the same as from the point of view of the aiding country. They need investment in private firms, which the private sector will

[12] *The United Kingdom's Role in Commonwealth Development* (Cmnd. 237, July 1957); *Assistance from the United Kingdom for Overseas Development* (Cmnd. 974, March 1960). The latter White Paper produces new estimates on a slightly different basis. It shows that aid is rising, though still not high. The estimate for 1959/60 is £100 millions from private sources, and £120 millions from government sources (about £40 millions of which are grants), only including funds going to under-developed countries, whether in the Commonwealth or outside. Adding in £20 millions going to South Africa and for " emergencies " in Malaya, Kenya and Cyprus, the total of £240 millions is about 1¼% of national income.

take account of. But a properly co-ordinated investment plan will not come about automatically through the market, and there will have to be a public investment programme both to fill the gaps left and also to provide those kinds of investment in roads, housing, education and social services which are never undertaken privately, but which, nevertheless, contribute to the growth of the national income. To meet these needs, their governments can to some extent borrow or tax locally. But they are likely to require help from abroad if a proper plan is to be carried out. They may be able to raise some money from private investors by floating loans on foreign markets; but this again will hardly meet all the need. Inter-governmental loans, whether from individual countries, or through the World Bank, can help much, but there may well remain a margin most suitably met by a pure grant, for which models exist both in the American Marshall Aid to Europe, and in the Colonial Development and Welfare Funds.

If help is to be given as required, and not merely according to the preconceptions of giving countries, we must look to this pattern of need in the developing countries. It is at this point that we need to challenge the policy of this country at this moment, and not only in terms of an inadequate total of aid.

Some of the factors in Government policy towards the under-developed countries were clearly revealed in the White Paper of July 1957 on Commonwealth Development.[13] While encouraging as far as possible the flow of private capital into the Commonwealth, whether through private subscription to overseas government loans, or through investment in the private sector, Government help was to be confined to technical aid, and, for the rest, largely to aid for colonial territories.[14] This raises three major issues: (*a*) how far technical aid without capital is adequate, (*b*) how far private investment can supply the needs of the poor countries, and (*c*) how far the distinction between the colonies and the rest is the appropriate distinction. Government policy on these three issues was very clear-cut in 1957.

[13] Cmnd. 237.

[14] Government help to non-colonial territories is afforded through Export Credits Guarantees, which are tied to U.K. exports, and through the sterling releases to the International Bank. The target for the latter was £60 millions for a period of six years from February 1953, of which about £45 millions had been authorized up to July 1957, and £55 millions disbursed up to March 1960.

(*a*) The provision of capital is but one part of Commonwealth development. The provision of all forms of technical knowledge whether financial, industrial or scientific is of parallel importance. . . . We place particular emphasis upon the provision of technical aid (paras. 3 (v), 64).

(*b*) It is through the investment of privately owned funds that the United Kingdom has made its most valuable contribution to development in other Commonwealth countries. . . . Private investment is better adapted to undertake the risk investment which often produces the most valuable addition to economic progress. . . . The Government does not envisage Government to Government loans as a normal means of assisting such countries [Colonial territories which have become independent]. Their interests can better be served if they build up their own credit and thus make use of the facilities for raising money on the London market or elsewhere (paras. 3 (iv), 14).

(*c*) The special responsibility which Her Majesty's Government has for Colonial dependencies ceases when they achieve independence. . . . In the Government's view the [Colonial Development] Corporation represents a valuable supplementary source of capital to ordinary private enterprise and has been able to make an important contribution to specific projects of Colonial development. . . . It should not invest money in new schemes in any territory after independence. In the view of Her Majesty's Government this would be inappropriate for a United Kingdom statutory corporation, particularly one whose essential purpose is the fulfilment of the United Kingdom's special responsibility towards its own dependent territories. . . . Since the United Kingdom is the only Commonwealth country which is a net long-term investor abroad, a Commonwealth Bank could do nothing to increase the total availability of capital for investment. A Commonwealth Development Agency which would lay down priorities for the Commonwealth as a whole would present insuperable difficulties for many Commonwealth governments of both a political and a practical nature (paras. 14, 30–1, 60).

It is clear that these policies benefit the British private investor, the City of London, and the richer Commonwealth countries, towards which there is a flow of private capital, as well as minimizing the burden on the British taxpayer. It is by no means clear that they suit the interests of the poor countries of the Commonwealth, such as India, and the newly independent countries, such as those in West Africa. The sudden cutting off of C.D.C. investment in new projects in Ghana came as much of a shock to public opinion as did a similar sudden cutting off of Lease-Lend to Britain at the end of the war.[15] The polite evasion of 'responsibility' for non-dependent territories was hardly happy.

[15] Existing projects of C.D.C. were not, however, affected.

The Montreal Commonwealth Trade and Economic Conference of September 1958 devoted a section of its report to development in the Commonwealth, and, reading between the lines, one can sense the frustration of the poorer members of the Commonwealth at the British Government's attitude. In fact, the report registers a retreat, if only on a small scale, from the 1957 dogmas. Thus, it generally recognized that

> the Commonwealth has a collective responsibility to do what it can to promote development in the less-developed areas. This is a human and moral responsibility which the members of the Commonwealth share with other countries and the ultimate object of which is to help raise living standards and provide a better life for the peoples of the under-developed countries.

But it specifically recognized that

> private overseas investment will have to be augmented by Government and international action, particularly in meeting the needs of basic development.

In practice, a few changes were made. Thus access to the London market was to be arranged for loans to local authorities, public utilities etc. in the less developed Commonwealth countries, further funds were to be granted to the Colonial Development Finance Company by the Bank of England, and Commonwealth assistance loans were offered both to independent countries and to colonial territories. But the Commonwealth assistance loans to independent countries were to be channelled through the Export Guarantees Acts as before and tied to British exports.[16]

Thus, in spite of some slight improvement, there is still a tendency to stress technical aid and private lending, and to distinguish between the colonies and independent countries. All these three points require considerable qualification. It is only too patently obvious, that they suit the political preconceptions of those who believe that government action is dangerous, that private enterprise can be expected to do all, or most, of what is required, and that taxation should not be increased. They tend to reduce the burden on the British taxpayer and the British consumer. For this reason we need to be particularly suspicious

[16] Cmnd. 539, Section III, 'Development'. Canada agreed to increase its contribution to the Colombo Plan at the conference. See also Cmnd. 672, op. cit., paras. 18–21, on the assistance loans to colonies.

of them, if they are in fact evasions of our obvious responsibilities to others.

(*a*) There is no doubt of the need for technical aid. It is as clear in the case of some countries that they are unable fruitfully to make use of new capital because they lack the technical expertise, as it is clear in others that what is required is capital. Generally speaking, capital and technical expertise go hand-in-hand. Nor is it only a matter of technical knowledge and know-how in the ordinary sense; perhaps more important in the case of most under-developed countries is the lack of business ability. Skilled engineers and funds to draw upon are useless without the business enterprise that can organize production and foresee the needs of the economy, whether this enterprise takes the form of private business or government planning. These are fields where the more developed countries can give of their wide experience, but they are not always substitutes for adequate loans and grants. The recent reports of the Colombo Plan Consultative Committee make clear that, as well as technical aid, finance is a bottleneck hampering the pace of development that many countries in the area would like to achieve.[17] It is not, of course, possible for the Colombo Plan Consultative Committee bluntly to state that inadequate aid from Britain and the United States and other richer countries is holding up the development of some of these countries, but the point is clearly implicit in many places in the reports, and it becomes explicit in the case of India.

> Recent developments have brought to the fore the problem of increasing savings in the economy and of conserving and enlarging foreign exchange resources. . . . In the near future, therefore, the economy will have to operate under some strain and the tempo of development will depend considerably on the success of the agricultural programmes and on the external assistance available.[18]

(*b*) A similar point can be made about the relative importance of private and governmental capital. Both are needed, and neither can be dispensed with. Comprehensive development both requires the provision by the government of basic facilities such as roads, ports, railways, hydro-electric and irrigation schemes, hospitals, schools, and agricultural research, and also the encouragement of private enterprise

[17] See 6th, 7th and 8th Reports.

[18] *Seventh Report of Colombo Plan Consultative Committee*, pp. 58–9.

in the more diversified industrial and commercial sectors. The encouragement of private enterprise in these sectors is required both to make fullest use of foreign experience, and to train people in the arts of business management. Whatever may be the case in the highly developed countries, in under-developed countries administrative skill is not available in sufficient quantity both for the government to undertake the necessary developments where government action is essential, and also in the sectors where it is not required. In theory, given sufficient administrative ability, governments could train men for business positions; in practice it is of course impossible. Wise governments in under-developed countries therefore welcome the contribution of private enterprise both from abroad and from home capitalists, while taking steps to see that this contribution fits into the general framework of development.

In the past, with colonial governments hide-bound by preconceptions of laissez-faire, the danger was that necessary public investment did not take place. In the present, in most under-developed countries, the danger is rather the reverse, that, through prejudice against private enterprise, governments will ignore its importance, and concentrate all available capital on the public sector. Development consisting entirely of hydro-electric schemes, railways and iron and steel works, without any corresponding expansion of consumer industries, is as unbalanced as the prevailing colonial pattern of development of agricultural estates producing cash crops for export.[19] Most under-developed countries have a large agricultural population, and the proper development of agriculture obviously requires close co-operation between the government and the farmer. This need for balanced development, as between different sectors of the economy, and as between different forms of capital, has again been stressed by the Colombo Plan Consultative Committee.

[19] Compare the report of the United Nations experts, which referred to 'the crowding of capital investment into a few sectors of the economy, to the neglect of other sectors, which is a common feature of under-developed countries' (para. 72). 'Under-developed countries have a great need for investment in the public sector. But they have an equally great need for extra capital in the hands of small farmers and in the manufacturing sector' (para. 129.). 'It is sufficient to record here the opinion that most development programmes accord too low a priority to investment in human beings, and provide correspondingly for relatively too high a priority to investment in material capital' (para. 166.).

But it still remains true that, if the capital requirements of developing countries are to be left to the capital markets of the West, without inter-governmental assistance, capital will not be able to be used in the most fruitful fashion. For example, the Sixth Report on the Colombo Plan pointed out that Indian plans required more foreign exchange. It is not obvious that the flow of private capital to India in all its various forms will necessarily make good this deficiency, and India had to obtain special international credits in 1958.

(*c*) It is clear that several independent countries in the Commonwealth are as under-developed as many of the colonies. It would be disastrous to our position in the world if we were to wash our hands of any responsibilities for these countries because they have become independent of our colonial rule, just as it is disastrous for us to confine our responsibilities to the Commonwealth, as if, in the one world in which in fact we live, what happens in Latin America were no concern of ours. The Colombo Plan indeed recognizes this fact of the mutual interdependence of Commonwealth and other countries and the close ties of the whole region with the 'western' world. The principle is not one for South-East Asia alone.

In fact, the independent countries of the Commonwealth include rich and highly-developed countries such as Canada, Australia and New Zealand, as well as countries such as Ghana and India. It is not obvious that we have responsibilities to provide capital for development in Canada and Australia in the same way as we have responsibilities for providing capital to the poorer countries of the world. If the matter is left to the market, capital will, in fact, tend to flow to Canada, Australia and perhaps South Africa (and, to the United States, if it were given a chance) for obvious reasons. But this is not how matters should be left. If necessary, deliberate steps should be taken to channel funds away from these rich areas towards the poorer areas of the world. Admittedly, it is not merely private interests that gain from investment in the richer areas, but also the British people as a whole, in so far as the profits and dividends help the British balance of payments. But if we are prepared to incur sacrifices for the benefit of the under-developed countries, this is one form the sacrifice will have to take.

In short, if we are really to help the under-developed countries, we will need not only to increase our aid, in all its manifold forms, to our colonial territories, and to the independent countries of the Commonwealth, but we will also have to expand our support of similar efforts by the United Nations in other parts of the world. The pattern of unilateral help is out-moded; it perpetuates the colony/mother-country complex which it should be our aim to dissolve, and it leads to mutual resentment. The Colombo Plan and the various U.N. programmes, which require to be considerably expanded, point the way to the kind of partnership in the development of the world's resources which is needed. It is a measure of our failure to meet the challenge of our time that we have held back in giving any sort of lead in this direction in recent years.

If we are determined to take the world revolution of the poorer under-developed countries seriously, what are the prospects? It is probably the case that the seriousness of the issues at stake is more generally accepted, and the issues themselves better understood than ever before. But it is not clear that our politicians are ready to give a real lead in explaining the sacrifices required, even if public opinion were ready to follow such a lead. They seem to prefer to outbid their rivals with offers of better standards at home. The Conservatives stake everything on reducing taxation, on the grounds that the crushing burden of taxation diminishes incentives, and that government expenditure is too high; it is an argument that must be met, though it does not convince me. They believe that investment abroad must be matched by savings at home, and are reluctant to increase these savings by increasing taxation; they prefer foreign investment to be left to private enterprise, and are not so happy about increasing government investment. Strangely enough, however, the election of 1959 seems to have produced a considerable change of emphasis.[20]

The Labour party, on the other hand, in principle favours government action, and a contribution by this country on a larger scale than formerly. But it is not so clear that it is really ready to make the sacrifices involved. This was shown clearly by the arguments used by Mr. Harold Wilson in the debate on the 1957 budget. Harold Wilson has written a book called *The War on World Poverty*,[21] and is

[20] See Cmnd. 974, op. cit.
[21] Gollancz, 1953.

not unaware of the economic issues involved. But when he criticized the budget proposals for tax relief on 'Overseas Trading Corporations' (which involves tax relief on private overseas investment), among other points he criticized them because they would increase investment abroad rather than investment at home, and would create balance of payments difficulties.[22] These criticisms equally apply to a scheme such as that of the Labour Party. Foreign aid will also compete with home investment if it is really to help countries like India. More atomic energy power stations in under-developed countries may mean fewer at home.

Are we ready to pay the price? No doubt the so-called middle classes do not give an adequate lead, and are as selfish as anyone. But in our egalitarian society more and more depends on the workers whose rising standards of living must bear some of the burden. As a Labour Party supporter, I am disturbed by the way in which some Labour leaders seem to be more concerned with what is in fact sharing among the rich (within a rich country like Britain) than with sharing with the really poor.[23] When the workers of the world really rise, they may be hard put to it to find their comrades in the West. This is surely a situation where Christians of every political party have something to contribute, even if they do not agree with the particular points I have made.

Much of this is agreed—at least when people give their minds to it. It is the lack of imagination that frightens one. Here is clearly a place where Christians can contribute something, so that we can try to see the world in some sort of perspective, appreciating what is happening around us, not merely looking to our own colonies or to our Commonwealth, considering the effects of our own policies on other countries, being ready to help where we can without taking the credit for it, and

[22] Third Reading, 19 July 1957 (*Hansard*, cols. 1537–1540). Earlier he had referred to the need to concentrate concessions on Commonwealth development (*Hansard*, 3 July, cols. 1245–1247; 17 July, cols. 1165–1170).

[23] It is however to be noted that at the Labour Party Conference in October 1956, when dealing with the party pledge to devote one per cent. of the national income to helping the under-developed countries, Mr. James Griffiths said, 'When we agree on these policies we must mean it. . . . When a Labour Government comes to power it means that if these people get it, we must go without it. If we are not prepared to go without it, do not let us pass resolutions that mean nothing. But we mean it. So let us be ready to stand up and meet the critics who say: "We should get this and not the blacks".' (Reported in *The Times*, 5 October 1956.)

in fact fulfilling all the traditional obligations of the rich, in a new context. Even if we are ready to give enough, we must be careful to give in a way that will not offend—as was true of the rich of the past, though it was a duty not always clearly carried out. This will probably mean being more ready to give full support to co-operative schemes like the Colombo Plan, and the various agencies of the United Nations, such as the Expanded Programme of Technical Assistance, and the Special Fund, which are starved by the miserliness of many governments.[24] There are in the world today many organizations designed to deal with the revolution that is sweeping the under-developed countries. Above all, what they need is money, as well as men. It cannot be said that the richer countries have shown themselves aware of the dimensions of the problem; and even where they show a verbal awareness, their very riches seem to blind them to the needs of action. It may be that, if we do not act, we shall be overwhelmed. We are after all in the rich West but a small minority of the ever-growing masses of mankind.

[24] For 1960, each will have about £11 millions though the Special Fund has a target of about £36 millions. Britain has promised £1 million to E.P.T.A. and nearly £2 millions to the Special Fund, both increases on the previous year (*The Times*, 21 January 1960.).

Chapter 6

CONFLICT AND CO-OPERATION

'Dr. Fisher, who was speaking at a luncheon given by the National Union of Manufacturers, said that size, with all the implications of power and organization that went with it, was not by itself the friend but the enemy of man. . . . He was convinced that there was a right size for schools, and he was quite certain that it was true of the trade unions. In the right-sized organization one could talk together as friends. "Anything is the right size just so far as it is a fellowship directed by persons who trust one another and appreciated by persons who trust one another."'—*The Times*.

'It is natural to fear large organizations, but it is not necessarily spiritual.'—BISHOP LESSLIE NEWBIGIN.

I. THE NECESSITY OF CONFLICT

I HAVE discussed the way in which a complex dynamic modern economy brings men together in the national community and has also broken through many of the barriers that formerly divided the world. These same forces operate throughout the whole world, making for greater uniformity and interdependence. Within nations integration leads to equality and uniformity; but differences still subsist. Men will never be entirely uniform—fortunately. Thus the varied fortunes of different groups lead to tensions and conflicts. It does not seem possible to envisage a period when incomes, even within one fairly homogeneous nation, will be exactly equal. But if this is the case, then, as we have seen, there will always be opportunities for dispute as to the share that it is proper that one group should have. There can be no absolutely right decision on this point that will commend itself to everyone, because, as we have seen, there is no universal criterion that can be applied. It may be that in a slowly changing world, of relatively static societies, it is possible to envisage a 'fair' distribution of incomes and power, which satisfies everybody all the time. But this is because people accept a common set of social values, in terms of which everybody judges. Today there is no such possibility even if we might think it desirable.

The issue is wider than that of incomes, and it is to these wider issues that I now want to turn. The essential fact is that we live in a plural world, plural both in the sense that people are attached to various different groupings which make up the complex pattern of their lives, and also in the sense that there is no uniformity of belief and desires. The varied groups to which we belong are an inevitable feature of a world organized on a large scale with division of labour and specialization. Nor can we ever envisage any continuous stability in the position of these groups as the economic system progresses and changes.

The additional feature of divergent beliefs in fundamental matters could conceivably be different. We may, perhaps rightly, hark back to some sort of Christian society where there might be a rough agreement about fundamental ends. But every church knows only too well from the bitter experiences it has suffered from the persecutions of rival Christian bodies how dangerous such a situation is for the good health of the Church. We know that Christians cannot be trusted to use any power they may have in a situation where there is general agreement about ends. We may therefore be grateful for the fact that we have to make-do, in a world where people do not agree, and where we have to put up with all the clashes and inconveniences which this affords. The longer-run questions as to whether this is the ideal form of society we may perhaps leave aside as too speculative to be worth considering.

In fact, then, we live in a society of differing and competing groups, which can only survive by taking realistic account of these differences and conflicts, and which may in the long run achieve some stability from the very fact of conflict, in that there is always the possibility of some new balance emerging, if the present one proves precarious. Judged by the rigid pattern of a simple society, modern society seems fragile, incoherent, divided, a mass of jarring atoms, inhumanly individualistic, and collectivist at the same time. But the rigid pattern of a simple society, satisfying as it may be so long as the pattern remains stable, may be forced into disintegration as soon as one element in the whole proves unsatisfactory. Thus it is alleged that some primitive societies fail because people cease to believe in the old religion, and, once the religion is lost, the society ceases to cohere. By contrast, a modern society is not so brittle. If its economic system fails to work satisfactorily, other elements do not automatically disintegrate. A failure of faith does not necessarily bring about a failure in the economic system. Political inefficiency may co-exist with economic success—one might refer to the American experience; but, on the other hand, economic failure may be combined with great political wisdom. Modern war has proved a disaster of such a cataclysmic nature that it is hard to believe that any society could stand it. But the fact remains that the fabric of European society survived two such disasters, that the economic damage was rapidly made good and the standard of living soon rose considerably above what it had been before the wars, and that apparent political stability, at least on a certain level, emerged fairly rapidly. The flexibility of modern society has proved of itself a factor of stability. Modern society is really remarkably tough and resilient. Man is a far more adaptable animal than one is often tempted to think.

It is a foolish apologetic, and a false pretence of prophecy, that contents itself with denouncing the elements of incoherence and instability in modern society, without looking deeper within. It is equally a superficial criticism that expects such a complex world to show forth the simple harmony and unity of small static societies, or the personal face-to-face relationships possible in small groups. Unfortunately, it is just this sort of criticism that appeals to ecclesiastical assemblies and their leaders, from which there flows a more or less constant stream of utterances, which are not merely foolish in their naïvety, but also positively harmful, because they distract attention from the real issues. The real issue is to see that differences and conflicts are so managed and balanced that they produce both the flexibility that can adapt to the changing problems of the times and also the richness that differing groups can contribute to the social whole. This issue is confused by the usual run of Christian anodynes.

The Lambeth Conference of 1958[1] devoted a considerable amount of attention to what it called 'The Reconciling of Conflicts between and within Nations'. This was the only section of the conference devoted to social questions, if we exclude the section on the family.

[1] *The Lambeth Conference, 1958* (S.P.C.K., and Seabury Press, 1958).

Whereas the latter report, admirably prepared by the preliminary study on *The Family in Contemporary Society*,[2] showed a real grasp of the issues involved, the sections dealing with conflicts within nations (and it is only with these that I am concerned) descended to a general level of bathos, perhaps because it was so overridingly concerned with racial problems, which are, indeed, of a different nature from the kind of conflicts with which I am concerned.

The resolutions of the conference on this theme started off as follows:[3]

The Conference is convinced that the Church's work of reconciliation must be powerfully expressed within the parish or local congregation. Consequently here it would lay emphasis upon the following points:

(*a*) There is a need for Christians to understand more deeply the meaning of God's providence in history and the ground of Christian hope, as distinct from a belief in automatic social progress. This needs to be emphasized in preaching and teaching.

I have suggested that the theme of providence is indeed one that requires further attention in the present world, but the real theme is the relation of this providence to the social progress that has taken place and is taking place. It may be doubted if many people seriously believe in any sort of automatic social progress today, and to set it up as a cock-shy merely provokes the suggestion that the Christians have really lost a meaningful doctrine of providence, and that the Churches have no positive contribution to make.

Lambeth goes on:[4]

(*d*) Where there are divisions in the local community, the Christian congregation in that place should face them fearlessly, and, by the action of its members, should serve as an agent of reconciliation.

(*e*) While there are many elements in the reconciling of conflicts, none are more important than the character and conduct of individual people. Success or failure in any particular instance may in the end depend on the individual: not only on his knowledge, his judgment, and his zeal, but also on the spirit of Christ mirrored in a life which bears the marks of the Cross and the fruits of the Spirit. . . .

The Conference calls upon all Christian people to strive by the exercise of

[2] *The Family in Contemporary Society* (S.P.C.K., 1958).

[3] Resolution 100, pp. (1), 52–3.

[4] Resolution 100, and Resolution 103, p. (1), 54.

mutual understanding, calm reason, and constant prayer, to reconcile all those who are involved in racial, political, economic, or other conflicts.

Nowhere is anything said about the proper part that is played by divergent views and groupings in the modern world. It is assumed throughout that it is the business of the Christian to reconcile, never that it may be his duty to take sides, or to break up a pretence of peaceful unity which is a sham. The statement that 'none are more important elements in the reconciling of conflicts than the character and conduct of individual people' will lead readers to neglect, as the Lambeth fathers themselves have, the importance of the institutional framework.

The committee report, on which these resolutions are based, did not entirely fail to notice these matters. It did clearly state:[5]

> The Church sometimes has to take the responsibility for creating conflict, never, legitimately, on its own behalf but to remedy injustice and to halt oppression . . .
>
> The Church has not infrequently failed to contribute to the resolution of conflicts in the social and political fields. Sometimes it has complacently and uncritically blessed an unjust *status quo* in the belief that the sinfulness of the world so easily leads to anarchy that any order, however unjust, is preferable to chaos. Sometimes it has confused social and political issues by proclaiming its perfectionist ethic as directly applicable to specific situations, and so has avoided the costly process of dealing with questions of relative good and evil.

But, having said this, it did not apply these insights to conflicts within nations, partly because it omitted to consider whole realms of life, which it should have considered under its general rubic, and whose absence is not adequately explained,[6] and partly because the title of the 'Reconciling of Conflicts between and within Nations' tends to preclude the consideration of conflicts which should not be reconciled.

It appears from the committee's analysis that conflicts arise largely from (*a*) 'a terrible insecurity' from which 'the long-established nations' suffer, which has 'led to a view of life that is essentially selfish'; (*b*) the fact that 'the generality of mankind, the West included, has no

[5] Ibid, p. (2), 121.

[6] A brief note that 'Although particular attention has been given to racial problems, the Committee is equally aware of the political conflict in the world' (with which it then proceeds to deal in less than two pages) hides the truth that the Committee in effect only dealt with racial problems adequately, and added almost as footnotes two sections on industry (pp. (2), 135–7), and political conflicts (pp. (2), 137–9).

firm philosophy of history to give it confidence in its destiny, or to justify the sufferings it must bear. Many, even in so-called Christian lands, had based whatever hope they had on secular progress. This outlook has been shattered by two world wars, and nothing has come to fill its place'; and (*c*) the further fact that 'the whole world has not only been profoundly affected by the dazzling material achievements of science and technology, but has been so progressively conditioned by a scientific climate of opinion that people come to look upon any knowledge other than that obtained by scientific method as suspect.' The result is 'an insecurity that breeds suspicion, finding its expression in a distrust of a class, an economic or some other group, or, in greater issue, a nation, an empire, or a race. . . . As a result people are pitted against people as all strive for significance. Fear is hypnotic . . . Group insecurity and frustration are not only external facts; they are generated from within. The germs of social disillusionment are found in individual disillusionment, and so are the germs of social antipathy and fear. Many an agressive move is born of insecurity. Many an accusation is the confession of unfaced guilt. Many a destructive hatred is the projection of a hidden mistrust of human nature, an unacknowledged mistrust of self.'[7]

It is not disputed that this is a lively account of some of the conflicts that can and do arise in society. But to admit that these general patterns of belief combined with such individual psychological motives may be important in creating conflicts in certain cases, is not to accept this as a general social explanation. These are only some of the many causes of conflicts, perhaps operative always to some extent in all conflicts, but not always the essential factors. To concentrate on these particular elements may be important in the case of such pathological social conditions as those existent in South Africa (the report seems to have had these in mind most of the time and to have generalized from them much too easily). It obviously serves very neatly the causes of Christian apologetic. But it misses some of the more difficult and important issues.

From this kind of analysis it follows naturally that:

> The true way of reconciliation . . . can only be achieved, however, when each party is prepared for the sake of some greater good to abandon and

[7] Ibid, pp. (2), 118-120.

offer up its own exclusive interest despite the contingent risks involved.[8]

In the Ecumenical Movement, as in the frank and friendly facing of the differences within our own Communion, we have learned that conflict can be constructive as well as destructive. When religious differences are accepted as tensions within a family, they can either be resolved, or, at the least, continue as differences within a loving brotherhood of believers.[9]

As has been said earlier in this Report, the conflict of ideas is often a means of growth; but there is a profound difference between those conflicts which can be resolved by peaceful means, and those where changes are made through civil strife or outside interference.

Even this poses the problem too simply. It is important to recognize the question-begging nature of a phrase like 'peaceful means'.[10]

Perhaps the most damnable aspect of this concentration on the Church's role of reconciling agent is the assumption that emerges that the Church has the answer. It is true that lip-service is paid to the thesis that Christians do not have answers to technical questions, but too easily this sort of pronouncement slips into the mistake of implying that in some way Christians are able to see the fray from above with an impartiality that is not granted to other people. Thus the committee says:

> At times of acute political conflict, the Church must keep before the people the principles of disinterested justice . . . It must also strive to keep the well-being of the community as a whole before the warring groups—the good of the whole community must come first, and party advantage must be kept secondary.[11]

Of itself this is unexceptionable, but it has certain undertones which may lead the unwary astray.

In the last resort, of course, the Church's task is one of reconciliation, but a too great concentration on ultimate issues in relation to immediate problems can be disastrous. The first question is not so much to resolve conflicts as to analyse them, and to see how far they are fruitful and necessary. Then one needs to see them in their institutional setting. Very often it is the institutions that need changing, not the people who use them. It is in this context that I want to consider some aspects of our contemporaty problems.

[8] P. (2), 120.
[9] P. (2), 122.
[10] P. (2), 137.
[11] P. (2), 138.

2. THE ORGANIZATION OF CONFLICT

The conflicts with which I am concerned arise fundamentally from three characteristics of our world: specialization of function, scale of operations, and continuous change. It is the combination of these factors which produces our peculiar situation.

(1) *Specialization of Function.* It is specialization that produces divergence of interest and often of outlook, whether at the individual or the group level. This is the most general factor producing 'class' differences, whatever may be meant by 'class'. We are here concerned with something much wider than purely economic differences, though it may be hard in most cases to disentangle the economic from other factors. Any simple Marxian, or other, attempt to relate such divergent attitudes purely to some economic criterion is doomed to failure. Nevertheless, it would not be exaggerating to say that many, if not most, differences in outlook arise from differences in behaviour and function in society. In addition, one can at least say that in modern society the economic factor is one of the most important in producing specialization in activity. It is not merely a matter of chance that, at the beginning of the development of modern economics, Adam Smith laid such stress on the importance of division of labour. It is indeed generally recognized that the division of labour lies at the root of our modern economic development.

But this division of labour inevitably brings in its train a divergence of interest, and encourages a divergence of outlook. We cannot escape from it. It is indeed beyond the power of any individual comprehensively to understand the complexities of modern society, in the sense of being able to enter sympathetically into the circumstances of other men. What we know of how other men live is inevitably fragmentary and narrow. It has, no doubt, always been so; but these fragments of knowledge were a larger part of the whole in simpler societies than they are today. One has only to glance through the list of industries in the Census, or the handlist of occupations provided for the same (itself a large volume), to realize how little one knows of what other people do. It is, however, to be noted that there is compensation for the fragmentary state of our knowledge in the variety of different experiences of others' lives we are likely to meet with in the casual chances of daily life. (That is to say, if we do not deliberately cut ourselves off from all but a limited sector of experience, as some people unfortunately try to do, though not always with great success.) We may be able to see less of the way different people's jobs make up the total pattern of society than people could in earlier societies; but we can see a greater variety of activities than our ancestors ever could. We have more opportunities to be made aware of the enormous range of what we call 'human nature' than they did, and the virtue of tolerance may, for this reason, come more easily to us than it did to them.

(2) *Scale of Operations*. It is possible that a small village community may be composed of individuals with highly specialized occupations; even within families there may be a great differentiation within the common family life. In such cases, conflicts may arise, and of course always will, so long as human nature is subject to sin. But they are conflicts of a different kind from those with which I am concerned; they are indeed the conflicts of the sort that the Lambeth report deals with. Though arising from specialization, they remain fundamentally personal conflicts, suitable for resolution on the personal level. This is true, as long as the groups in question, within which the conflicts arise, are small. But it is quite different when we have to deal with the interconnections of large numbers of people, and when each special group may itself be both large in numbers and organized in a complicated way. Problems of quite a different character then arise. Here again, modern economic methods rely on the advantages to be gained from such large-scale operations, so that a modern economy inevitably produces such problems. We cannot go back to a small-scale world, even if it were conceivable that the world's population should shrink to what it once was.

(3) *Continuous Change*. A world of specialization even with large-scale organization might not produce conflicts requiring any special method of resolution. That is to say, it might be possible to imagine a situation in which such conflicts of interest were definitely resolved by a particular social pattern. In a static world, one can conceive a stable balance of forces; indeed it would seem necessary for any sort of static society, if we mean by this a society that is unchanging in important respects. Even if we confine our attention to an imagined

world where only technology and economic organization is stable, it is possible to consider such a complex, specialized world, organized on a large scale, and yet still harmonious in the sense that it has achieved a balance between the divergent economic interests and outlooks of its members.

Needless to say, we are not dealing with such a world, but it is useful to notice that it is the combination of continuous economic change with specialization and large-scale organization that produces our peculiar problems. These problems are inherently connected with the facts of economic progress and the growth of wealth. They are linked with the necessary development of abstract relationships between people, which means that not all relations with others can be of a face-to-face nature, as they largely can be in small-scale primitive societies. It is the relative decline in such face-to-face relationships that is perhaps the most important factor leading to the constant complaint of 'dehumanization'. I am not here, however, concerned with such complaints, but with how the conflicts of interest that inevitably arise in our large-scale, specialized and changing world are in fact dealt with, and whether there is any better way of dealing with them.

There are in fact roughly two ways by means of which such conflicts can be organized, both ways well-known in history, but both more highly-developed and self-conscious today. I refer to the market mechanism, and to political organization. Both are essentially mechanisms, and their successful use therefore depends on their being properly 'set up' in the first place. But both are at the same time natural to man, in the sense that they arise spontaneously without conscious forethought as human societies develop. Both have advantages and disadvantages and each has peculiar merits for dealing with specific situations.

(*a*) *The Market.* Markets arise naturally in human society as things are bought and sold at a price, and payments are made in money. Such activities go back a long way in the history of civilization, and without them it is doubtful if there could be any civilization, except at the most primitive level. Essentially, markets settle the conflicts of interest between different groups through the process of price changes and the consequences that follow from them. When prices change, people have to adapt themselves to the situation. They may, of course, be able to use some sort of political pressure to alter prices, whether the pressure takes the form of guild regulation of economic activity, or the modern 'pork-barrel' politics, by which governments step in to help particular economic groups in the community. But the market is then superseded by politics—which may, or may not, be a good thing, depending on the situation. Essentially, the advantage of the market mechanism is that it forces men to adapt themselves to an objective factor in the situation, the prices that face them. No conflict arises between persons or groups. You have to accept a change in the market price; there is no one to blame, no one to fight with.

But in this also lies the disadvantage of the market mechanism. If the market can be understood to represent an acceptable objective force, then it may in fact be accepted objectively. But this requires a high level of maturity, even if the changes in market price do in fact represent changes that are objectively desirable. Many people prefer to kick out at someone when something goes wrong. It is an easily observable phenomenon that young children tend to blame their parents and hit out at them, when they accidentally fall and hurt themselves and when the said parents happen to be near at hand. This refusal to accept the objective nature of the world in which we live is equally observable among adults, who often prefer to blame someone, against all the evidence, rather than adjust themselves to awkward facts. Many of these absurdities are to be seen at their most striking in the processes of law. The legal system has, among other more adult functions, that of being the repository of the childish impulses of the community to hit out at someone, when something goes wrong. (Which is no doubt one reason why judges have generally been found opposing changes that would lead to greater rationality in our social arrangements.)

These advantages of the market mechanism can clearly only be realized if two conditions are satisfied, first, that it does in fact perform a useful social function of signalling to particular groups the changes that are required in their conduct, and, secondly, that people are more or less ready to accept that this is so. As far as the first point is concerned, I do not propose here to discuss this in all its ramifications, but merely to state that the market mechanism or the price system, or whatever it is called, is one of the most useful achievements of human inventiveness; but not, it may be added, one to be accepted uncritically in the precise form in which it has in fact developed historically.[12] The mechanism is not one suitable for dealing with all human problems; it has distinct limitations even within its special field, and as a whole it has to be subjected to political control. The framework within which the market may be allowed to operate must be a political creation. It is the failure fully and clearly to understand this simple point that led to the distortions of *laisser-faire* on the one hand (in the sense of a belief that somehow or other the ideal use of the market comes about without any human action at all), and, on the other hand, to the uncritical attacks on markets, prices, economists and bankers, which have been all too common among some Socialists and many Christians. If the market is used, and not abused, essentially what it can do is to register the reactions of large numbers of people, in a situation where quantities are involved, more delicately than can any other electoral process. Thus its fundamental function is to register what consumers want to buy within the limit of the incomes they possess; it is thus necessary in a world where men are rich and choice is considerable. On the other hand, the market cannot deal with choices such as that about the use of atomic bombs, nor even can it solve traffic problems, if it is assumed as axiomatic that people cannot be charged for the use of the roads. I accept then that within certain limits the market is a highly useful and desirable mechanism.

But, though objectively useful, it might still be useless in practice, if people were not ready to accept it. At times of serious crisis our complex economic system has almost collapsed precisely because people have ceased to believe in its rationality. Such was the state of affairs in the Great Depression of the 'thirties in many countries, and such is the state of affairs in many under-developed countries emerging from stagnation. In the Great Depression, however, the fundamental problem was not that people failed to believe in a rational system, but that the system was in fact irrational, and that its high-priests did not know what to do about it. That particular problem of mass unemployment due to deficiency of overall demand has been analysed and explained by the revolutionary work of Keynes. We now know how to deal with it, and that same situation should not arise again. But other cases are more complex. There is no guarantee,

[12] See *Christianity and Economic Problems*, Chapter 9, 'The Price System.'

when important groups are faced with market signals which record bad news for them, that they will react rationally to the objective situation. There are frequent examples to be found in the pages of economic history textbooks where such groups have reacted in ways that gave them social satisfaction at a cost of a worse economic future than they would otherwise have had to face. I am thinking of cases where a declining industry, by gaining political and artificial protection that appears to satisfy it immediately, in fact hastens its own decline. Admittedly there are times when action of this sort can benefit one particular group at the expense of others in the same society, or at the expense of the long-run disadvantage of everybody. (Such questions are very much to the point when we are looking, for example, at the future of the cotton industry in Lancashire.) It might be too extreme to say that every attempt to deal with a declining industry through control of its prices and output will make matters worse, but it is much nearer the truth than is often allowed by those who blindly rush towards more protection.

But to fall back in this way into the arms of some controlling authority is the human reaction, and it is not to be expected that people will react to situations which threaten their livelihood without some emotion. A wise society tries to take account of the situations where human beings are seriously threatened by the action of market forces, so that proper adjustments can be made to help them. Hence we have, not only all the apparatus of the welfare state for dealing with the inevitable ups and downs of human life, but also the development of policies designed to 'take work to the workers', and to deal with declining industries by means of temporary subsidies and arrangements, during the period of readjustment. The growth of trade unions is, of course, due to these same human reactions. The problem of our time then, as of all times, is to see that special action is taken to deal with the critical situations, where the workings of the market, though in themselves satisfactory, lead to human reactions which are disruptive. This is, of course, in addition to dealing with situations where the market does not work satisfactorily. Often, in fact, as in the cases mentioned of location of industry and declining industries, the human reactions are strongest in cases where in fact the market does not work satisfactorily of itself.

(*b*) *Political Organization.* Political organization is something wider than politics in the normal sense. The problems of power, parties, sovereignty, choice of leaders and effective representation are all to be found, in one form or another, in all organizations from tennis-clubs to churches. In our large-scale world we solve our problems and meet our conflicts in and through multifarious organizations, as well as in and through market mechanisms. If we are to solve them adequately, we need to have an understanding of the functions these organizations perform, and on that understanding to base a morality which will help us to act responsibly in our modern world. Here I can only make a few remarks on this theme. Properly to discuss it would require a far wider knowledge than I possess of modern society, and than perhaps any one person can possess, as well as particular knowledge of particular institutions, which one can state dogmatically that no one person can have, and also an understanding of the special approaches of the sociologist, the student of politics and administration, and the lawyer, as well as the economist.

There is a thesis persuasively argued by an American Quaker, a Professor of Economics of distinction, Kenneth Boulding, that the growth of organizations in the twentieth century (he calls it *The Organizational Revolution*)[13] is a disaster, creating problems rather than solving them, and leading us away from their true solution, which is rather to be found in the market than in the growth of associations and organizations. A similar harking back to some more or less idyllic world where there were real individuals and a real and effective market might be thought to lie behind W. H. Whyte's satirical analysis, *The Organization Man.*[14] In its extreme form, this doctrine seems to rely on a myth, both in its belief in some pristine state of grace before there ever appeared such things as organized vested interests, and in its belief that the market can cure all. It would be unfair to state that Professor Boulding or Mr. Whyte believe this myth. But there are others as well who have a tendency to look in this direction for a cure of our problems. No overall solution of all our problems is to be found in this direction. We have to live in a world of organizations, because human beings want them, and because some problems can only be

[13] Harper & Bros., New York, 1953.
[14] Simon and Schuster, Inc., New York, 1956.

solved in and through them. There is no real choice between the market and organization in general; we need both. In particular cases, on particular issues, the choice has certainly to be made, but it is a choice at the margin, not a question of all or nothing. And there still remain many questions about organizations.

(1) *People and Organizations.* The responsibilities of people towards and in an organization are different from what they are in the case of personal relationships. If the ends of an organization are right, if it is playing its proper role in society, and functions so as to serve the common good, clearly the individual within the organization has the duty to see that these ends are realized most efficiently and easily. He has to ensure that the organization does serve the common good in the way it is intended to do. If it does not, he has to work to reform it so that it can perform its function more effectively.

Responsibility is primarily something that is due from people. Organizations have ends and functions, for which their members are responsible in varying degrees. It is only in a secondary sense that we can say that organizations are responsible, or fail to meet their responsibilities, though Christians and others do sometimes talk as if personal morality applied to institutions in the same way as it applies to persons.[15] If we make the judgment that organizations fail to meet their responsibilities, we may be saying one of two things, either that the members of the organization have failed to exercise their responsibilities in the institution, or that the institution is badly devised to achieve the aims it should be achieving, or was devised to achieve (or indeed a mixture of both). In the latter case, what needs changing is the structure of the institution, which may certainly be a primary responsibility of those in the organization.

If institutions are created or allowed to grow with ends that are contrary to the Will of God, or that clash with the requirements of society as a whole, no amount of responsibility by the leaders and members of the organizations will by itself serve the public interest without some reform of the institution. Rather the opposite; the more devoted and responsible the members are within it, the more will society diverge from its right ends. The same goes for an organization

[15] An interesting exponent of this view today is Mr. George Goyder, some of whose views are to be found in *The Future of Private Enterprise* (Blackwell, 1951).

with right ends, but which is badly devised to achieve them. In both cases what is wanted is the fashioning of a new structure, and not merely responsible action within the structure; sometimes deliberate sabotage of the organization may be required, as in the case of the soldier refusing to obey 'superior orders', which require him to commit 'crimes against humanity'.

(2) *The State, Society and Organizations.* The right structure of organizations in society is clearly partly a matter of the general health of society, which spontaneously produces, or fails to produce, the kind of institutions which are needed. Indeed, the growth or languishing of such institutions in response to changing needs may be one of the best symptoms of social health. But the growth of organizations cannot be left entirely to *laisser-faire* any more than can the market. The state has the general function of regulating them, licensing them, forbidding them, and ensuring in a general way that they meet the needs of the common good. Whether or not the state fulfils this function properly is clearly a matter of the greatest importance.

It is perhaps necessary to state this very obvious truth because there are people who have argued, in Christian terms, that the State has to leave natural groups to grow on their own, and that too much State interference is a sign of the very weakness of society and the failure of the natural health of its organs. This thesis has often been brilliantly argued by Professor V. A. Demant. It is not disputed that a society may be ailing because it lacks natural groupings of sufficient variety and vitality; nor is it disputed that the State can act too cavalierly in destroying them and taking over their activities itself, when it would have been wiser to leave them to subordinate bodies. Many particular political disputes about education, health services, local government, national insurance and so on are indeed about this particular issue. But in general it would be as true to say today that the growth of state action leads to, or is accompanied by, a similar spontaneous growth of other organizations, as to state that the growth of state action leads to their supersession. The state acts because these organizations are lively, and it has to act, because otherwise their actions would not meet the needs of the community, and in many cases could not exist at all without the appropriate framework being provided by the state.

This can clearly be seen in the economic field, where the activities of the state cover an enormous range. On the one hand, the state lays down the pattern to which institutions of various kinds must conform, as for example the regulation of financial institutions of various sorts through the Bank of England, the regulation of companies through Company Law, the control through registration of others such as insurance companies, friendly societies, building societies, co-operative societies, and trade unions. It interferes with them by means of Factory Acts and laws about employment, and, more recently, prevents them, through the Monopoly and Restrictive Practices Court, from following various kinds of non-competitive actions. In other cases, it imposes detailed regulations, as in the case of transport, and even enforces non-competitive actions. All I wish to stress here is the wide range of interference with institutions of various kinds, which we have to accept as right and proper in our complex world. Nor is it merely a matter of interference with healthy and spontaneous growths; the examples quoted show clearly enough that the growths are not spontaneous and cannot be. The modern company and the modern building society, as institutions, are creations of the state; without its action they could not, and would not, exist. The moral seems to be that if we want multifarious institutions in a complex society we must have a complex machinery of state action to control them, just as the healthy working of the market depends on the state fulfilling its function in regulating it. (Indeed, it will be seen from the above examples that one of the major issues is the extent to which organizations are encouraged to react to the market, or discouraged from doing so.)[16]

The questions that Christians have to face here have nothing to do with the behaviour of people, or with morals in the ordinary sense. They concern the proper ends of institutions and the framework within which they can be expected to fulfil them. What is required is detailed and careful study of the ends of society as a whole, and the contribution which these various organizations have to make to the whole. In the main the institutions which I have mentioned are concerned with the increase of wealth and the welfare of consumers and producers. They have to be judged by their contribution to the general ends outlined earlier in relation to progress, wealth and human welfare. We can

[16] Nothing said here is meant to preclude the possibility (and desirability) of direct action by Government. This issue is not discussed here.

criticize the general balance of society in so far as, for example, it lays too much stress on creating wealth (or too little), or gives too much or too little attention to proper forms of human security, or debases or enhances the cultural tone of society. We can also criticize its particular dealings with special branches of society, such as building societies, or trade unions, in so far as it helps them, or hinders them, in fulfilling their proper ends.

One particular function of the state is necessary in a changing world where institutions often, if not always, change less rapidly than the social and economic realities. We have to be flexible in such a world, and such flexibility requires that institutions should never be allowed to exist merely because they have served a function in the past. One of the problems of maintaining flexible growth in a complex society arises because institutions rarely, if ever, die. Universities are one example, companies another. New universities are created, old ones do not die, though some are still-born. Is it not time we thought of killing off one or two? The same problem arises from the fact that the really large company has a built-in capacity to survive (or so it seems today). And yet the successful growth of a modern economy was always premissed on the decay of some businesses as others proved more successful. It may indeed be the case that companies of the size and complexity of I.C.I. or Unilever have achieved justified success and proved themselves more efficient than their rivals. But we cannot yet be sure of this, any more than we can be sure that the numerous ancient charitable institutions in this country serve useful purposes, merely because they have survived through the centuries. One major exercise of government should be to ensure that institutions should not continue to exist merely because there is no way of getting rid of them. This is doubly necessary where the existence of these institutions creates conflicts which would not exist were they not in existence; the mere existence of an institution creates an interest, and a potential conflict. In these cases, the conflict does not need to be faced, but the institution should be buried.

3. SOME GENERAL PRINCIPLES

Much has been written on these issues—and wisely written—in terms of the problems of controlling power and achieving justice in the conflicts of our time. Sometimes justice has to grasp firmly the nettle of power; at other times, power is best allowed to dissipate itself unnoticed. Sometimes a powerful institution can best be controlled by 'the countervailing power' of another institution in potential, if not actual, conflict with it; in other cases, powerful institutions have to be destroyed. Justice will always face up to the fact of power. Fundamentally, what the Lambeth Conference failed to do was to take adequate account of these realities and of the need to ensure a proper framework according to principles of justice, before there can be any question of that solution which Christian love can alone ultimately provide.

Is there anything we can say in general on these questions?

(1) Though society exists, and can only exist, when men live together with some common ends, so that political and social organization exists to serve some 'common good', yet this common good is not something entirely above, and different from, the common goods of the people who make up the society. It is people in all their relationships with other people with whom we are concerned, not some non-existent abstraction we may call 'nation', 'society', or 'the state'; these words are used for convenience to describe the complex realities of human living, they do not refer to entities whose interests we have to consider.

(2) In the modern world people are divided in their fundamental attitudes, so that we cannot assume any common religious scale of values. We have to adapt ourselves to a world where people differ radically in their standards of value, and yet have, somehow or other, to live together. One might add that in fact they find it stimulating and worth-while to do so, in spite of many disadvantages.

(3) A fully human society is one where people belong to all sorts and kinds of groups in which they find their fulfilment at different levels. It is as idealistic to look back to some norm of rural community life, as it is to look forward to a world filled with nothing but large-scale planning organizations. A realistic Christian assessment of human nature recognizes that men require many different kinds of groupings, communities and organizations and that their requirements will change as circumstances change. A human society requires a rich variety of changing organizations and communities.

(4) Power is a reality of the world, morally indifferent of itself, but liable to be abused by sinful men. All politics is concerned with power, and politics enters into all organizations. There are many well-tried expedients in the history of the West for dealing with power, which have proved more or less successful. The basis of them all is the recognition (which is fundamentally a theological recognition) that power is always dangerous and can corrupt the best of men.

(5) In a complex world, men inevitably have differing interests which will clash, and clash in different ways at different times. It is right and proper that they should organize to ensure proper representation of these interests. Unorganized interests are likely to be neglected, and the interests of all legitimate groups have something to contribute to society. It is idealism of the most fanciful kind to ignore the existence of these interests and their need to be organized. Those who think they can be trusted to look after the interests of other men for them are the most dangerous of men, because they are unaware of their own liability to corruption.

(6) The appropriate form of organization is not necessarily a special institution. The interests of consumers may be better represented in a properly organized market than in so-called consumers' committees (which have not proved particularly important, even if valuable in a humdrum sort of way). (A specialized consumers' research organization, such as that which publishes *Which?* is obviously more useful than the follies of a 'Housewives' League'.) The relationship between groups of people or institutions may be more important than any particular institution. Much attention has often been given to the legal framework of a society. Outside the ranks of economists it may be doubted whether people have paid enough attention to the structure of the market (or the price system). This is perhaps particularly true of political philosophers, lawyers and theologians.

(7) The complex modern world in which we live is not only a world with highly developed markets, but also with great institutions representing the interests of different groups. Many of these institutions often fail to adjust themselves to the realities of the changing world around them. But even if they are adjusted, they inevitably clash with other institutions. It is the business of the state to ensure, as far as possible, both that particular institutions are adjusted to present

realities, and also that clashes with other institutions serve 'the common good'. That is to say, the state must see that the balance of the struggle, in so far as struggle is necessary, is so arranged as to serve the most general interests. The state must do this, because only the state can. But this does not necessarily imply that the state has to act and to be operative itself. It may only be active in the sense that it permits a certain balance of forces, which will work themselves out in due course, or prevents the development of certain accumulations of power, which would prove disastrous.

(8) It should be surprising to many of our moralists that the modern world works, in spite of the fact that it does not correspond to their ideal of a world with a common morality, harmony of interests, and co-operative or compromise solution of conflicts. The unity of mankind is tougher than is implied in the denunciations of some of our prophets. In the last resort we are made to realize the profundity of the remark of F. D. Maurice, 'Competition is put forth as the law of the universe. That is a lie'.[17] But what is true of the profoundest levels must not be taken necessarily to be true at the everyday level. The framework which binds us together in our complex world is much more subtle than to be comprehended in some simple principle. Just as modern society does not cohere because of a common set of beliefs, and gains much from the richness of conflicting beliefs, so there is no one principle of organization, whether the market or some ideal structure of organizations, such as theorists of 'distributism' or 'the corporate society' hanker after, which can assure the cement of social order. The stability and humanity of our social order gains much in the sphere of organization, as in the sphere of belief, from the conflicts and incoherencies of our world. It is not that there is virtue in conflict and incoherency for their own sakes. But they do allow for flexibility and adjustment to change, and they do express something of the richness and variety of the lives of the men who make up our society.

[17] *The Life of Frederick Denison Maurice*, ed. by his son Frederick Maurice, Vol. 2, p. 32.

Chapter 7

CAN WE CONTROL THE ECONOMIC SYSTEM?

Mr. Featherstone on Bulstrode the banker

'You'd sooner offend me than Bulstrode. And what's he?—he's got no land hereabout that ever I heard tell of. A speckilating fellow! He may come down any day, when the devil leaves off backing him. And that's what his religion means: he wants God A'mighty to come in. That's nonsense! There's one thing I made out pretty clear when I used to go to church—and it's this: God A'mighty sticks to the land. He promises land, and He gives land, and He makes chaps rich with corn and cattle. But you take the other side. You like Bulstrode and speckilation better than Featherstone and land.'—GEORGE ELIOT, *Middlemarch.*

Bank Failure in 1825

Mr. MacFungus:

'A weel sirs, what's the matter?
An' hegh sirs, what's the clatter?
Ye dinna ken,
Ye seely men.
Y'ur fortunes ne'er were batter.
There's too much population,
An' too much cultivation,
An' too much circulation.
That's a' that ails the nation.
Ye're only out o' halth, sirs,
Wi' a plathora o' walth, sirs,
Instead of glourin' hither,
Ye'd batter, I conjacture,
Just hoot awa' thegither,
To hear our braw chiel lacture:
His ecoonoomic science
Wad silence a' your clanking,
An' teach you some reliance,
On the principles o' banking.'

THOMAS LOVE PEACOCK, *Paper Money Lyrics.*

I. A SYSTEM OUT OF CONTROL?

SOME people may be dissatisfied with what has been said so far about our twentieth-century economic and social system. It may be thought that I have been far too optimistic and complimentary about our achievements and far too ready to accept them uncritically, while evading the heart of the criticisms of our society made by profounder prophets. I gave warning at the beginning that I would tend to concentrate on the positive element in our world. What I have said has been concerned with a limited number of problems, and it might be thought that, on the one hand, there has been too much detail on specific issues for the really fundamental questions to be raised, and, on the other hand, too much vague generalization on other questions. It is difficult to see how such a situation can be avoided in dealing with such a world as ours. A *Summa Sociologica* of our world would be beyond the powers of any man, and, even if achieved, would be out-of-date as soon as written. It is probably inevitable that what one has to say will appear to be impressionistic in general, with curious patches of Pre-Raphaelite realism.

The picture that emerges, however, may be said to be much less satisfactory than is implied in the various comments made at intervals about our world. We have to live in a world of continuous change, which is both stimulating and unsettling; in a world of superabundant wealth, surrounded by the agonies of those who strive to rise out of age-long poverty; in a world where men are brought to realize their common humanity and their equal status as men, and yet which can find no obvious means to express these facts; in a world where men face a rich and bewildering variety of opportunities, and yet where there is no possibility of finding any solution to apparently ceaseless conflicts between differing groups and interests. Is this the best that men can expect? In one obvious sense, there can be no other answer than 'Yes'. The best that men can expect is what they find around them.

But, in another sense, one can rightly ask, whether our system could be improved in its pattern and outline, without requiring of men that they should cease to be the restless sinners that they are. It is no adequate defence of the *status quo* to argue that the only reform possible is the conversion of all mankind into saints; such an argument suggests not merely profound theological error as to the nature of man and sin, but also such a conformity to the ways of the world as to deny to the speaker any right to his hearers' attention. There can be no economic and social system so good as not to require improvement, improvement which is within the bounds of realistic action in a world where men can be presumed to remain the sinners they have been and are. To fail to face up to this fact in the various ways required of us is to fail in responsibility to man and God. It is my contention that the churches and the Christians today do largely fail of their responsibilities in this field, especially in Britain, and especially in the Church of England, to which I belong. In my last chapter I will discuss this in some detail.

If there is no social system so good as not to require reform, the converse is equally true. There are few, if any, social systems so bad as not to show some elements of a proper human order. But there is a great deal of difference between a system where the required improvements are possible and indeed allowed for in its very pattern, and a system where reform is only possible by the total overthrow of the system itself, either by a complete recasting of its institutions, or by the total removal from power of the particular groups who exercise it. There are some who would appear to argue that our social system is of this kind, and it is with this argument that I am concerned.

I do not intend to deal with the arguments of those who believe that our economic system is so inhuman and so inefficient that it requires total overthrow and that the only solution is to be found in a completely socialist society where there is no private sector. The arguments for and against this view are to be found in a wide range of literature by economists and others. It is a view that hardly requires serious discussion today, when we have experience of what can be done in a system of welfare capitalism, using post-Keynesian means of control; which is not to deny that it was a serious issue to the 'thirties. My own views, which I have expressed elsewhere,[1] are that a completely socialist society in this sense is unnecessary to achieve the essential humane ideals for which socialism stands, but, on the other hand, unlikely to prove the disaster that the old guard would have us believe it might be.

Nor do I intend to deal with the outbursts of those who find the last

[1] In *Christianity and Economic Problems*, *passim*.

enemy in some 'Establishment' or other. Various paranoid explanations of social phenomena unfortunately are all too easy to littérateurs, philosophers, and theologians, not to mention their appeal to the simple-minded and to cranks and psychotics. It is human to blame the Jews, the capitalists, the Bank of England, the Fellows of All Souls, the Foreign Office, or whatever group in society one dislikes or from which one feels cut off. It is very easy to dilate these feelings into a complete and simple social explanation. But society is not so easily explained. There is, unfortunately, no simple key to unlock the complexities of our times, or the depths of our ills. We shall not understand without hard work, patient study of the facts, and an open-mindedness which is ready to discover that our preconceived ideas were wrong all the time. (I hold no particular brief for the institutions mentioned, and am inclined to believe that the Bank of England, the Foreign Office, and the Fellows of All Souls (the latter in so far as they can be regarded as an institution at all, rather than a collection of persons of varying distinction) are institutions that are unnecessarily ingrown, ripe for reform and unadapted to their position in modern society. But to say this is not to accept any myth of the 'Establishment'.)

The criticism with which I am concerned is most commonly found among literary writers and among philosophers and theologians, in so far as it can be located at all. It argues that we live in an inhuman world that is in some sense uncontrolled. Not merely are human beings subject to forces of daemonic intensity, and de-personalized by the machinery of life, but also these forces are in some sense inherently out of control, at least as we find them around us. The solution, it is said, requires some return to a human scale, some humanization of a technological world. This may be envisaged in terms of a break-up of our great concentrations of power and organization and a return to something simpler and more humane. Or alternatively what is demanded is a democratization of economic life, which will bring economic forces under human control.

It is with these questions that I want to deal, vague as they may seem to be, firstly, in terms of the effects of what is sometimes called the 'technological revolution', and then in answer to the question whether our economic system can be democratized, and what form this should take. Finally, I will try to deal with the question whether it is possible for men as they are in reality, little men with narrow horizons, to live a properly human life in the complexities around us.[2]

2. THE TECHNOLOGICAL REVOLUTION

There is to be found among Christians, and perhaps others, a liking for the description of our world as 'technological'. It is often said that we live, and have lived, through a technological revolution. Technology is said to be the dominant force of our times, which determines the pattern of our world. Technology is a force, it is said, which is both creative and daemonic; it makes and breaks human society. It has a dynamic of its own, which carries us on almost irrespective of our plans and hopes. It is not merely neutral, because it shapes human lives in ways that affect their inmost personalities and intimate social relations. It is not merely a matter of techniques that can be accepted or rejected in order to achieve given ends. It determines human ends as well as means. The technological revolution is one of the major revolutions of history. We have to come to grips with it.

This thesis can perhaps be seen most clearly stated in the World Council of Churches' study on 'Christians and the Prevention of War in an Atomic Age—A Theological Discussion'. This is a most admirable study of the Christian approach to war, but my concern is confined to certain passages, which express views about our technological world.[3]

35. There is serious reason to believe that technological society in its present forms is a society in which impersonal and indiscriminate behaviour in social relationships is more dominant than discriminate moral purposes. The impersonal character of urbanization, the mechanization of much of private and social and economic life, the highly complex interconnection of economies throughout the world and of the factors within domestic economies, the relatively high degree of standardization in products and communications and taste, the ability especially through communications to control and shape opinion and action—these are all based in large measure upon the fact and influence of technology. Moreover, in our present society, men have not

[2] 'We must preserve the possibility of a satisfying life for "little men in big societies".' (Report of Section III, 'The Church and the Disorder of Society', Amsterdam Assembly. *The First Assembly of the World Council of Churches*, ed. W. A. Visser 't Hooft (S.C.M. Press, 1949), p. 77.

[3] This report was offered to the churches by the Central Committee of the W.C.C. in 1958 as 'a contribution to Christian research and inquiry'.

learned that it is in a certain sense non-technical to use technics to the full. . . . The chief problem of technological culture is that it contains something within itself which, in spite of its achievements and in part because of them, tends to establish the impersonal, the mechanical, the indiscriminate as that which is dominant.

36. How may this element be analysed? It is composed of various factors interacting upon each other. The first concerns the nature of science and technology. These words denote essentially a process which produces results. . . . On the one side, as related to human minds and wills, these processes are not neutral but, like all human works, ambiguous, especially as regards their application and use. On the other side, so far as they are objective, the processes of science and technology contain their own inner logic, independent of individuals and groups. This inner logic is revealed most vividly in the fact that the scientific method is irreversible and unpredictable in its results. There is a dynamic in the march of scientific discovery and technological advance which seems to defy the decisions of men.

37. Moreover, many of our present forms of technological culture contain within them an attitude on the part of the population which is an idolatry. For the ordinary man, the mystery of scientific achievement and its obvious benefits have the appearance of a source of salvation. Progress in the human race is defined in terms of the plenty and peace which science and technology can produce. . . .

38. A *process*, which is ambiguous and which contains its own dynamic, which is irreversible and produces unpredictable results, which already has greatly benefited mankind and promises to produce greater welfare, is at present regarded idolatrously by men as the principal source of plenty, security and well being. This means that deep within technological society, indeed in one sense as its mainspring, there is a powerful, impersonal element. It means that men do not control the total processes of their technology, not so much because men are unable to do so, as because men have surrendered to them. Moral and ethical purposes are more formed by technological society than in control of it.

39. This analysis leads us to the conclusion that there can be no effective discipline for the control of any large single part of technological culture unless there is a comprehensive discipline also whereby the essential development of technological culture is subject to the ethical and moral aims. . . .

40. Three elements at least should form the basis of this broader discipline.

41. 1. Christians must make every effort to insure that in their own thought and scale of values there is no element of the popular idolatry of science and technology, no borrowing from the philosophy of scientism. . . .

42. 2. A discipline of mind and spirit is required which is able to analyse the ambiguity involved in the scientific and technological process, and able to control the evil of the ambiguity and to use the good. There is scarcely a single discovery or a machine which is not subject to this ambiguity, or which does

not call for decision as to how its evil uses may be curtailed and its good uses promoted. . . .

43. 3. A third discipline is that of self-sacrifice in relationship to the benefits of technological society. . . .

44. . . . What is required is a certain humanism, embodied in disciplined living, and directed toward the particular spiritual and ethical needs of technological society.[4]

There is first the question of words to be considered. 'Science' means knowledge; in this context, knowledge of natural phenomena. 'Technology', from its root, and by analogy with other similar words, also means a kind of knowledge; the *Concise Oxford Dictionary* (3rd ed.) defines it as 'science of the industrial arts; ethnological study of development of arts'. In the normal and primary English usage, it is a solecism, therefore, to talk about science and technology as 'denoting essentially a process'. We do not talk thus about theology or the study of the classics. It is equally a solecism to talk about a 'scientific society' or a 'technological society', though this usage has become more common. Would we normally describe Tibet or medieval Europe as 'theological societies'? Did Old Stone Age man live in a 'geological society'?

In departing from the primary usage, which is in itself an entirely legitimate matter, the danger is that ambiguity enters. I suspect that this whole use of the word 'technology' is a case of a definition which implicitly prejudges a case that requires argument and proof. I take it that a 'technological society' or a 'scientific society' means a society in some sense dominated by 'technology' or 'science'. In the case of 'science' there is less ambiguity. It is fairly clear that modern science, as developed from, say the seventeenth century, can be treated as a new and unique phenomenon in human history. But 'technology' is neutral in the sense that one can talk of 'Stone Age technology' as properly as of 'modern technology'. Presumably it is the latter that we are concerned with. But a question immediately arises. The implication of the phrase, 'technological society', is that modern technology dominates society in a way that Stone Age technology did not dominate Stone Age society. To say that modern society is scientific in a way that no other society has ever been is obviously right; but to say that technology

[4] Pp. 23–6. The conclusions are admirable, and there is no quarrel with them.

dominates society today as never before is a highly dubious proposition. It would be possible to argue, not without plausibility, that Stone Age society was far more technologically determined than modern society, precisely because there was not the opportunity to choose alternative techniques to achieve given ends. It seems doubtful whether anyone really wants to assert that modern society is more determined in this way than earlier societies.

It may be said that the whole point has been missed. 'Is it not clear that what is meant by "technological society" is a society dominated by gadgets, mechanical processes, etc., in effect by modern technology as it has developed with the aid of modern science?' Unfortunately, the question is then wholly begged. It is a tautology that modern society uses modern technology. If it is not true that modern society is more dominated by its technology than previous societies were by theirs, then there is no point in talking about a 'technological society', unless we specify some particular aspect of modern technology, which is different from previous technologies, and which we believe to characterize modern society. When the question is put this way, it becomes clear that the fundamental differences are to be found in the application of science in modern society, and the complex of social and economic changes we call the industrial revolution.

Modern society is characterized by the application of science and 'the industrial revolution'. It is these that produce the 'impersonality', the 'mechanization', the 'complex interconnection', the 'standardization' and so on. Many of these things I have discussed already. It is not clear that there is any simple relationship between the development of science and its application, or between the application of science and 'the industrial revolution'. Even if we take the application of science in its widest sense and include the kind of technical improvement that requires no knowledge, it is clear that many of the characteristic features of modern society and much of our capacity for economic growth depend on purely economic and social factors, such as the development of a certain type of business-man, the growth of markets, capacity for organization and so on. The matter is highly complex, but it is not clear that much is gained by labelling the whole complex of social and economic processes as 'technological'.

If not much is gained, not much would be lost, if the use of this particular label did not lead to the almost unnoticed insinuation of further theses. It is natural to talk of a 'scientific process' or a 'technological (or technical) process'. The normal meaning of these terms would be to describe a set of operations either as they occur within a laboratory during a scientific experiment (or which make up a model of what is believed to occur in nature), or such as we find within a factory or some other human group where complex means (usually including machinery of some kind?) are used to achieve some human end. Thus the *Concise Oxford Dictionary* includes under 'process' the phrase 'method of operation in manufacture, printing, photography, etc.' But when it is said in the passage quoted above that 'these words ['science' and 'technology'] denote essentially a process which produces results' clearly something else is meant. It is clear that the only kind of process which can be meant here is a social process; they are indeed described later as 'like all human works'. What kind of social processes are involved? This is never made clear. Nor is it made clear why social processes require to be described as 'science' and 'technology'.

It is at this point that the essential confusion arises. It is much more plausible to describe science and technology as having 'an inner logic, independent of individuals and groups', which is 'revealed most vividly in the fact that the scientific method is irreversible and unpredictable in its results', and as having a 'dynamic, which seems to defy the decisions of men', than it would be to say the same about social and economic processes, in which men would inevitably be involved at all stages, even though perhaps unable to control them.[5] It thus becomes plausible to say that 'deep within technological society, indeed in one sense as its mainspring, there is a powerful, impersonal element'; this would require much more elucidation if it were rephrased in terms of social and economic processes. 'The technological process' is in fact a sort of Platonic entity, which has no real existence; as a shorthand phrase to describe certain features of the modern world it is misleading, though it could be used legitimately if the features in question were

[5] There is a certain ambiguity in the text between 'a dynamic . . . which seems to defy the decisions of men', and the assertion that 'men do not control the total processes of their technology, not so much because men are unable to do so, as because men have surrendered to them'. The argument may be that, when men surrender to these processes, they then appear to them to be outside their control (in accordance with the traditional doctrine of original sin). But there are certain phrases which seem to imply that there is some inherent uncontrollability in the processes themselves.

specified at the outset. If it is thought that there is something real going on in the world, that could be simply described as a 'technological process', in the same sort of way that one can talk of a process of capital formation, or a process of replacement of status relationships by contract relationships, all I can say is that I do not know what this process is. It is up to those who use these ambiguous phrases to explain them by reference to the real world; otherwise we shall be forced to assume that they are talking about unicorns or other monsters from some modern theological bestiary.

Let me try to outline the social and economic processes that these misleading phrases seem to be describing. That they are misleading becomes clear once the realities are described for what they are.

1. There is, firstly, the social process by which scientific discoveries take place and are propagated through universities, research institutions, learned societies and 'the commonwealth of science'. Similar social arrangements exist for technological studies. The existence of these social arrangements, with the climate of opinion they produce, stimulates scientific discovery, given the natural human desire for knowledge. It would no doubt be impossible to prevent people from studying and making discoveries. But the organized arrangements for these studies, which alone make possible the continuous extension of scientific knowledge, depend entirely on the social institutions which train people, provide equipment for experiments, and publish the results of scientific discoveries. There would be no difficulty in producing a Dark Age in scientific as in other studies, if it were desired to do so. But so long as the facilities are available, it is clear that there will be a constant stream of scientific discoveries.

2. When we come to the application of basic science to industrial use, the social processes are more obviously important, and more difficult to specify. We enter upon a field where there is a great deal of discussion, and where only recently has there been any attempt to discover what actually happens.[6] Some of the social processes in question are the forces leading young people to study science, the way they select the jobs they take afterwards and the attraction that industry

[6] E.g. Ministry of Labour, *Scientific and Engineering Manpower in Great Britain* (H.M.S.O. 1956). C. F. Carter and B. R. Williams, *Industry and Technical Progress* (O.U.P., 1957). J. Jewkes, D. Sawers, and R. Stillerman, *The Sources of Invention* (Macmillan, 1958). C. F. Carter and B. R. Williams, *Investment in Innovation* (O.U.P., 1958).

exerts on them, the use industry makes of scientists and technologists, the availability of scientific results to that public which can make use of them, the 'climate of opinion' which leads people to welcome scientific contributions to practical life, and the economic processes which induce business-men to improve their methods, or dissuade them from doing so.

3. This leads to the third process, that by which business-men apply scientific discoveries in their businesses. Here we come upon all the traditional themes of Religion and Capitalism, the profit motive, the individual's desire to adventure, the willingness to undertake risks, the capacity to foresee a future different from the present, and all the complex social forces which have led to the emergence of a business class, such as we know it in the West. Given such a class, much depends on the economic climate, whether of competition or restriction, and the governmental environment.

4. The application of the particular techniques available in the modern world has hitherto led to the investment of resources in large blocks of capital equipment which human labour uses and with which it co-operates. The steel-mill, the continuous assembly plant, the power-station, the oil refinery, the railway, the large liner or tanker, are all examples of the kinds of capital equipment which embody modern technology to serve the ends chosen by our economic system. The units are large, and often require a large assembly of human labour. In the more fully automatized factories, there may be less labour employed, but its conditions may be even more narrowly circumscribed by the requirements of the plant. Here men may be said to be 'mechanized', and relations within the plant may have to be impersonal, though this need not always be the case.

5. Then there is the 'impersonal character of urbanization', which is brought about by the growth of population, the development of transport, the advantages of industrial and commercial concentration, and so on, as described earlier in chapter three.

6. Another aspect of these changes is specialization of activity, and the narrow limitation of an individual's occupation, which is, however, associated with a greater choice of job than was possible in more primitive and less specialized societies, as was referred to in the last chapter.

7. The mere fact of size is a separate factor. The large scale of the modern world leads both to large units, whether industrial plants or large cities, and to 'the highly complex interconnection of economies throughout the world'. The former may lead to remoteness of the individual person from those who make the final decisions affecting his life, while the latter leads to those feelings of subjection to vast impersonal and uncontrollable forces which the market mechanism tends to produce (and which were discussed in the last chapter).

8. The business-man shapes our tastes and our manner of life in so far as he moulds our activities by advertising and produces certain kinds of products which we are cajoled into buying. This is the 'standardization in products and communications and taste' referred to above, and which I discussed at some length in my third chapter.

9. As a result of all these and other processes we live in a world of continuous change, as never before in human history, as earlier described in my second chapter.

It would seem that these are the main social and economic processes which are in question when we talk about our society as in the passage quoted above. No doubt there are others linked with them, or which would be distinguished from them in a more careful and detailed analysis. But to make such a brief and summary list shows that we are dealing with a range of different phenomena, no doubt interconnected, but involving different aspects of life.

Our concern is with persons in this world. All societies under the impact of original sin tend to dehumanize man. Men are dehumanized in any activity in so far as they give themselves totally to it; even the simple all-round life can become dehumanized. Every institution is capable of being perverted, however primitive it may be; the mere complexity of an institution is not of itself a sign that it suffers from a greater measure of corruption. Our problem then is to humanize our particular world, with all the peculiar opportunities it offers to us.

To bring the large-scale, the impersonal, the mechanical and the complex within the range of human comprehension, it might be thought odd to start at the top, where the complexity inevitably resolves itself into an abstract pattern. If we look for understanding of a wide-ranging and varied world in a simple theme or set of patterns, the only understanding we shall achieve will be highly abstract and impersonal. Similarly, if we try to control such a world through some single centre of power, or some single idea, the idea will be abstract and the power centre will deal with relationships at their most abstract and impersonal. Such theoreticians and such administrators are not those best suited to see matters in human terms on a human scale.

But if, on the other hand, we start with human beings as we find them, then we have to deal with the particular situations outlined above. It is possible to understand much of what goes on in an industrial plant, without reference to the whole of our civilization, and equally decisions have to be taken within it independently of what happens elsewhere, though no doubt determined by the framework within which it works. Similar considerations apply when we turn to city life, consumption patterns, advertising, taxation, and so on. If we turn to particular problems, we can begin to see how these aspects of life affect people concretely. There is a chance that we may be able to deal with them by themselves and thus humanize particular areas of life. It may indeed be the case that there are some areas of life which cannot be humanized so long as they have to operate within a particular framework. Nothing that I have said is to be taken as meaning that piecemeal concern with a narrow sector of life can be justified where what is required is an alteration of the structure. But much can be done within particular sectors, and, where the structure is right, this is where we have to operate. It is here that men exercise responsibility, and each man's is inevitably limited.

What I am suggesting is that to break up the different aspects of modern society into manageable subjects for study and to deal with them in turn is likely to lead to a fuller sympathy with people in their real human relations and a deeper grasp of what is required to humanize these relations, than is a concentration on overall slogans, which purport to explain the total picture, but in fact fail to do so. The human way to study human society is to proceed in the limited terms possible to the human mind; the same applies to reform which aims to bring society within a human scale. Once again I suggest that it is those who talk in terms of these vast impersonal forces who are themselves dehumanized; a dehumanization which results from a Promethean desire to comprehend all society within a formula patent to their inevitably limited minds.

In proceeding as I have done by dealing with a limited number of aspects of modern society, and analysing them separately, it has been possible to show something of what goes wrong in these particular fields, and what can be done about them. Nothing can be done about a 'process with an inner logic, independent of individuals and groups... irreversible and unpredictable'. Many theologians have drawn the conclusion, in their obsession with phrases such as these, that there is little, if anything, that can be done in modern society. They cease to offer guidance of any relevance to those engaged in the practical process of living, and the Church becomes a ghetto. But, if we deal with the particular aspects in turn, we find that there is much that can be done. In the course of these chapters, I have dealt more or less summarily with most of the matters mentioned above, with specialization, city life, advertisement and consumption patterns, with economic growth and the large scale of modern society.[7] Because they have been dealt with *seriatim*, they may appear not to fit into a pattern, and to miss the trends of our time. But on the contrary it might be argued that, if the detailed suggestions I have made at intervals were really practised, and if we really visualized them, the world, though altered piecemeal in a number of different respects, would look a very different sort of world. A painting is not merely made up of a blur of colours seen from a great distance; it is also made up of a mass of detail which fits into the pattern of the whole. Too great a concentration on the detail may indeed lead us to miss the beauty of the whole, but not to look at the detail is to ignore how the whole is fitted together.

3. DEMOCRATIC CONTROL OF THE ECONOMIC SYSTEM

There is an interdependency in a modern social system, and, however much particular sectors can be dealt with separately and the pattern altered by altering the details, people still feel that the system is beyond them. Is it not possible to subject it to control in some way that will make it more democratic? It used often to be said that what was required was to introduce democracy into industry or into economic life, in the same way that it had already been introduced into political life. Is this possible?

[7] The biggest gap concerns the problems of industrial management and community within industry.

It is not realized clearly enough, or widely enough, that the market system, perhaps better described as the price system, in so far as it works, and is properly used, rather than abused, is a form of democracy, by which people express their wishes in many important fields of life. There are many, who ought to know better, but who continue to perpetuate gross and simple errors about these matters, which a little consideration would remove. There are large numbers of educated people, whether scientists, philosophers, lawyers, littérateurs or theologians, who do not make the minimum amount of mental effort to understand the realities of economic life, which they would make as a matter of course in any other matter about which they thought fit to speak. A more widespread understanding of how the price system works, and where it can be expected to work well and where badly, would remove some of the helplessness people feel about the world in which we live. We do in fact today live in a world where the market is controlled and, on the whole, used rather than abused. There is no possible going back to the world of *laisser-faire*, though there may be much disagreement as to where exactly intervention is required. We do not live in a world of uncontrolled economic forces, which no one understands, and with which it is for some reason impossible and totally forbidden to interfere. We do interfere, we do control, and we do, more or less, understand what the market does. If it is left to do its job, it is because it does it well, or because people, misguidedly, think it does its job well. If we disagree, we have to show that there is a better way to achieve the same desired results (or to show that we do not want these results at all).[8] There are indeed many reforms which I would favour, but it is not the place here to discuss them.

But is this enough? Is it not possible to break down our complex economy into more manageable units? Is it not possible to recreate some of the small regional areas as suitable for control of the system? It is at the local level that people can properly participate in democratic life. Can there not be local control of economic life? There is no question that, if we were able to achieve more in this direction, we would have a more humane and Christian society. It is equally clear that we suffer from a haphazard, unplanned and ill-directed system of local government, which is, in many ways, quite unsuited to deal with

[8] See *Christianity and Economic Problems*, Chapter 9, 'The Price System'.

the problems of the twentieth century. Because of the political pressures of the existing institutions, whether county boroughs, county councils or other forms of local government, it has hitherto proved impossible (or beyond the courage of politicians) to provide even the minimum of reforms. At the moment, these matters are being comprehensively reviewed by a Commission, which might, possibly, produce some worth-while reorganization. It is not the place to go into these matters here, but what can be clearly seen is that the growth of the large conurbations of our time, and the development of comprehensive town-planning on a regional basis (quite apart from developments in the fields of health and roads), require new units of government more appropriate to the realities.

The question then arises: 'How far could reorganized regional or other appropriate forms of local government control and plan the economic life of their areas?' To begin with, it is clear that there are many more powers that could be given quite appropriately to local authorities. Already local authorities are permitted to spend money on the encouragement of art and culture; how many make use of their powers? Are Christians active in persuading them to do more, or to do it more effectively? Or are Christians to be found in the vanguard of those who decry the spending of public money on 'lumps of stone' and 'daubs of paint'? This is but one example among many of the creative powers that local authorities possess, but which are used haphazardly and without thought, or not used at all. Determined local action could do a great deal to develop the use of powers (that already exist) in order to enrich the quality of local life.

If we are concerned to humanize the complexities of life as far as possible, it is desirable that local authorities should be given opportunities to control those aspects of economic life that they suitably can. Much is, in effect, already done through the operation of local planning powers. Probably more could be done to decentralize, to regional authorities, powers now exercised centrally by the Board of Trade in the matter of location of industry, and in giving grants for the proper distribution of industry. There are many local organizations concerned with local or regional economic development, such as the Scottish Council (Development and Industry) and the North-East Development Council. There could no doubt be more with greater powers. But in this, as in other such matters of local government, one overruling problem requires to be solved, namely the avoidance of local corruption. The more economic powers are given to local bodies, the more important is it to create the machinery for ensuring that they are not merely used to foster the interests of particular persons or groups.

Overall powers of control or encouragement of economic activity are bound to be limited in a complex interrelated economic system such as that existing in Britain. But there is no reason why local authorities should not have powers to run commercial enterprises on a local scale, if they can compete satisfactorily with private business. The advantage of having local enterprises run by local councils is, firstly, that many who would not otherwise have experience of business may learn something of it through their local council; it is to be noted here that, in this respect, nationalization of gas and electricity represented a net loss to democracy. Secondly, it may well be that there are local fields of enterprise where, for various reasons, private business fails to meet the public demands. It would seem entirely reasonable that local authorities should be given powers to undertake this sort of enterprise, subject to limitations of the amount of subsidy, if any, that they may be permitted to grant from the rates, and to proper commercial accounting. Why should private business complain of such enterprise, if competition is on fair terms, when it believes that private enterprise is more efficient than public? Why do Conservatives, who believe this, oppose the granting of such powers, which should conclusively disprove the arguments of socialists, if their beliefs are true? Why do booksellers oppose the development of university bookshops? In a world where we are trying through anti-monopoly legislation to encourage competition, such local experiments in commerce as the opening of local authority cinemas, theatres, restaurants, public-houses, and (why not?) ordinary shops, should surely be encouraged, at least by Christians who believe that human responsibility is important. It is clear that the public needs to be protected from the development of inefficient local monopolies, but it is not beyond the powers of social invention to ensure that many of these dangers are avoided.

When all is said and done, however, the extent to which economic life can be reduced to regional or local terms is limited. An illustration of the naïvety of some of those who advocate such action can be seen in the Scottish Covenant movement, powerfully backed by Edinburgh lawyers and others innocent of the realities of economic life. At one time the Covenant movement attracted a good deal of support in Scotland (at least in the form of signatures), and its sponsors actually worked out the details of an arrangement for a Scottish Parliament. It was here that there appeared a failure to appreciate the limits of possible regional action. For, on the one hand, the Scottish Parliament was to have powers to control wages in Scotland, but national insurance, including unemployment benefits, was to be a matter left to Westminster.

I take it for granted that Scotland is essentially a poorer country than England, and that economically the benefits flow from England to Scotland. That is to say, the payments from the Exchequer to Scotland in the form of grants to local services or particular activities, and by means of national insurance and assistance payments, are proportionately larger than the amounts collected in taxes in Scotland. In other words, an entirely independent Scotland would be a poorer country than it is at the present (as it was poorer than England before the Act of Union of 1707, and indeed has been since, but with a narrower gap). This thesis is indeed disputed by the supporters of the Covenant, but many of their arguments are fairly obviously fallacious when subjected to economic scrutiny, and others remain unproven. The balance of informed opinion, and of probability from what evidence there is, does not support their thesis.

If we then accept that Scotland is essentially a poorer country, and admit the fairly obvious fact that politically Scotland is more radical than England, we can envisage an intriguing situation emerging from a Scottish Parliament established as the Covenanters would like it. Such a Parliament, with its powers to control wages, could set Scottish wages at higher levels than those in England (whereas at present, in so far as there is any difference, wages and earnings in Scotland are lower than in England); the result would naturally be that industries in Scotland would be unable to compete as successfully as before with industry in England, and a certain amount of unemployment would follow. But England would have to foot the bill! There would be a steady stream of national insurance and assistance payments to Scotland, the extent of which would depend on the difference in the wage-levels in the two countries. Either Scotland would, in effect, be forced to follow the national trends, or Westminster would have to pay for the follies of the Edinburgh parliament (a situation which would hardly be stable). Admittedly, the situation would be different if Scotland were entirely independent. As an independent country, it would be forced to pay its own bills, if it wanted to raise wages in this sort of way, and would pay the price in the form of an adverse balance of payments or a devalued Scots pound, leading to higher costs of imported goods.

The purpose of this argument is not to meet the substantive question whether Scotland would be better or worse off if it were an entirely independent country, but to show that there are narrow limitations on what can be done by regional or local action in important economic matters within the context of a unified economic system. There is no overall solution in this direction of the dilemmas of a complex economy unless we are ready to face the consequences of a deliberate return to a primitive economy with the low standard of living that it involves.

This is not to deny that there are many fields where more efforts could be exerted to increase the range of human responsibility, or what may be called democracy. In particular, there are many opportunities open within industrial units, whether they are large or small. Men spend the larger part of their waking life at work, and it is here that they have to exercise their responsibilities. This is a field where we can be grateful that the Church as an organized body is beginning to work seriously, though Christians have long been active within their jobs and professional organizations. Again, I merely mention this field, though its importance is clearly immense.[9]

4. THE HUMAN SCALE

I have argued that something can be done to bring economic life within the human scale by 'democratization' within industry, by enlargement of the powers and activities of local government, and by a

[9] Christian work here has a long history, for example in the Industrial Department of the Student Christian Movement. See also Sir G. Schuster, *Christianity and Human Relations in Industry* (1951); E. R. Wickham, *Church and People in an Industrial City* (1957), *The Task of the Church in Relation to Industry* (Church Information Office, 1959); *The Church and Industry* (British Council of Churches, 1958).

wider understanding of the use (and abuse) of the price system. But these matters are limited, though important. Our economic system remains complex, large-scale, and subject to forces of national, and indeed international, range. These forces cannot be understood by the ordinary man in the street, and even experts can only see the picture as a whole in the most abstract terms, thus ignoring the impact of the forces on particular men and women where they are most keenly felt. Is it possible to live as men in such a world?

An answer can only be properly given to this question by those who live and work with men in their different lives, and not by an academic economist. A Christian would normally expect to go to the parish clergy in order to know where the shoe pinches. But one may, unfortunately, suspect today that this would not always be the best place to find the right answer. Partly this is because the parish clergy are out of touch with most aspects of people's working lives, and are themselves merely another kind of specialist with all the disadvantages of the rather academic role they play. Secondly, this view is based on the empirical fact that the kind of criticisms of our modern social order one finds arising from the clergy does not seem to be really based on concrete knowledge of the facts, but often seems rather to stem from a sort of generalized 'theological' approach, such as I have pilloried in my analysis of the concept of 'technological society'.

An academic economist cannot be expected to know the realities of the situation, but can merely record an impression that the situation is not really as bad as it often seems to be. A fearful picture can be painted by means of abstract generalizations, but there is no need for us to frighten ourselves with phantoms. The witness of those laymen active in their various fields of life as Christians, and not unduly insensitive to the pressure on men, tends to suggest that the outcry against dehumanization is a myth of academics or clergy, and that the impact on men of a large-scale world is not so devastating as it appears when considered in the abstract.[10] After all, men are not confronted with the vast complexity of inter-related forces which can be conjured up by an economist or a sociologist. They are faced with pressures at their work, on their way to work, in their homes, in the way they spend

[10] See, however, *Casualties of the Welfare State* by Audrey Harvey (Fabian Tract 321, February 1960).

their money and their leisure time, and what they do about their holidays. Men have always been faced with pressures from outside in all the various activities of living. In the past, they were tossed about by what appeared to be divinely ordained harvests, or plagues, about which they could do nothing. Today, they may be forced to change their jobs, because (in some way mysterious to them) the price of the product they have been producing has fallen, and their firm has to contract, or become bankrupt. Even the most understanding are constantly subject to forces only half-understood. This is part of the mystery and ambiguity of human life. It may be as Promethean to try to reduce everything to the human scale as to try, as a mere man, to rise to the heights of total comprehension. It is not at any rate clear that either programme in its extreme form is suitable for Christian endeavour. Some of the things Christians *should* do will be the concern of my last chapter.

NOTE ON 'TECHNOLOGY'

The peculiar usage of words recorded in the text seems to be due to J. H. Oldham under the influence of Karl Mannheim. Mannheim's *Man and Society* (1940) considered the influence of '*social techniques*' on the whole of social development.[11] 'The technical management of human affairs did not merely produce a new style of thought, it was also combined with a philosophy which declared technical inventions to be the dynamic factor in the making of history. The significance of technics first became obvious in the field of economic production. . . . There is no reason why technology should be significant only in the economic sphere and should be the sole factor decisively influencing the framework of events.'[12] He went on to explain how the word *techniques* had to be widened from its attachment to machines to include *social techniques*. 'These techniques, which set their seal upon mankind, are not merely accidental, but form part of an entire social and cultural system.'[13] Earlier, he had talked of 'aspects of nature which

[11] See the Table of Contents for Part V, particularly Section 1.
[12] Op. cit., pp. 242–3.
[13] p. 247.

have come under the domination of technology.'[14] One of the themes of the book is the wide-ranging influence on the whole social framework of modern technical means of control, and of the conscious application of functional reason to the solution of human and social problems.

J. H. Oldham referred to Mannheim's book in the *Christian News-Letter* of 5 June 1940 (No. 32), where he seems to have accepted that a 'planned society' would inevitably continue after the end of the war. Two supplements of 18 June and 1 July 1941, on 'The Predicament of Society and the Way Out' (*C.N-L.* Nos. 86, 88) were no doubt written, partly at least, under the influence of Mannheim. They talk about 'vast, mechanical, impersonal forces which deprive the majority of men of real existence as persons'. 'It is only by such [rational] planning that the complex forces of modern society can be directed to desirable ends . . . . The drift towards rational planning seems irresistible.' The only way to overcome the dangers is '*consciously to plan for freedom*' (a phrase from *Man and Society*). Later we are told that what is wanted is 'a conscious common purpose, on a scale far greater than anything that exists at present . . . which the historian of the future will recognize as having a comparable importance in history to the rise of the Communist and Nazi movements.'[15] It all reads rather strangely in 1960.

On 22 October 1941 (*C.N-L.* No. 104, Supplement), Oldham summarized the issues raised by *Man and Society* with a good deal of discussion of the problems of social techniques.[16] On 6 May 1942 (*C.N-L.* No. 132, Supplement), in reference to other books, he comes back to the question of 'technical production and social living', and here I find for the first time the use of *technological* as an adjective used of society in the phrase 'the question of the stability of our modern technological civilization'.[17]

A second stream of influence leading in the same direction comes from Lewis Mumford, the American sociologist/town-planner, whose *Technics and Civilization* appeared in 1934. Many of the ideas were also

[14] p. 155 n.

[15] There is also a discussion of the decay of community, the dominance of 'mass-man', the loss of meaning in life, the decay of organic communities in favour of Leviathan etc.

[16] See also *C.N-L.* No. 135 (27 May 1942).

[17] Mannheim further elaborated his ideas in *Diagnosis of our Time* (1943), to which Oldham again devoted a supplement of the *C.N-L.* (No. 174 of 24 February 1943). See also No. 180 of 21 April 1943, p. 7.

to be found in its sequel, *The Culture of Cities* (1938), which perhaps had a wider influence, with the distinction between 'eotechnic', 'palaeotechnic' and 'neotechnic' phases of civilization. Mumford seems clearly to have influenced Philip Mairet, whose essay 'A Civilization of Technics' appeared in *Prospect for Christendom* (1945).[18] Mairet also talks of 'our technological civilization,'[19] and similar phrases were taken up by other members of the 'Christendom Group',[20] and gained wider currency elsewhere.

The phrase became internationalized at the Amsterdam Assembly (which founded the World Council of Churches), when, after Greek and Latin, English became the third world-language of the Christian Church, and was destined as a result to suffer the same course of evolution and degradation. Oldham's influence was seen in the introductory volume on *The Church and the Disorder of Society* (S.C.M. Press, 1949), with chapters on 'Technics and Civilization' and 'Personal Relations in a Technical Society'. In the Report of Section III on this theme, it was accepted that 'society as a whole, dominated as it is by technics, is likewise more controlled by a momentum of its own than in previous periods', though 'there is no inescapable necessity for society to succumb to undirected developments of technology'.[21] The report talked more or less indistinguishably of 'the technical society', 'technical civilization' and 'technically organized communities'.[22] Similar arguments and phrases were to be found in the reports of the Laity Committee and the Youth delegation, and in speeches by Mrs.

[18] Mairet defines his theme as 'a social order so shaped and adapted that it can make the fullest use of the solar energy stored up in mineral form as coal or oil, or obtained by distillation from vegetable substances'. (p. 70 n.). This seems to confound Mumford's distinction between the palaeotechnic coal-and-iron phase and the neotechnic phase based on the motor-car and electricity (particularly hydro-electricity) (see *Culture of Cities* (1940 ed.), pp. 340, 344), while drawing too narrow a boundary round its subject, which should surely include hydro-electricity and atomic energy, which may well supersede coal and oil one day.

[19] p. 83.

[20] E.g. V. A. Demant talks of 'our vast technical civilization' in a supplement to the *Christian News-Letter* of 3 April 1946 (No. 257, p. 9). The phrase recurs in the Index of *Theology of Society* (1947), with 'a cosmopolitan civilization of technical means' in the text (p. 45), from an essay of 1944. Later examples can be found in *Frontier* (1950–2), edited by Philip Mairet, and in his report *The National Church and the Social Order* (1956), pp. 144–9.

[21] *The First Assembly of the World Council of Churches*, ed. by W. A. Visser 't Hooft (S.C.M. Press Ltd., 1949), p. 75.

[22] ibid., pp. 75, 76, 77.

Bliss, Professor Ellul, Bishop Runestam, and Reinhold Niebuhr, from England, France, Sweden and the United States.[23]

Thus it seems that this misleading set of neologisms, unknown to the Oxford Dictionary of 1934, entered the international babel from England, where their birth was assisted by sociological midwives from America and Germany. But the responsibility for paternity seems to rest squarely with J. H. Oldham.

[23] ibid., pp. 36, 37, 86, 155, 178, 192.

Chapter 8

THE CHRISTIAN IMPACT

'Observed truth is a servant of moral truth and every man must secure as much of it as he needs and can use. But to regard the search for factual truth whether in science or history as an end in itself, to be pursued without regard to human ends and God's purposes, seems to me to be a great mistake. . . . As an end in itself it is no more (and no less) significant than, shall I say, stamp-collecting.'—ARCHBISHOP FISHER.

'The Christian must welcome truth from whatever quarter it comes, for his Lord is the Truth as well as the Way and the Life. A sound Christian theology insists that the love of truth is as important as the practice of truthfulness.'—ARCHBISHOP RAMSEY.

I. THE SITUATION IN BRITAIN

IF we look for the reasons why the Christian impact has been so inadequate in the economic field in the last fifty years, and in particular in the post-war period, we are driven to look at three sets of factors. (*a*) There is little literature to guide anyone who wishes to think about these problems. (*b*) Church leaders have not been trained in the relevant fields. (*c*) There are practically no teaching posts in Christian social ethics. This is both a major cause of the lack of literature and ignorance, and also a result of having leaders ignorant of the discipline in question.

(*a*) *Literature*. If we look for books which might inform a Christian public (and perhaps others), we find remarkably little. There is a fine Anglican tradition of social concern in the twentieth century, characterized by the writings of Scott Holland, Gore and William Temple. Both Scott Holland and Gore belong more properly to the world between the Jubilee and the First World War than to the twentieth century. But the tradition is continuous that culminates in William Temple's *Christianity and Social Order*, a war-time Penguin, that may be regarded as one of the foundation piers of the Welfare State. This tradition was prophetic, critical of a complacent world and concerned to establish the proper Christian emphasis on men as essentially beings who live in a social order which could never be outside the Church's concern with all human life. In principle, this claim has been admitted everwhere and fails to arouse the bitter feelings it once met with. In practice, the particular issues on which battles were fought have largely ceased to be relevant, and, in any case, the tradition was more successful in establishing principles than in any concrete contribution to practical problems.

In the inter-war period, the tradition was carried on in various ways. Perhaps the most dominant and formative influence was that of the 'Christendom group', working through the Church Union Summer School of Sociology (started in 1925, and still continuing), the journal *Christendom* (1931–1950), and the varied writings of a brilliant, if wayward, group of theologians, philosophers and historians. Their ideas have percolated deeply into the thinking and pronouncements of the Church of England, even if explicitly accepted only among small groups. These ideas were to be found in the report of the Malvern Conference 1941,[1] in the work of the Industrial Christian Fellowship, and in various statements issued by the Church Assembly as reports of particular committees.[2] More weakly some of these ideas have percolated into Lambeth reports and pronouncements by ecclesiastics, who may be unaware of their origin. What characterized the writings of this group was a brilliance of intellect and imaginative grasp of problems unhampered by any solid knowledge of the realities of the issues with which they tried to grapple, and any willingness to learn from experts. As a result, they naturally failed to say anything of significance on economic matters.[3]

If we turn to look at the recent literature published in Britain on the relation of the Christian faith to economic matters, it is obvious how little there is. In the tradition of William Temple and the Christian Socialists, we find the works of Professor R. H. Tawney. His *Religion and the Rise of Capitalism* is a classic in the field of economic history, though it no doubt had a wider impact in opening people's eyes to the concern of the Christian faith for economic matters. *The Acquisitive*

[1] *Malvern, 1941: The Life of the Church and the Order of Society* (Longmans, 1941).

[2] E. g. *The Church and the Planning of Britain* (1944) (C.A. 753); *Towards a Common Life* (1948) (C.A. 877); *The National Church and the Social Order* (1956).

[3] For justification of these harsh criticisms, see the references in the footnote on p. 3.

Society (1921) and *Equality* (1931) belong to the great tradition, and no doubt can still be read with profit, but much of the world with which they deal has passed away, as has been admitted by their author.[4] Another set of Scott Holland lectures following soon after *Religion and the Rise of Capitalism* has perhaps not been noticed as much as they deserve, A. D. Lindsay's *Christianity and Economics* (1934). This small volume does not say much, but it does at least show a serious realization of the scope of economics and the problems that are raised.

The man who wrote most on this subject in the inter-war period was Sir Josiah, later Lord, Stamp, a distinguished economic statistician and writer on economic questions. In a series of books he discussed the relation of the Christian faith to economic problems.[5] It is perhaps not surprising that they have not been more seriously considered by Christian writers, in view of their rather out-of-date Puritan/Victorian individualism, and their narrow conception of the Christian faith. As their titles suggest, they are exaggeratedly concerned with personal motivation. 'Those who envisage a truly Christian order assume that existing economic incentives can be replaced entirely, in so far as they are hedonic, by altruistic and public service ideals.'[6] It is not clear that this is at all true of the most severe Christian critics of an industrial order. Parallel with this goes the following definition of the Christian faith:

> I am old-fashioned enough to believe that the value of Christianity consists in the case of a single man raised from sin to conquest, from feebleness to moral strength, from meanness to beauty, rather than in a 'clear programme' of action for unemployment or exchange control.[7]
>
> The Christian ethic does not validly express itself in practice by laying down schemes of society, which involve many other factors than human relationships, such as geographical situation, racial inheritance, natural resources, human temperament, and scientific potentialities, but by informing and vitalising the individual man with particular ideals and motives.[8]

But of course the Christian faith is concerned both with individuals and

[4] See *The Webbs in Perspective* (Webb Memorial Lecture, 1952. Athlone Press, 1953), pp. 13–21.

[5] *The Christian Ethic as an Economic Factor* (Epworth Press 1926, 1927); *Criticism and Other Addresses* (Ernest Benn, 1931); *Motive and Method in a Christian Order* (Epworth Press, 1936); *Christianity and Economics* (Macmillan, 1939).

[6] *Motive and Method*, p. 49.

[7] ibid., p. 48.

[8] *Christianity and Economics*, p. 177.

with social orders, and both in a different sense from that which Stamp seems to imply. Nevertheless, particularly in the later *Christianity and Economics*, there is that from which Christians could profit today, though there is much that would need re-writing in a post-Keynesian world.

More recently and fully up-to-date is John F. Sleeman's *Basic Economic Problems—a Christian Approach* (S.C.M. Press, 1953), which admirably sets out the main issues and relates them to the problems of planning and free enterprise. The mammoth undertaking of the American churches has been referred to earlier.[9] Varied in quality, wide-ranging and comprehensive, the series does not seem to have attracted much attention in Britain, partly no doubt because so much of the discussion is American in tone and relates to American conditions. But this would be less disturbing, if there were any comparable literature to be found in Britain.

Much is owed in Britain to the work of Dr. J. H. Oldham, and his offspring, the Christian Frontier Council, has kept alive a serious and detailed concern for everyday problems among Christian laymen whose business takes them among them. The *Christian News-Letter* and its successors under different names and formats (at present *Frontier*) from 1939 to date have provided a forum for Chistian discussion of these issues at all levels. In their pages is to be found an immense amount of wisdom and practical sagacity, and there could be few better antidotes to pessimism about Christian thinking than to re-read the back numbers. From the same source have come a number of books treating different aspects of contemporary life. But it would not be unfair to say that the economic field is one where the contribution has been most inadequate and ineffective. In the files of *The Christian News-Letter* or *Frontier*, it would not be possible to find as much coherent guidance to our economic problems and perplexities as to other aspects of life.[10]

[9] See footnote, p. 6.

[10] Reference should however be made to the following supplements to the original *Christian News-Letter:*

'Changing Industry and Moral Decision', by W. G. Symons (No. 124, 11 March 1942).
'The Profit Motive in Industry', by Basil Smallpeice (No. 152, 23 September 1942).
'Christians and the Beveridge Report', by J. H. Oldham (No. 178, 24 March 1943).
'Responsibility in the Economic Sphere', by a group (No. 190, 8 September 1943).
'Responsibility in the Economic System—Government Regulation', by the same group (No. 204, 22 March 1944).

(*b*) *Church Leaders.* Ignorance of the elements of economic thinking is a widespread disease in Britain, probably more serious than the more publicized ignorance of scientific knowledge among 'Arts' people. Nevertheless, there are many people to be found without specialized knowledge who are not entirely unaware of the significance of such matters as the balance of payments, monetary policy, or the level of investment. Among Church leaders, however, such a limited familiarity as this is so rare as to be a matter for surprise. It is not to be explained by general ignorance or by an unwillingness to learn about the modern world. It is a peculiar fact about the habits and traditions of our leaders, which requires some explanation.

No doubt, bishops and other church leaders live extremely busy lives and have little time to read. Nevertheless, one is impressed with the range of reading and knowledge that many of them possess, though there are notorious exceptions. There are many bishops who are knowledgeable on education or Communism. One would not be in the least surprised to find that many of them had recently read some book on modern science. But I would be extremely surprised if more than two or three bishops could be found who in the last fifteen years had read two books on economic matters, such as Beveridge's *Full Employment in a Free Society*, Shonfield's *British Economic Policy since the War* (Penguin), or W. A. Lewis's *Theory of Economic Growth;* or even any serious government White Paper, such as the Radcliffe report on *Monetary Policy*, the reports of the Cohen Council on *Prices, Productivity and Incomes*, or any of the annual *Economic Surveys*. On the other hand, I would be equally surprised to find that there were not half a dozen or more bishops who had read Deutscher's *Stalin*, or one of the volumes of Churchill's War History. It is not a question of the literate and the illiterate, but of what people read about.

The reasons are to be found quite simply by examining the back-

'Responsibility in the Economic System—III: The question of Ownership', by the same group (No. 242, 5 September 1945).
'Full Employment and the Responsibility of Christians', by Civis and Metoikos (Nos. 229 and 230, 7 and 21 March 1945).
'Some Reflections on Industrial Relations', by L. John Edwards (No. 261, 29 May 1946)

The three supplements on 'Responsibility in the Economic System' are perhaps the most valuable, and represent the desirable kind of concerted approach, which does not seem to have been repeated.

ground and training of church leaders. We take the case of bishops in 1958, the year of the Lambeth conference. There were 43 archbishops and diocesan bishops in that year in the provinces of Canterbury and York.[11] The average age of 41 of them was 61, and only two were under 50.[12] The Secretary of the Central Board of Finance comments that 'most of the dignitaries of the Church of England—Bishops, Deans, Provosts, Archdeacons, Canons, Rural Deans—are men in the prime of life. . . . They are grouped fairly closely round the age of 58.'[13] Perhaps the 'prime of life' has a rather different meaning in Church House from what is normal outside; it is, however, clear that the average age is higher than one would expect to find in comparable occupations outside, whether in business, the civil service or the universities. Age explains a good deal. All the 1958 bishops were born before the First World War, and a large number were educated in that period. Twenty-one went to Oxford, and Modern Greats was a new post-war phenomenon in the 'twenties when the youngest were educated. Most people from the kind of schools to which bishops went studied Classics (in the form of Honour Mods. and Greats at Oxford). The figures bear this out. Of our 43 bishops, 18 went to 12 well-known Public Schools—Eton, Winchester, Rugby, Marlborough, Malvern, Shrewsbury, Repton, St. Paul's, Westminster, Merchant Taylors, Haileybury and Bradfield. Of the rest, all but three went to (mostly well-known) minor public schools and grammar schools; of the three, the education of one is unrecorded and the other two went to a secondary school at Brighton and Cambridge County High School. With such a beginning, it is not surprising that 21 went to Oxford, 17 to Cambridge and only 5 to other universities; of the latter 1 each went to Manchester, Durham and King's College, London, and 2 to Dublin. Information is only available as to the subjects studied in 35 cases, but of, these, 15 studied Classics, 10 History, 3 Theology (as a first degree; several went on to study Theology after Greats at Oxford), 2 Science, 1 English, 1 Oriental Languages, 1 Law, and 2 Modern

[11] Some of the following information comes out of *Facts and Figures about the Church of England* (Church Information Office, 1959), giving information for 1958. Other facts were culled from *Crockford*, *Who's Who*, and University Degree lists. Reference may also be made to an article in the *Economist*, 20 October 1956 (pp. 214–5), giving some interesting sociological data about bishops.

[12] *Facts and Figures*, Section C, Table 13.

[13] ibid., p. 2. In fact out of 1,101 such dignitaries, only 222 were under 50.

Greats. That is to say that only 2 out of 35 studied any of the social sciences, and neither of the two who took Modern Greats obtained more than a third class.

An analysis of suffragan bishops produces very similar results. There were 77 suffragan and assistant bishops at the end of 1958, of an average age of 62, only 9 being below 50.[14] Of 54 for whom information about schools is available, 16 went to the 12 public schools, 1 to Harrow, and all the rest, except 2, to minor public schools and grammar schools; the two remaining went to Uxbridge and Woking County Schools. Details are available about the university education of 66; 27 went to Oxford, 22 to Cambridge, 5 to Durham (one took a degree externally), 3 to London, 3 to Dublin, and one each to Glasgow, Liverpool, and Sheffield.[15] There were however 3 who went to no university, one having been to the Royal Naval College, Dartmouth. Out of 45, 8 took Classics, 20 History, 7 Theology, 5 Science, 1 English, 1 Geography, 1 Philosophy, 1 Law and 1 Modern Greats. There was thus a slightly broader sweep than in the case of diocesan bishops, but again a predominance of the more ancient disciplines, with a striking concentration on History.

One would expect to find similar results from a study of Deans, Canons and other ecclesiastical dignitaries. No doubt the pattern of leadership in the Nonconformist churches and in the Church of Scotland is different; there one would expect a much lower proportion of old public school boys, a higher proportion from modern universities, a wider range of studies and perhaps a lower average age. The balance would no doubt be more representative of modern society and less heavily weighed down by the influence of the traditions of the classics. But would it be all that different? The non-Anglican churches in Britain have made a better showing in their knowledge of modern society, but the tone of British Christianity has still been set by the Anglican tradition.

It is not surprising that the dominance of the classical tradition has led to a lack of concern with the specific problems of modern society, because this is one of the unfortunate results (today, though not in

[14] ibid., Section C, Table 13.

[15] One distinguished himself by going to Manchester after a First in Honour Mods. a Oxford.

earlier societies) of what would otherwise be an admirable education.

(*c*) *The Study of Christian Social Ethics.* Very little literature has appeared in Britain of recent years on Christian ethics, much less on social ethics, and, as we have seen, practically nothing on economics. On the whole, it is not too far from the truth to say that books are only written when there is some institution which pays people to produce them and encourages people to study the subject. If there are no paid teachers in a subject and no students, subjects are not studied and nobody bothers to write about them; with no established market for such books, publishers will be less interested, and readers will be unaware that there is any knowledge that they lack.

Why is there no professional study of Christian ethics, and in particular of social ethics? There are a considerable number of chairs of Theology in Britain; non-Christians are often ribald as to the ratio between professors and students in some universities. But by and large theological teachers study the Bible, Church history, Christian doctrine (up to some decently remote period, such as 461), and perhaps the philosophy of religion. The number of posts in Christian ethics is lamentably few. There is a Professor of Moral and Pastoral Theology at Oxford; there is to be a new chair of Social Ethics at King's College, London; there is a lectureship in Christian Ethics at Manchester. At other English universities no doubt the subject is taught somehow or other. In Scotland, there are Professors of Pastoral Theology in the four universities, but they have to cover a very wide field which only includes ethics among other subjects. Nor is it surprising that the theological colleges cannot specially provide for the subject in view of all their other commitments. It is thus not surprising that there is practically nothing to read on Christian ethics; but it is perhaps surprising that the theological departments of the various universities have done so little to re-group their forces to meet this obvious gap. The situation is entirely different in America, where there are large numbers of teachers in the field of Christian social ethics, who are to be found in most universities, and a growing literature and practical concern with the world of the twentieth century.

With the recent disappearance of the paper in Christian ethics in the General Ordination Examination, the Church of England has openly proclaimed that it does not require its priests to know anything about it. This understandable response to an over-loaded syllabus can hardly reflect a considered opinion that the problems of ethics in our modern world are simple and require no special study. It may, on the contrary, be due to a recognition of the complexity of the problems that modern men have to face and to a lack of books or teachers to guide students. But the result of the abandonment will still be disastrous. In a world of professionalism, it is natural that the main burden will have to be borne by the laity, but they need guidance, as do the clergy. If there is to be no guidance, professional ethics take the place of considered Christian ethics, and a professional clerical ethic is likely to be as one-sided as that of any other profession.

2. WHAT THE CHURCH COULD DO IN BRITAIN TODAY

There are those who argue that the less said by ecclesiastical assemblies or by church leaders on social matters, the better. It will be clear from various statements which I have criticized that I do not think very highly of the quality of many of the utterances by those in positions of distinction. Those who would prefer our leaders in church matters to remain silent appear to believe that we can expect nothing better. If this were so, I would agree that it would be best that there should be no such statements. There is no gain to anybody in the publicizing of platitudes or nonsensical remarks, which may mislead the faithful and encourage those outside the Church to believe that church leaders are as incompetent in their own fields as they are in their incursions into others. Furthermore, there is positive gain in the reminder that silence often better becomes the Church of Jesus Christ than too much talking; a lesson it might well learn from its Master, though a very difficult lesson for all those, whether academics or clergy, whose profession involves public utterance.

Nevertheless, I am not convinced by these arguments that there is no place in the Church's work for public statements at the highest level on matters of public importance. These would serve two rather different purposes: firstly, the clear proclamation of prophetic witness to the state or society as a whole, on matters where Christians are clearly agreed and where a positive policy is required; secondly, the enlightenment of Christians on complicated matters with which they should be concerned as citizens or members of particular groups in society. If those outside the Church listen in to this second kind of utterance, so much the better. But the function of this statement should be primarily to clarify the Christians' own approach to the world in which they live. It is this second function I am mainly concerned with.

The mere fact that we live in a most complicated world, each of us in his own very different compartment, makes it the more necessary that we should have guidance about matters that are not within our immediate purview. It may be that the guidance will take the form of a definite statement of policy; it may be that it will be a matter of putting forward several points of view, each of which it is possible for Christians to adopt. It may be that all that is needed is to point out how limited are the moral and human issues involved in a particular matter, where at first sight deep emotions appear to be aroused. But, whichever is the appropriate method, it will serve its purpose in giving guidance to Christians likely to be bewildered in our ever-growing abundance and complexities. Nor need the guidance be confined to Christians; it may help others also.

Is not this done elsewhere? What need is there for Christians to undertake it? In so far as it is adequately done elsewhere, there is certainly no need for Christians to repeat it. It is quite likely that the kind of educative formulation of the issues may in certain fields be provided by secular bodies; so much the better. Often there will be no further need for specifically Christian formulation, once the issues are clearly laid bare. But in other cases this will not be so. Only too often the discussion at this sort of level is carried out by political, or semi-political, propagandists, and the ordinary man may find it difficult to disentangle the important from the irrelevant. This is not to the discredit of the propagandists, who are fulfilling a valuable function in society. But however helpful are the works of the Bow Group or the Fabian Society, the Acton Society Trust and writers like C. A. R. Crosland, or the authors of *Twentieth Century Socialism*, there may still be a place for a definite attempt under Christian auspices to disentangle the moral issues and the fundamental assumptions about the nature of man which lie behind their differences.

For example, in recent years, if the Church had been able to draw on the available *expertise* to clarify the issues behind the different policies for dealing with inflation, it would have been able to perform a most valuable public function. In all the expert and political controversy, there has been practically no educative endeavour to make clear to the public just where the experts differ because they do not know enough, and where differences arise because different social and political aims and preferences are involved. It is not beyond the wit of man to show some of the complex interrelations between these matters, but it requires an honest confrontation of different points of view, which does not commonly arise in public controversy.

This can be illustrated by the history of the Cohen Council on Prices, Productivity and Incomes, which was apparently designed to fulfill this function. Its abysmal failure, at least as shown in its first two reports, provides a signal lesson. The 'Three Wise Men', who could have performed a useful function in discussing the disagreements between economists and their political background, preferred to state a dogmatic view, which was not acceptable to a large body of economic opinion, and was politically rejected by a large part of the population. This was indeed a view which needed to be presented, among others, but when put forward alone, with some rather naïve 'refutations' of views held by distinguished economists, it was not surprisingly dismissed, by those who disagreed with the arguments, as the biassed pronouncements of three old Conservatives. If the government thought that, by appointing an *ex parte* group to support their economic policies, they were likely to commend them to any wider public, they clearly miscalculated. More seriously, the result was to discredit what could have been a most valuable exercise in public education on serious and difficult issues.

Regrettably, at the time of the appointment of these 'three wise men', church leaders, as diverse as the then Archbishop of Canterbury and the then Bishop of Chichester, saw fit to accept the thesis that complicated economic problems could be left to a group of wise men to settle on behalf of the nation as a whole. They were rightly rebuked by *The Times* for their naïvety.[16] Far more valuable would it have been, if the Church had itself taken up the challenge and shown how it would have been possible to present a report outlining the different approaches and making clear to the public what would have been involved in each of them. It is my conviction that this was not beyond

[16] Editorial in *The Times*, 9 December 1957.

the bounds of possibility. There are in fact enough economists who would have been able and willing to perform such a function, and rare though Christian economists are, it would be possible to find a group to make such a report. What is required is not, as the Archbishop of Canterbury envisaged the role of the wise men, 'an attempt to restore a sense of moral authority and an idea of moral obedience in a field from which moral law as a guiding principle has been almost wholly dismissed';[17] but rather a matter of disentangling the complex technical issues from the political, social and moral choices which lie behind them and in their midst. Anyone who has looked at the controversies about inflation cannot fail to be aware of the moral questions mixed up with them, which exacerbate the discussions. What is needed is not a dose of moral authority, but a careful discrimination to discern the real moral issues involved.

Even if it were granted that Christians had little to contribute to the general discussion of these issues—and it is not entirely clear to me that we need take such a pessimistic view—the need would still remain to clarify the issues for the ordinary man in the pew, who wants to have some idea as to how these matters tie up with his Christian faith. It seems to me, then, that there is a place for statements which aim to educate people to the fundamental issues which lie behind the current controversies which they cannot evade, and to show how these issues are related to the essential tenets of the Christian faith. How is this to be done?

If the organized Church is to speak in this sort of way, clearly there must be some machinery enabling it to do so with reasonable competence. It may be fanciful idealism to expect churches in the twentieth century to adapt their organizations to the times; but it may equally be improper despair which asks for nothing more than what we have. At least, I would like to outline what, in my view, would not be beyond the bounds of possibility, within the particular church of which I am a member, the church of England. (It may be that other churches organize these things better; some certainly do. But I will speak of what I know.) It is, as I see it, largely due to a failure of organization that we are where we are, and organizations do in fact alter as times change.

[17] Quoted from *Diocesan Notes* in *The Times*, 23 August 1957.

Perhaps the fundamental failure is the failure to see that the problem is one of organization. Too often the Church strikes the layman as a set of one-man competing shows, each run by one man, good, bad or indifferent. In simpler societies, no doubt the parish system was well-devised to deal with the realities of those societies. Today, it needs, at the very least, to be supplemented by something different. In fact, one of the virtues of an episcopal system, as is clear to anyone who has lived in Scotland, is that it enables experiments to be carried out under the aegis of the Bishop, by special people appointed for the task, whereas a presbyterian system, whose ministry is essentially parochial, is not well-equipped for dealing with the kind of problem I have in mind. But not all bishops realize the advantages they are blessed with, and too many seem to run a diocese as a larger one-man show, a sort of large-scale parish. But no modern organization can be run in this way today.

Let me start at the top. Essentially what is needed is a set of advisory committees of laymen and church leaders concerned with particular problems. Only very recently has the Church of England set up a Department of Social Responsibility with a full-time secretary and a Board to guide it. This is a beginning, and a very valuable one, when one realizes how much of the effort involved in such social concern as has previously existed, such as the Malvern Conference of 1941 and reports produced by the Church Assembly,[18] was the work of a few devoted enthusiasts. What is needed is continuous study, by groups of laymen and others, of the background to particular issues, groups who would be able and ready to comment on particular problems put up to them, and would be able at the same time to work out a common Christian mind (or a set of differing Christian approaches) to the issues of our time. It is not because church leaders are particularly foolish that they make foolish statements, but because they fail to make use of expert advice, which could be available to them if they asked for it. No business-man, no politician, no academic engaged in serious matters, tries to think out answers to all the problems he is confronted with, without taking advice from those he knows to be experts. He does not need to follow the advice given him, but at least he makes up his mind after hearing what the expert has to say. Church leaders all too often do not seem to feel any need to do the same, even though many

[18] E.g. *The Church and the Planning of Britain* (1944).

of them sit in the House of Lords and have a say in many of the complicated affairs of the nation.

If there were such expert advisory committees, by and large they would tend to make an impact. In some cases, it may be that church leaders are congenitably incapable of listening to others and making use of advisers. I am not inclined to believe that this is numerically a large problem; rather I would think that it is the sheer lack of machinery that has led to the present situation. This can be shown by the fact that, in those fields where there is the machinery, much better results are achieved. On the whole, when Anglican leaders speak on matters of education, the family, and relations with churches overseas, they speak knowledgeably, wisely and convincingly, even to those who disagree with them. This may be partly because these are matters more within their own sphere of experience. But it is mainly because for many years the church has had specialized bodies of experts discussing these matters, formulating policy and engaged in continuous study of them. I am asking for no more than that the same technique should be applied in other fields.

The fact that there is organization in these fields and not others has led to the curious anomaly that, in so far as there is a specifically Anglican approach to current social problems, it tends to lead to a concentration on educational and family matters. But these are by no means the only, nor necessarily the most important, matters of social concern. There was a certain element of comedy in the way Church of England representatives at the Evanston Assembly of the World Council of Churches seemed at times to be a 'family' lobby, in the way that others represented a farmers' or a trade union lobby. In so far as this has led, for example, to attempts by the Moral Welfare Council to dominate the Social Responsibility Department of the Church,[19] it can be seen to be a most dangerous tendency, which could lead to stultification of the whole of the Church's leadership in the twentieth century. In saying this one does not need to deny the value of the work the Moral Welfare Council has done in its own field. The preparatory report for Lambeth on *The Family in Contemporary Society* is one of the most striking achievements of the Church in this field. It exemplifies the way in which a group of experts meeting with theologians can

[19] Attempts which, at the time of writing, seem to have been disastrously successful.

clarify problems and provide guidance to church members in a particular field. Would that we had more such reports!

The recent development of an industrial secretariat should lead to similar valuable study and action. But again there is the danger that this may be merely another field of action added to the already ploughed fields of education and the family. There are many political, social and economic problems that do not fall within any of these rubrics. But at least the right principle of action has been accepted.

The point was clearly made in the Family Report:

> The bearing of the Christian faith on many matters can only be worked out by sustained co-operation between experts in various fields of study. The present Group, for instance, has been compelled regretfully to abandon fruitful lines of inquiry for lack of opportunity to pursue them further. It may be that in the future the solution of this kind of difficulty will be found in the establishment of permanent Commissions between one Lambeth Conference and the next. . . .
>
> The great value of permanent Commissions sitting between successive Lambeth Conferences, since the bearing of the Christian faith on practical behaviour is something which can be worked out only as the result of co-operative study between experts. Certainly it would seem in our own time to be a theological, philosophical, and practical necessity, and we should like to recommend that the Bishops give earnest thought to the practicability of providing opportunities for such discussion in which churchmen would join with others, not all of whom would necessarily profess the Christian faith. Whether within this formal framework or not, only in this way in the present complex situation will religion succeed in supplying a cohesive bond.[20]

Nor need this method of action be confined to the central organization of the church. It can also be applied in each diocese, as indeed it often is. But there must be many dioceses where the Bishop would be immensely helped, if he were to make use of advisory committees of laymen and specialists in particular fields. There are dioceses where such committees exist, for example in the industrial field, bringing together trade unionists, industrialists and academic specialists. There are others where industry is also prominent, and where such committees would be looked upon as either odd or unnecessary. I am not suggesting that there is any one desired pattern of organization. All I would suggest is that, in a world of complex large-scale organizations,

[20] *The Family in Contemporary Society* (London, S.P.C.K., 1958), pp. 121, 160.

there may be need of not entirely dissimilar organization to deal with these problems.

In one area what may be needed is a committee of town planners, social workers and clergy to discuss the problems of the growth of new communities. In another area it might be concern with the political responsibilities of Christians in local and central government. Elsewhere it may be a matter of a particular industry or profession, steel, banking, agriculture or medicine. Sometimes the best machinery may be a local Council of Churches, elsewhere it may be the appointment of a particular man to specialize in a particular field. Or it may be that what is needed is the creation of a voluntary association not too closely linked with the official machinery of the church. With imagination, there are many opportunities that open before us.

Already I have moved from the official level to the more or less unofficial. Nothing that I have said about the value of central organization or official statements is to be taken as meaning that this should be the only, or necessarily the most important, element in the church's activity in the world. But some of those who have rightly stressed the importance of the activity of laymen in unofficial 'frontier' groups have been led to what is, to my mind, an unnecessarily negative approach to more general action by the organized church as such. It would be disastrous to go to the other extreme and deny the importance of these lay activities.

Any coherent guidance in our complex modern world must come from those actually at work in it. But it is unlikely to come unless those people in their daily jobs can contact others in different positions, and also talk things over with others similarly placed. Lay groups of various kinds are needed, and lay centres, where these matters can be fully thrashed out. The Church already has such centres, as for example the Royal Foundation of St. Katharine, William Temple College, and the Iona Community. But it is not clear that all that needs to be done, and could be done, is being done. There may still be a place for a wider Institute of Laity to serve as a focus for the many varied groups at work throughout the country.

In the last resort, it is the dialogue between people of different backgrounds and experience that is required. As the former Bishop of Chichester said:

I suggest that the Church, and by that I mean the Church authorities, must recognize that the most rewarding method is that of encounter, and the Church should make some plan or arrangement by which the moral philosopher, the pastoral theologian, may encounter the scientists and technologists. All this requires a new strategy and the providing of some place in which such encounters can take place, and in which research can be undertaken. This is beyond the resources of the parochial system as it now stands but it is of very great importance.[21]

The same point was made again in the report on *The Family in Contemporary Society:*

We believe that a Church which hopes to make any impact in its local situation must set its theologians and its administrators to work with the men and women of integrity (be they Christians or not) engaged locally in academic study, field research, or administration or community service; in order, first to understand what the situation really is, and then to order Church life and activity within it accordingly. . . .

Cathedral foundations in particular (which in the past were the nurseries of schools and hence sometimes of universities) might well take the initiative in fostering such co-operation, and thus again offer a more ample and reasonable service to God and men.[22]

In short, there is a great deal that could be done, even with the limited resources available to the churches today, if they were to use them more coherently and responsibly, and with more imagination.

3. TOWARDS A CHRISTIAN SOCIAL ORDER?

I set myself the task at the beginning of looking at a limited number of problems of our day—and it will now be obvious how limited are the problems with which I have dealt—in terms of a number of questions. These were to ask what are the trends, what is positive in them, where God is to be found at work, and what we are to do to make his Will more manifest. It has not always been possible to take up all these questions in relation to every topic, but they have provided a background to what I have had to say. A clearer pattern may emerge if I now summarize the trends and realities that seem to be visible, so as to show where the more positive elements are to be found and to

[21] Speech by Dr. G. K. A. Bell to the Upper House of Canterbury Convocation, reported in *The Times*, 3 October 1957.

[22] Op. cit., p. 23.

make clearer what sort of a world we might live in, if we were more faithful to the Will of God.

We live in a world of change, rapid change, which will continue for as far as we can see ahead. This presents us with ever-widening opportunities to give glory to God, as we discover more of his unsearchable wisdom. It gives us opportunities to break up the rigid patterns set by sin, and to create more worthy institutions and a more humane environment. But it equally sets us problems. We may chase novelties without discrimination, and we may create a life so restless that men do not have those basic securities without which human personality cannot flower.

Much depends on the development of business enterprise. Christians have failed properly to appraise the creative activities of business-men in our modern world, and, because of this, they have often misread the dangers, which are as great as the opportunities. Business enterprise is essentially fluid and adaptable, and its forms change, even when people pretend that they remain the same. If we avoid the dogmas of right and left, we will see hope precisely in this fluidity with the occasions for experiment that it opens up to us.

Our wealth is overwhelming; only let us be careful that it does not overwhelm us! A society in which, for the first time in history, the common man has the chance to enjoy the fruits of the earth, as formerly only the rich and leisured could, reveals to us new horizons on which we should not turn our backs. It is easy to be contemptuous of our modern vulgarities. It is much more difficult for Christians to create a pattern of living in the twentieth century which is neither irrelevant nor escapist. But it is even more difficult to embody in institutions the checks on mass vulgarity which the dangers involved in our culture plainly require. We *could* create beautiful, efficient and humane cities in place of megalopolis; we *could* use and not abuse the opportunities with which the motor-car presents us; we *could* grapple with the monsters of advertisement, mass-circulation newspapers and vulgarized culture. But it will not be without much hard thinking and much patient work behind the scenes. Neither is much in evidence.

Modern civilization inexorably draws men together in unity and equality. It levels down as well as levels up. The forces are too strong for those who rather feebly try to resist them. Their resistance, however, creates untold harm in bitterness, sectionalism and unnecessary conflicts. There may be some who see in these trends something to be resisted in the name of God. On the contrary, my argument leads to the conclusion that they are to be welcomed as expressing in concrete form the fundamental theological unity of mankind. If we are thus led by God towards a new equality in community, we shall be sensitive both to the new dangers of vulgarity and mass-pressure which lie before us and also to the ugly temptation to delay the process so as to gain immediate advantage for ourselves. There are many indications that the serious charge to be laid against modern conservatives is not that they deliberately try to conserve the best in past traditions, but that, rather than trying to express these in the new context of our expanding and egalitarian economy—which would of itself be a major endeavour—they merely try to retard a process which they know to be inevitable, by throwing out a few sops to the less privileged, and by competing for the support of the common man on the level of *panem et circenses*. In this there can be little that is creative, and it is a creative equality towards which we should look.

A more equal society which embodies a rich diversified community, where men count for what they are worth as men, and not because of any badge of class or wealth that is given to them from outside, will be much more sensitive about inequalities of income and capital than is our present society. To say this is not to deny that we have gone a long way in the last thirty years; but we still have far to go. Above all, we have to go much further in recognizing the social revolution that is taking place in the world as a whole, which is the dominating fact of our time. If we have achieved much in breaking down the barriers to community within the highly developed Western societies, the gap between these few privileged groups and the mass of starving mankind remains staggeringly large, even where it is not actually increasing. We are called again and again to recognize the reality of this world revolution, which represents man's refusal to accept the present state of affairs as permanent. The tragedy is that so often our very riches blind us to the needs of the outside world. Judgment rests on our society at this point, and it could be disastrous. If we are not ready to share our riches, it may be that we shall be forced to share poverty. The power of modern weapons suggests that recovery from another war will not be so easy as it was in 1918 and 1945. Soon these weapons may be in the hands, not only of Russia, America and Britain, but also of desperately poor countries struggling with intractable economic and social problems, with little to lose and much to gain.

In the last resort, what we have to offer the world is not so much our riches as the kind of life which is embodied in our society. We shall be judged by what we make of our own social order, and by its success in providing a humane pattern which others can follow. This is the ultimate weapon against Communism, and the only decisive one. Such a humane pattern is not an alternative to economic and social aid to developing countries, but it inevitably includes this aid in all its forms.

The quality of living in modern society is not merely a matter of individual standards, nor merely a matter of central government action, important as both of these are. It also depends on the health of all the intermediate groups and organizations to which people belong, and in which they find varied social satisfactions and significance as persons. The balance of these organizations of all kinds is a cardinal factor in creating health in society as a whole. This balance requires a proper mixture of co-operation and conflict. It is not something that comes about automatically as a result of holding the right beliefs, nor is it something that can be merely created by state fiat. People have to act in and through organizations, and often against organizations; at the same time, the state has to act in various ways to encourage, purge, control and direct. The pattern cannot be fixed for all time, but new situations will bring new institutions, and, it is to be hoped, the death of some old ones. In this variety and in these changes there is always hope, though there is no guarantee that changes will inevitably be for the better.

A complex society, such as our own, with its network of relations between huge populations organized in many complicated ways, requires the use of the market mechanism (or the price mechanism). But the market mechanism has to be understood and appraised for what it is worth; it is neither a monstrous impersonal force to be denounced, nor an idol which will solve all problems. It is a serviceable mechanism, which can serve men, if properly used and not abused. It provides no complete substitute for organized action, whether through institutions, or by means of government action at the central or local level. But the proper combination of organized action and reliance on market forces is a continuous test of statesmanship.

There still remains the problem of fitting our vast world into a human pattern, a pattern within which men can live with all the narrow horizons and limits that circumscribe all of us. To give each man his proper responsibility, neither too much nor too little, is a task of enormous difficulty. Modern industrial organizations do not seem to have discovered any generally valid patterns; the worst have much to learn from the best, and the best do not go very far. We should distrust any attempt to provide any single cure, as we must recognize that the conflicts of interest and need which differ according to place and time prevent any perfect solution. But we can admit that both within industry and in the framework of local democracy there remains much to be done in the way of creative action.

In the end we can say that, in spite of all the difficulties of a rapidly changing, large-scale world, there is no more reason to suppose that it is impossible to create a human environment today than there was in the case of other societies. We have to face difficulties never faced before, but we have matching advantages with which to meet them. We have opportunities never before known in human history, and the greatest opportunity of all, in that we can see ever-widening horizons before us.

It is among other things the mission of the Church to transform the world. This is a mission of the whole Church, and not of one part of it, clerical or lay. It is a mission without bounds. There is no area of life, no part of human experience, no geographical area which is excluded from this mission. This follows from the very nature of the Church as the hands and feet of God in the world. There are no limits to God's concern and no limits to God's activity. The whole world is God's, difficult as it is for mortal and limited men to appreciate the full significance of this fact. We are always tempted to interpret God's interests as narrowly as our own are circumscribed. Perhaps it is true to say that the more deeply religious a man is, in the sense that his understanding of God and his apprehension of him is the more vivid and central to him, the greater is the danger that his apprehension will be associated with the limited symbols and experience of his own life. It is no accident perhaps that the mystics who have made most clear to us something of God, as man in this life can experience him, have been so extremely narrow in the range of their imagery. No one need be misled by this, though there are some (both religious people and Freudians) who seem naïvely to assume either that the only pattern of human response to God is one closely akin to the personal relations between the sexes, or, on the other hand, that mysticism is merely an erudite sexual abnormality. The treasures of God are poured into earthern vessels, and any human understanding of God, for all the revelation in Jesus Christ, is bound to be filtered through our limited minds. Through the very intensity of our limited concerns God comes to us, and in this intensity we may find him. But he is more than they.

There are thus no specifically religious concerns (though of course the worship of God involves particular buildings, particular ceremonies, particular people, and particular times set aside for prayer, public worship and so on). The religious man is not a man who does one thing rather than another; for example a teacher rather than an industrial manager, or a tennis-player rather than a football-watcher. There are no concerns more particularly Christian than others, though Christians often give the impression that they have a particular corner in gambling, drink and sex, and perhaps smoking (in some circles). But there may rightly be specific matters with which particular Christians should concern themselves, and there may, at any given time of history, be a need for Christians to concentrate on some special issue which seems especially urgent to them.

If I were asked what were the major issues on which I should like to see the churches concentrating their thought and efforts (in the kind of field I have been discussing), I would answer that it was the question of the use and abuse of our rich expanding economy, on the one hand, and, on the other hand, the problems of the poverty of the mass of mankind. I would be bold enough to state dogmatically that I am sure we would be more nearly obeying the Will of God for us in our generation if we were to devote to these matters a tithe of the effort and resources we now devote to other concerns; I am thinking only of effort and resources within the Church, whether organized or among ordinary Christians.

Of course, I may be wrong, and may be merely led astray by my own particular interests and concerns. More importantly, it is clear that these are among the concerns which should be worrying Christians, as they are among the concerns of God. Above all, we need to be clear that the whole realm of the social and economic order is something of concern to God. Even if Christians fail to think about it, and fail to act responsibly within it, it still remains God's order. He is at work in it, even if we are not always clear how he is at work. The more we can relate what we think and do in these fields with what we know of God, the more will we carry out his will for us and our world. Then the more will we be able to give to him the glory that is his due, and the more will we be consciously transforming this world into what he wills it to be. Nothing less than this is what is demanded of us.

It is at this point that we set our sights too low. It is hard for many Christians to avoid the Platonic heresy which regards this world as a sort of testing-ground for another, and this world's concerns as to be despised in favour of another world. But this world's concerns are God's concerns, and the next world is not other than God. If we want to escape from this world into another, we are trying to escape from God, and the next world to which we want to escape is none other than Hell. We have not to despise this world, but to see it and appreciate it as God's 'creature', in so far as we can; that is, to see God in it and to make it more of a mirror of God to men. If there is a subtle Platonism in much Christian piety, which fails to appreciate the grandeur of the Incarnation and what follows from it, there is, of course, an opposite worldliness, which so rejoices in the world as to fail to see the sin in it.

The Christian has to steer between these two extremes. Life in Christ means bringing, so far as we can, all our life and our surroundings to be transformed, as human life has been, in principle, transformed once and for all in the Resurrection and Ascension of Jesus Christ. Perhaps in the Western church we do not sufficiently glory in the transfiguration of our world that has already taken place. Certainly, it is this transformation of our world that is our daily task, as individuals and as members of Church and society.

What I have tried to throw light on in this book are some of the ways in which it seems to me that God is in process of transforming our economic order, and some of the ways in which we can, and should, participate in that activity.

Appendix A

CHRISTIANS AND ECONOMIC PROGRESS

(See Chapters 2–3)

A talk given to the Edinburgh Congress of the Student Christian Movement in April 1958. (Reprinted from *The Student World*, Third Quarter, 1958.)

During the last two hundred or so years, in the Western world, for the first time in all the hundreds of thousands of years that man has lived on this globe, there has been continuous economic progress. This is one of the most striking events in all human history, and by and large Christians have utterly failed to appraise it at its proper valuation. Many wise things have been said about progress in general, and about the relations between Christianity and culture in general; but little has been said of value about economic progress. What has been said has tended to be negative, and much of this negative valuation has been based either on sheer ignorance, or on false comparisons between the economic and other fields, social and ideological. What I want to do is to try to present some of the issues we have to face; what I have to say is necessarily sketchy, fragmentary, and incomplete. I have no well-rounded scheme into which everything can be fitted; I doubt if one is possible. I find as a Christian that I am more baffled than clear about what is expected of us; and I distrust many of those who seem to find a ready answer to our uncertainties.

I

Firstly, we need to be clear about some of the things that are involved in economic progress, before we can evaluate it at all.

1. Economic progress means the continuous growth of income per head. It is this continuous growth that is new in the world of the last two hundred or so years. There is a simple measuring-rod for this growth, the changes that occur during the lifetime of a human being. Never before have human beings seen so many changes in the environment of their lives in the course of a lifetime.

2. The growth of income per head basically means an expansion of choice for human beings. There are more goods and services available from which to choose, and life is enriched. It would be utterly wrong to see this merely in terms of a greater abundance of material goods. In a highly developed economy services expand more rapidly than goods, and expenditure on reading-matter, concerts, holidays, and travel expands more than expenditure on food and

clothes. (A cynical commentator said to me the other week in America: 'The recession must be getting serious. People are cancelling their trips to Europe.') It is a primitive, and meaningless, distinction popularized by Adam Smith, that divides the 'productive' from the 'unproductive'; today it is only found useful by Marxists and some Christian theologians.

3. Economic growth also means more leisure for recreation, and less subservience to back-breaking toil. It means more opportunities for varied jobs, less crippling pain, and longer lives in which it is *possible* to grow more wise.

4. Historically, and to some extent inevitably, the expansion of choice for the many means less freedom of choice for the few. The development of modern economies seems in time to break down the class barriers that in most human societies have buttressed the riches of the few from the poverty of the many. As societies become more integrated, and power more widely diffused, incomes are redistributed by taxation, and the rich become sometimes, not merely relatively, but absolutely, worse off. That the so-called middle classes in Britain today (in fact the richest 5–10 per cent. of the population, with the exclusion of the highest 0.1 per cent. or so) are sometimes worse off than they were before the War, or in those blissful days before the First World War, and have less freedom of manoeuvre than they had, is a consequence of the enrichment of the ordinary man-in-the-street. (It is also aggravated by the rise in prices of services, particularly domestic service, that accompanies economic growth.) Greater choice for the many can mean more restricted choices for the few.

I, for one, am not prepared to hark back, like the so-called 'wise men' who advise us on inflation, to the pattern of income-distribution of pre-war days. I fail to see any Christian justification for the inequalities of income that exist today, not all of which are necessary from an economic point of view.

5. The opportunities of choice that economic progress makes available involve concentrations of power; opportunity means power. Who holds it? It is not true that the greater power of choice made available by modern economic development is always available to everybody. In the economic field, the pioneering inventions are made by a limited number of people, and the new products are sold to us by powerful business-men, who condition our responses by advertisement. I will come back to this problem.

Much economic advance required the use of large blocks of capital, which have to be centrally controlled, whether by the monster car firms of the United States, or by a powerful Atomic Energy Authority. We have not devised any certain system of control for monopolies, whether private or public; this still remains a problem. But the danger is not fundamental in that the price we have to pay is not, as some extremists seem to think, the danger of domination of our lives by these 'managers', or whatever you call them, but more the danger of their inefficiency, lethargy, and failure to fit into the total pattern of society. They may restrict our choices by making us less rich than we otherwise would be, but this is a danger that greater riches will overcome; we can afford the wastes of monopolies better today than we could in the days of Charles I. Those who would like to see a little more stability and dislike most the restless change that competition brings, should perhaps welcome the flabby conservatism of the large economic unit. In short, the problem of monopoly power is a serious economic problem, but a problem of limited importance.

6. It is also true that, in the political field, the choices are so vast that the man-in-the-street may be pardoned for thinking that he counts for little. Many of the most important decisions are made by government corporations, by experts (whether scientists or economists), by civil servants, by political cabals, over which we seem to have little control. Nevertheless, though the political decisions are not made by the man-in-the-street, he does have some sort of say and some sort of check on the wild misuse of power. It is not my business to discuss *how* political decisions can be influenced; but it is important to be clear that many of the things we complain about, and in particular, many of the things that Christians complain about, could be changed by political means, and are not out of our control.

By and large, and taking account of all the limitations put upon us by the political realities, the hell that we have created from the tremendous opportunities that are offered to us is of our own making. By and large, it is not due only to wicked men, whether powerful business men or entrenched trade unions. It is not, by and large, due only to the wickedness of secular men who have turned their backs on God. It is not, by and large, due to some sort of 'materialism' that has infected men. Christians cannot pretend that they are not to blame—in the way that they can (to some limited extent) claim that they are not to blame for the unbelief in the modern world. In spite of their beliefs, they have not shown much, if any, greater discrimination in these matters than their secular friends. (It may be indeed that the lack of discrimination is a sign of a deeper unbelief that is the real cause of men's alienation from God; but that would take us beyond our present concerns.) All too often Christian witness in the economic and social field is like the protest of the Angry Young Men, who want to be angry, but cannot find anything to be angry about, and so become even more angry because they can see nothing to be angry about. In fact, there is a great deal to be angry about, and what is required is the anger that points out where action is required, and what kind of action is required. It is here that we need to exercise our discrimination.

Let me illustrate with the case of advertisement. How frequently have Christian bodies denounced the evils of advertisement! But how rarely have Christians done anything about working out the legislative steps that are required to stop these evils! Advertising exists because we tolerate it; it can be stopped if we want it to stop. I have not seen any suggestions by Christian bodies as to how the Sale of Goods Act 1893, or the Merchandise Marks Act

1953, might be suitably amended, or, perhaps more importantly, how these and other similar acts might be properly enforced by the creation of an adequate inspectorate. If Christians would devote the energy they devote to such causes as Sunday legislation or gambling to lobbying about advertisements and to examining how the local control of advertisements is exercised under the Town and Country Planning Acts, they would be able to achieve a great deal. This is what I mean by saying that our Christian witness is often like that of the Angry Young Men.

In other words, if business-men alter our pattern of living with the new products they have put on the market, and if they debase our tastes with their advertising, it is because we have allowed them to do it. The contrast between the blaring advertisements of America and the more sober aspect of our cities (ugly as they are) is evidence that we do not need to make ourselves slaves to business interests.

7. There is a wider sense in which the pattern of economic development shapes all our lives. Economic progress involves change, and social change as well as changes in habits of living. It depends on urbanization and industrialization; it involves the growth of impersonal relations between large masses of people, living in large-scale units; it seems to lead to the emergence of powerful organized social groupings, such as farm organizations and trade unions, which create new problems.

These things are indeed what we mean by economic progress. Without them enrichment of choice is impossible. What is difficult is to see how far the way in which these processes have in fact developed, with all the cramping effects they have had on human beings, is in fact necessary to the process itself. We have all of us seen enough glimpses of how cities can be built and lived in with a really human graciousness to know that city life is not of itself of the devil, but can be offered to the glory of God. The same is true of industry. Nor need we be distressed about the impersonalization of relations between people, where this is a necessary part of the fulfilment of a proper function; men have always spent a good deal of their lives manipulating brute matter, and this has not always been in circumstances where personal relationships were possible. What is necessary is that we should treat people personally where personal relations are required, and perform our impersonal functions efficiently. (By contrast, it was always possible for the Assyrians, as it might be, to treat people as cattle; and it is not desirable that persons driving a motor-car should devote the attention to personal relations that should be devoted to careful driving.)

The same applies to all these other social aspects of economic progress. Of themselves they are neutral; what matters is what kind of cities we live in, what kind of industry we work in, what kind of organizations we belong to, and what kind of network of relationships makes up the fabric of our society. There are great problems here to which Christians need to give attention; there is great scope for the exercise of Christian discrimination.

8. Economic progress is, of itself, a very limited matter. It neither involves progress in morals, taste, humanity, sensitivity, or any other more fundamental human value, nor does it preclude any of these. It is perhaps much more distinct from the various social, moral, and ideological changes that have accompanied it than we often think. It is so easy to argue that, because the modern world has seen a vulgarization of taste, the wasteful destruction of social tissue in the emergence of a proletariat, the decline in Christian morals, and the emergence of shallow this-worldly interpretations of human destiny—that *therefore* all these things are inevitably linked with economic progress. There are complex inter-relationships between all these things, and it is the height of folly for Christian apologists to pretend that they are all tied together. Let us learn a lesson from those cheap apologists of free enterprise, who managed to convince themselves that economic progress was dependent on the independence of the business-man, and then turned round and argued that the justification of a free enterprise system was to be found in its rapid rate of economic progress. The consternation that the sputnik caused in America to these simplicities should give pause to the theologians who all too frequently fall into similar errors. Economic progress has not been proved to be inevitably linked with the evils with which it has been associated in the West. We do not know enough about it to be able to dogmatize on these matters.

9. Lastly, the tremendous riches of our present-day choices need not blind us to the fact that there are limits to choice. We cannot choose to buy goods that are not available, or, to put it more concretely, if goods are really costly in terms of human effort, there is no economic trick that will make them cheap. (For example, it may be that we are offered a choice between a society where domestic service is cheap for a minority of the population, because human labour is cheap and most men live lives that are nasty, brutish, and short, and, on the other hand, a society where most men live at a fairly high standard of living, but domestic service is dear even for the privileged few, precisely because human labour is now dear, not cheap.) If so, we must make the choice as it is presented to us, and there is no place for repining that we are not put in a world where there are no hard choices. I am afraid that Christian prophets today often spend their time repining that the choices with which they are faced are not the ones with which they ought to be faced. And, of course, we all of us do that most of our lives. But it is not very heroic, and certainly not prophetic.

II

I now turn to the second part of what I have to say. Basically, economic progress means enlargement of choice, and the expansion of opportunities. These greater opportunities do not of themselves bring men nearer to God; they do not of themselves make them more wise, or even more happy. Do we then want these greater choices? Should we throw away these opportunities? There are quite a few theologians who in one way or another tell us to do this, though they are not always clear as to what they are telling us to do. But in effect they are frightened that men may misuse their powers, and want us to go back to a state of society where they cannot be misused, because men do not have them, or where the power is kept safely in the hands of those who can be trusted, as it is thought, to use it well.

Let us be clear about the theology of this. There seem to me to be two fundamental points.

1. Man was made by God to 'be fruitful, and multiply, and replenish the earth, and subdue it' (Genesis 1. 28). In the last two hundred years, for the first time in all the hundreds of thousands of years that man has lived on the earth, he has begun to fulfil the divine injunction. It is somewhat ironical that the theologians do not like it, and seem to prefer a world in which men were not so fruitful, and were unable to subdue the world. Today we have the opportunity (and I repeat the opportunity, I do not say the achievement) to glorify God by the control of natural forces.

2. The extraordinary thing about the biblical narrative from beginning to end is the patience of God, and his refusal to destroy the freedom to choose which he gave man at his creation. There is perhaps no greater contrast between Christ and his Church, as it appears on earth, than that between his refusal to force men to choose by even the lightest form of psychological pressure and the constant bullying, nagging, preaching, and misuse of secular power that has characterized the working of his Church's leaders. (This is not something that can be laid only to the charge of Catholics, whether Roman or Anglican. The Kirk of Scotland has quite as bad a record, and does not always seem to have thrown over its heritage; and I note that Evangelical bishops in the Church of England plead for the maintenance of legal penalties for adult homosexuals. Sabbath legislation provides another example.)

It is the destiny of men to subdue the earth; it is the responsibility of men to use their freedom to glorify God. There is no guarantee against the misuse of the enormous powers we have today; the same free choice that can be used to glorify God can be used to build a hell on earth. Men are sinners, bound together in original sin, and we have had considerable experience in this century, and indeed in the last few years, as to what this hell on earth means. But let us be clear that the powers are God-given and the freedom to choose part of our creation. When we condemn the misuse of the gifts of God, let us not, like the Grand Inquisitor of *The Brothers Karamazov*, malign God for his graciousness.

If you accept my point that we are not in the grip of forces beyond our control, or subject to some inexorable laws of history or technology or economics, our problem is to persuade people of the sort of society we want to see. Before we can persuade, we need to be clear what sort of society it is that we want; we need some sort of vision as to how God can be glorified in the abundance of a fantastically rich society, which becomes continually richer as the years go by. It is this vision of what might be that we lack, perhaps because we fundamentally lack faith in the effectiveness of God's grace. We Christians so often look back to visions of societies that are dead and gone, or content ourselves with niggling grouses at the more obvious vices to which, as comfortable, nice people, we are never tempted. Perhaps it is because we have not the vision that the people perish.

I do not claim to have any great vision to communicate to you. I merely want to point to a number of places where Christian discrimination needs to be exercised.

1. The world of enriched choices that is opened to us is not merely for the Western world. Whether we like it or not, the whole world is awake to the new technical forces, and demands a share in the riches it sees the West to possess. Surely part at least of the mission of the West is to share in the development of the wealth of the whole world and the awakening of the masses of mankind out of centuries of slumber, so that God may be glorified in his works. This is at least part of what is involved in God's covenant with Noah and Abraham, 'the everlasting covenant between God and every living creature of all flesh that is upon the earth' (Genesis 9.16). Nor should we be frightened to act imaginatively, because the West has in the past so fearfully abused its trust, and still does so, in the false imperialisms and colonial settlements, where white people have dominated, and still dominate, over coloured people. More recently we have shrunk into a lazy unwillingness to pay the price that is required in terms of increased taxation for economic aid for developing countries, or a selfish refusal to face the problem as one of international scope, and not merely a matter of unilateral hand-outs. The test of our real concern for the development of the world is whether we are ready to pay the price in terms of lowering our standard of living below what it would otherwise be, and whether we are ready to work as partners in this world-wide problem, in a partnership where we may learn much, as well as perhaps having something to offer in addition to our money.

2. Though there is little, if any, gross poverty and unemployment to be angry about in most of the Western world, there are still the under-privileged in our welfare society. Our society is still class-ridden, and it is still not true that the ordinary worker has his proper share in the responsibilities and privileges of our civilization. A great question-mark still remains to be put against the two-stream system of education in England, which perpetuates the barriers between social classes, and delays our new and slowly growing sense of community. (In saying this, I do not believe that priority in the schools should be given to social adjustment over and above education. One of the fundamental requirements of our society still remains to educate well those who can benefit from it, and the public schools of England have set high standards for others to follow. Scottish education, admirable as it is in its

democratic flavour, seems to be half-way to the American system, where schools have given up the idea of teaching anyone anything, and confine themselves to adjusting students to the American way of life. We need both quality and the abolition of class barriers.)

But it is not only the over-all class divisions that we need to be sensitive about. We need to be sensitive to the small groups of people who cannot fit into our high standards of living, all those who fall by the wayside of modern industrialism: the mentally deficient, the mentally ill, the old, the erratic, the eccentrics, and all the queer people whom we tend to overlook in our generalizations. There is a danger that the welfare society may have less place for the odd and peculiar than other, less well-adjusted societies.

3. Economic progress means change. By and large human beings, though of all animals they are the most adaptable, resist change beyond a certain point. Security is a necessity for proper human development, as well as a danger that can lull to sleep. We need to be discriminating in distinguishing between those elements of security that are good for man and those that merely put burdens on other people. To illustrate, one should distinguish in the realm of full employment between the security that enables a man to settle in a given place, without having to uproot himself every time a particular industry declines, and the security that comes from a guarantee of a particular job in a particular firm or industry; the latter involves too high a price for a country like Britain to pay.

Christians need to be sensitive to the adventurous possibilities in our world, which depend on a readiness to accept new techniques, new materials, new kinds of work, new gadgets, new means to glorify God. Does an electronic computer glorify God less than a clerk laboriously totting up figures? Does a washing machine do him less honour than a woman painfully scrubbing her washing in a sink or stream? But if we need to be ready to adventure, we also need to be sensitive to the point beyond which people cannot bear change. There is a pace of change that can be too rapid for human beings to bear. We know that, in the case of individuals, people become neurotic when the changes are too rapid for adjustment; but, in the sphere of social relations, we do not know at all where that point is to be found. One may guess that in Britain, and in Western Europe generally, we are too frightened of the changes we could well bear, whereas in America they are perhaps too insensitive to the damage produced by perpetual social movements.

In the last resort, there is nothing Christian about change any more than there is anything Christian about stability. It is what use we make of them that matters. The test for Christians is the humanity of a given society, which depends on a proper balance between a multitude of different forces. Both a static and a dynamic society can glorify God, and both can be perverted.

4. Above all, what matters is the quality of life in our rich and expanding world. This is a matter both of the private pattern of our living and of the

public activities in our national life. The Church and the Christian have much to do in working out a proper pattern of private living for the twentieth century. (Why is it that so often Christian belief is associated with the stuffiness of nineteenth century social conventions?) In the field of national life, we have a right to expect more of our national leaders, particularly in political life, than the demagogic debasement of taste which they encourage. (I am thinking both of the way they think it necessary to play down to the public, and the demagogic way in which recent governments have preferred to reduce taxes rather than incur necessary expenditure on cultural objects.)

One could give many illustrations of our failure to achieve a quality of living commensurate with our opportunities, a failure for which we are all to blame in some measure, whether Christians or non-Christians, leaders of opinion and taste, or merely followers. Whether it be a matter of advertisement (which, in my view, could be much more drastically curtailed than is at present possible), or of the degradation of the press (which could be stopped tomorrow if there were a Press Council with teeth in it, instead of a body of white-washing newspaper men who prefer to turn their attack on politicians, and to play down the evils of the press with a rather sickening hypocrisy),[1] or of the failure to spend more on culture, whether in the arts, music, or broadcasting, or of the deeper failures to achieve an adequate community life in our cities or our places of work, or a pattern of personal living that is both true to the twentieth century and that gives glory to God—all these failures are the responsibility of all of us, and perhaps most of all of those who are leaders, or potential leaders, of our national life, which means *us*.

What I have said may at times have sounded unduly dogmatic and critical. You may think I have been excessively optimistic about the opportunities before us, and at the same time excessively critical about some aspects of our affairs, perhaps about the wrong things. It would be surprising if everybody agreed about these matters. The exercise of Christian discrimination, in front of the situation as we have it today, involves no easy answers. If I have sounded dogmatic, it is not because I know the answers, but to clarify some of the issues, and to provoke thought. I remain as uncertain as anyone. The pattern of a Christian society in the modern world is not something of which we can have any clear view; at best we may glimpse fragments of a vision.

Secondly, though I have laid stress on our responsibility, and what we can do, on our freedom and our failures, I do not want to suggest that for Christians our freedom is anything other than secondary to the grace of God. A Christian society will be accomplished fragmentarily, if at all, only when we act in obedience to the grace of God. We cannot glorify God except through his

[1] See *Reports of General Council of the Press*, I, pp. 27–28, and Appendix VI; II, pp. 6–8, 24–25; III, p. 31 and Appendix V; IV, p. 2 and Appendix V; also correspondence in *The Times* about the B.E.A. crash at Munich, and in particular the letter by Mr. Max Aitken.

grace. But perhaps our failure today is largely through our failure to see his grace at work in the opportunities offered to us.

We live in a rich world, growing richer from year to year. I have stressed many of the positive things we can do with our riches. But we cannot neglect the warnings of the New Testament about riches. Our whole Western world lives under the condemnation of Dives. In our comfort and relative freedom from pain, we often find it hard to realize the significance of the crucifixion. But we may perhaps take two points that seem to follow from it. (1) In all our appreciation of our tremendous opportunities, we need to practise some form of detachment, that we may not lose sight of the glory of God amid the glories of his created world. (2) In all our stress on the achievements of our world, we need to remember that as Christians we are inescapably bound to a perpetual life of protest and rebellion, that will continue until the Last Day. There will be no society so good that it will not need to be leavened by the Church.

But the crucified Christ rose again on Easter Day. The crucifixion was not an end in itself, as Western Christians have so often seemed to make it. It was the necessary means by which the resurrection might be accomplished. God came to earth that he might take men up to God; the resurrection is the pledge of that hope, and it is a pledge that bears on our social life as much as on our personal hopes. The twentieth-century world of electronic computers, automation, aeroplanes, and atomic energy, the world of cities, factories, blocks of flats, and motor-cars, all this world has been, potentially, taken up to God in the resurrection of the body of the man, Jesus Christ, who in himself alone comprehended all the hopes of Israel and all the covenants of God. The grace of God is not limited by the bounds of our imaginations. Perhaps we find it hard to visualize God and his works except in the dress of the Middle Ages or the ages of the Reformers. But he is no less calling us to new opportunities in the twentieth century, and his grace is as much at home among our modern riches as among the hovels of the Roman Empire. God grant that we may be more sensitive to it.

Appendix B

THE USE OF THE RESOURCES OF THE WORLD IN STEWARDSHIP FOR THE WHOLE OF MANKIND

(See Chapter 5)

A paper prepared for the Thessaloniki conference on Rapid Social Change (World Council of Churches, July/August 1959).

1. SOME THEOLOGICAL CONSIDERATIONS

There is a crude and sane realism about the Bible's view of man's relation to the world in which he lives. The world, though itself the creation of God, is to be used and enjoyed by man. Thus Genesis provides in the creation story the archetypal picture of what man is to do with the world: 'Be fruitful, and multiply, and replenish the earth, and subdue it; and have dominion over . . . every living thing that moveth upon the earth. . . . Behold, I have given you every herb yielding seed, which is upon the face of all the earth' (Gen. 1.28–9). The Bible presents us with a world in which man is to be active, not a world whose set pattern is to be contemplated, and whose 'nature' is untouchable. Which is not of course to deny that the world is a fit subject for meditation on the glories of God, as in Psalm 8: 'When I consider thy heavens, the work of thy fingers, the moon and the stars, which thou hast ordained'. But the same psalm goes on to stress man's dominion: 'Thou madest him to have dominion over the works of thy hands; thou hast put all things under his feet.'

In the New Testament there is little directly bearing on this theme, but there is no contradiction of the Old Testament. On the one hand, we are warned against the barrier that riches set up between man and the Kingdom of God, and reminded of the way they distract men from the central concerns of faith, but, on the other hand, the parable of the talents suggests that a too careful placidity is not what is required of man.

In Christian tradition we find a twofold attitude to property—and what is said about property as between one individual and another clearly applies as between individuals of different nations and continents. On the one hand, property is good and necessary for man, because only through appropriation of the means of life can man exercise a truly personal responsibility and be fully a man. On the other hand, no man has any absolute right to own what happens to be his. Property is held in trust for the good of all. Not only does this imply personal responsibility for what is under one's control; but it also implies that society has a responsibility to see that property arrangements are such as to satisfy the good of all. A too great stress has often been put on the personal responsibility of property owners, where it has been desired to preclude criticism of the arrangements that society makes. But social arrangements are themselves not given matters, but can be changed by human action, and both the arrangements and the changes are subject in principle to criticism according to Christian standards.

In practice, however, Christian principles cannot prescribe any particular property arrangements. These must depend on what is possible and achievable in any given society, on the brute facts of sinful human nature, the knowledge available at any given time and the traditions that limit human imagination. What is desirable at one time will not be desirable at another, as the technical and economic possibilities alter.

What has been said about property has perhaps sometimes tended to be limited to a confined list of problems. People think of the ownership of assets, such as land, houses, stocks and shares, and industrial capital. But it applies also to income of all sorts. There is no simple relationship between ownership of assets and income deriving from them (as is seen by the enormous variety of different patterns in different societies); there is no simple and clear distinction possible between capital and income (economists have spent a great deal of time discussing the metaphysical complexities of the problem, and tax collectors, in trying to draw a line somewhere, have given a great deal of work to lawyers and ended up with a tangle of absurdities); nor can we clearly distinguish different forms of capital and income (personal abilities, from which a man derives income, are a form of capital, and few men receive income in which there is no element of profit or monopoly return). We have no more absolute right to the income we chance to receive than we have to the property we happen to own. In both cases, we receive what we do through the effort of others, through luck, and through social arrangements that are always more or less inefficient and more or less unjust, as much as from our own efforts. (Nor is it obvious, morally speaking, that men should be paid for effort, a point which is indeed suggested by the parable of the labourers in the vineyard.)

We tend also to limit these considerations to policy within a nation, where indeed power today largely resides and decisions have to be made. But in principle there is no validity in such a limitation. There does not seem to be any theological or moral principle that states that income and property must be distributed according to justice (and a proper expediency) within a nation, but that a nation has an absolute right to distribute among its members those resources over which it has control. Nations may indeed be in some sense part of God's providential pattern for man (though it could be disputed), but the absolute claim of the nation-state to control and disburse what it happens to possess is as illegitimate as the erstwhile claims of the property-owner.

It is a secondary fact that there is no machinery for ensuring a just distribution of resources between nations, just as there was a time when it was not possible (either because of technical limitations or lack of proper political institutions, or because it was then outside the reach of human imagination) to distribute the resources of individuals within a nation except according to the traditional rigid patterns of property ownership. In these circumstances, there is the more need to stress the responsibilities of those who have the means to use them for the good of all, in terms of proper stewardship. Thus we need to speak to the rich nations of the West, and to those countries which find themselves in the possession of rare and valuable resources, such as oil.

But it must be clearly stated that such stewardship is no substitute for proper arrangements by which a just distribution of resources is assured by political institutions. Christians in the West are kidding themselves if they think that economic aid to underdeveloped countries is a matter which their own countries have a right to decide according to how they conceive of their responsibilities as stewards or their leanings towards charity. Admirable as their decisions may be, they should not be theirs. The aim should clearly be such international arrangements that nations may be taxed according to what is just and expedient. Stewardship is no substitute for taxation. Just as property owners cling to the idea of stewardship in order the better to fight the justice of taxation of wealth, so there is a danger that nations may try to justify their possession of what they have by exercising what they conceive to be a right of stewardship on behalf of others, when justice insists that they have no such right.

So much for principle, which is more helpful negatively than positively. If we wish to consider what positive distribution of wealth and resources is desirable at a given point of history, we have to consider expediency as well as principle, and much more when we are considering what political arrangements are required to ensure it. We must turn to the nature of economic resources today.

II. ECONOMIC RESOURCES

A. We tend to think in this context of natural resources provided once and for all by nature in the form of land or minerals. But from the economic point of view this picture is highly misleading.

(1) Resources themselves have no value, but only become of use when they are in the right places and have been properly processed. (Coal is of no value in the earth, but becomes valuable in a fire or a power station; copper ore is useless until refined.) The value of resources thus depends on the capital and labour applied to them, either in extracting them, transporting them, or processing them.

(2) Some resources first become valuable when new methods of production are discovered, or new techniques emerge. Oil was largely useless until the internal combustion engine was discovered; copper ore was worthless until

Bronze Age man discovered how to smelt it, and only came into use on a large scale with electricity; the application of natural rubber is a matter of recent history, but is already in process of being superseded by new techniques of artificial production. If technical and economic progress makes old resources valuable, it equally makes others valueless, as circumstances change. As one resource becomes scarce, its use is economized, and substitutes are found. Unwise action to push up the price of a commodity may only hasten the use of a substitute and destroy the basis of a country's economy.

(3) We know little about the resources available in the world. Even in highly developed small countries such as Britain, new deposits of well-known raw materials, such as coal, are continually being discovered. This quite apart fom the existence of resources which are of no economic use today, but may become so with new technical means (e.g. uranium in the recent past).

Two conclusions might be drawn from these facts:

1. A concentration on conservation of resources, such as has sometimes seemed attractive to Christians, has little to commend it in a rapidly changing world. It is one thing to condemn a ruthless cutting down of timber (such as occurred in the exploitation of the American continent), when it is known that it takes many years to replace it (and this is one of the few natural resources which can be harvested in such a way as to maintain output constant over time), and when the uses of timber are manifold and likely to continue over time as far ahead as we can see. It is rather different to conserve coal stocks when we can see possibilities of substitutes over the horizon. We must discount the future in a world that progresses technically at a rapid rate. How much to do so is a most difficult problem.

The economic problem is one of finding the right rate of interest that will do justice to today's and tomorrow's citizens, and that not merely from the point of view of the individual, but also of society as a whole, and of the world as well as a particular nation. At least we can say that it is no valid criticism of the Western world that it is using up the natural resources of the world as known today at a very rapid rate, though it might be a valid criticism that it is discounting the future at too high a rate of interest. (To put it simply, the future will be better served if we exhaust the coal reserves of the world and in doing so discover a better method of heating, such as atomic energy, than if we carefully husbanded our coal reserves for the benefit of future generations, and still left them to be heated by an inferior method. The problem is not entirely unlike that outlined in the parable of the talents!)

2. No very clear line can be drawn between 'natural' and man-made resources; which leads on to the next point.

B. The second major form of resource in the world is the capital inheritance of the world, in which are embodied the technical inventions of past ages. Techniques and capital equipment are more important than 'natural resources'. By and large those we have that are most valuable today have come down to us as a result of the historical development of the Western Christian world as a whole, into which pattern we have to fit the growth of nationalism, the development of scientific enquiry and technical invention, the growth of individualism and profit-making, the expansion of the activities of the business-man, the industrial revolution, and all that makes up the modern world of economic progress. Though now spreading over the whole world, these complex interrelated processes are a product of a limited part of the world in a limited period. It is, historically, not surprising that the fruits have largely accrued to the people living in the countries which developed in this kind of way. Before discussing this, I turn to the third main form of resource.

C. If natural resources are useless without capital and technical knowledge, capital and technical progress do not come about except as a result of human labour. By human labour is meant not merely that of the ordinary worker whose toil is necessary to produce the finished product, but also all the complicated labours of those who have invented machines, and controlled their development.

All have received some of the benefits of the development of resources in the modern world, and the application of capital to production. How far is it just that the workers in the West should have received the main benefit of their efforts? How far is the distribution of world income in any sense fair? If we could answer this question, we could quite simply know the main lines of a proper distribution of the world's resources. But the question cannot be answered. There is no absolute standard of fairness, except perhaps complete equality, and this is impossible in practice, even though, as Evanston suggested, it is a standard always to be borne in mind. All we can do is to outline a number of the relevant practical considerations that have to be remembered.

III. PRACTICAL CONSIDERATIONS IN DISTRIBUTION

A. There may be a clash between the best form of distribution of wealth and the maximum production that is possible. Neither is an absolute goal, and compromise is often necessary. Thus it may be that it is to the interest of the world that oil should be extracted at the maximum rate from certain countries, but that this can only in practice be done if the incomes accruing from the operation are unfairly distributed whether between countries, or between different groups within a country (the oil companies and the oil consumer, or the owner of a tract of oil-bearing land and the inhabitants of the country in general).

B. To be more particular, incentives are necessary in some form or other, though we do not know a great deal about which are essential and which merely conventional. A price may have to be paid by the rest of the world for the continuance of Western progress.

C. In general, it is not to the interest of the world that Western progress should be restricted and hampered, even if it creates more glaring divisions between rich and poor countries. To put it at its lowest, there will be more crumbs falling from Dives' table the richer he is. (It is assumed that the rich countries do not merely become richer by impoverishing the poorer. By and large, there is no evidence that this has often, if ever, happened. That an undue share of the gains may come to rich countries from exploitation of resources in poor countries may indeed be true. But the whole argument here is that there is no way to decide by principle what is 'undue gain'; it is a matter of what is fair taking into account what is expedient and possible in the circumstances).

D. What is required in the long run is not aid from richer areas to poorer countries, but such a development of the poorer countries that they cease to need such aid. Aid is therefore better when it takes the form of building up capital resources, whether in the form of educated, healthy, technically competent people, or in the form of roads, dams, and factories, than when it merely provides food to save people from starvation.

E. Just as even within the richer countries themselves, poor regions exist, which do not disappear naturally without special efforts, and without continuous economic aid and stimulus, so, in the world as a whole, as long ahead as we can see, the same kind of aid may be needed.

IV. FINAL PRINCIPLES

A. It is impossible clearly to distinguish natural from man-made resources. The resources of the globe that we have to use for the benefit of all mankind include the products both of labour and of nature. Thus, if natural resources are undeveloped in many parts of the world, so are men. And further, even if all the riches men enjoy in the West were entirely due to their own efforts, they would have little more right to them than if they were entirely the result of a lucky find of precious stones.

B. The development of all these resources is a task for all men. In so far as the development of resources in so-called underdeveloped countries, so that they can make a start on the process of economic growth, is a major issue today, resources from the richer countries must be devoted to this end.

C. The West has a major responsibility in this field. Its specific temptation is likely to be the assumption that the full development of its own resources (which are the most important in the world context) can only come about, if it takes for itself the major share of the fruits—a thesis which is quite unproven.

D. On the other hand, underdeveloped countries may be tempted to hamper the development of their own resources for the benefit of all, because they claim a share of the benefits which is so large as in practice to prevent the use of the resources, or because they set political goals above economic possibilities. (E.g. Is a country which is itself unable to develop its resources justified in refusing to allow foreign management to help under suitable conditions? *N.B.*—This is not the same as the further question about suitable conditions for foreign private enterprise, as countries can hire foreign management to run industry for them.)

E. If the final goal is the development of all resources everywhere, the aim must be to ensure that this is done as far as possible under conditions similar to those within a country. What is needed is a form of international taxation. Meantime, countries should do nothing to undermine what international organizations are already doing in the field.

F. The responsibility of Western countries, in the present situation, is clearly to be ready to give multilaterally, continuously and without too much looking backwards, in the hope that in time it may be possible to consider the question in a true world spirit. Meantime, so much needs to be done, that there is no question of our moving too fast and setting too high goals.

Appendix C

THE TWO-FACING ROLE OF THE BUSINESS-MAN

(See Chapter 6)

Reprinted from *The Journal of Religion* (Chicago, January 1959). A contribution to a symposium on the stresses of business-men.

It is not Christian to be unrealistic but Christians are always tempted to unrealism. When moral demands seem almost beyond the reach of human endeavour, and the vision of what the grace of God can accomplish is so different from the bleak realities and possibilities of our human situation, Christians are tempted either to retreat into a combination of *Realpolitik* and pietism or to escape into the illusion that, by some ideal reorganization of our affairs, the dilemma will be resolved. The latter is represented by those who assert that, by the abolition of the 'profit motive' in industry, the problems of a complex industrial system will be solved; the former class includes those pious business-men who believe that there is nothing wrong with the business system as it actually functions, except for the lack of piety of the individual. The pious easily come to comfort themselves with the belief that God prospers in business those he favours and that his overruling Providence has created the system for the blessing of all mankind. This comforting thesis is not only blatantly untrue (many of the most successful business-men do not obviously seem to be the kind of persons we would recognize as entitled to a first place among the saints, and it is not obviously clear that the American business system, or any other for that matter, is incapable of improvement); this thesis is also plainly un-Christian, in that it implies that any actual system of social relations as it has developed is in accordance with the will of God. (If not the Nazi system or the Communist system, why the American business system?).

We need a Christian critique of any social system or method of economic organization. But equally clearly there is no 'perfect Christian system', in which all will be love and friendship, with no conflicts and clashes. Complex social systems are not families and cannot be made into 'happy families' by any sleight of the hand or over-all reorganization. A good deal of the unrealism, which I am concerned to attack, is due to the application of the family model to the industrial system. In a complex social system there inevitably exist partial organizations whose proper functions are precisely to balance, correct, and check the activities of other organizations. Tensions and clashes are part of a functioning social system. The same is, of course, true in its way of a 'happy family', which is not one in which nobody ever speaks a 'cross word' but one where the legitimate tensions between the different members are recognized and overruled by common affection. But common affection, which each member of a family can feel in his or her different way, cannot be felt in society as a whole. No one has the range of knowledge or imagination to play all roles at once; nor can a particular person in a particular role be always looking over his shoulder to take account of the interests of everybody else. It is not the business of the chancellor of the University of Chicago to be considering the interests of Harvard, Yale, or the University of California. If, in fact, by aggressive competition with the prestige of Harvard, Yale, and other universities, he damages the interests of university education generally (which is not necessarily the case, of course; it may benefit all universities), then the appropriate remedy is not to appoint representatives of all universities to the offices of each but to provide by some set of general rules for this disaster to be averted. (It could be, for example, by some limit to the numbers at particular universities or to the salaries that could be offered, as is roughly the case in Great Britain.)

The general principles that need to be kept in mind are threefold: (1) Tensions and conflicts between different interests are an inevitable part of complex social arrangements. They not merely are inevitable but also are often, though of course not always, desirable. (2) A well-ordered society is not one in which there is harmony everywhere but one in which the tensions and conflicts are organized so that they serve the common good as best they can. This means that artificial conflicts should not be encouraged by an inappropriate framework, as, for example, appears to be the case to the layman in the organization of the armed forces of most states into navies, armies, and air forces. On the other hand, it means that real conflicts and tensions should be appropriately channelled to serve society as a whole. It would be going too far to say that all real conflicts and tensions should be 'organized', as it often appears to be the case that conflicts and tensions are best solved by subtle processes of evasion, though others are best brought to the surface. (Part of the difference between American and British ideas of democracy is perhaps that the Americans prefer their tensions to be manifest in the market place, whereas the British think they have found by trial and error that some tensions are best politely ignored and assumed not to exist; both systems have their obvious defects.) (3) The aim of a Christian critique should be to assess how far the social structure as a whole meets the needs of men as human beings. Christians therefore ask whether a particular set of organizations encourages artificial conflicts, whether it properly deals with the fundamental conflicts, and whether it takes account of the realities of human nature as the Christian faith knows them. The Christian critique is therefore more concerned with the general balance of any society than with any particular arrangements which, unsuitable in this particular society, might be entirely suitable in another. But it can neither criticize the general balance nor provide any hints for particular organizations unless it is entirely realistic as to the functions of organizations and the actual historical situation.

I come at last to the business-man. My main proposition can be stated quite simply. It is that the business-man has a two-facing role between producer and consumer and that there is an inevitable conflict between the interests of producers and consumers which is focused in him. It is therefore not the case that, if only the profit motive were abolished, the 'artificial' conflict between management and labour would disappear. 'Harmony in industry' is not necessarily the best social arrangement; it may indeed rather represent the pathological situation of the family where 'never a cross word has been spoken', which often means a situation where one partner has so successfully dominated the personality of the other that the marriage has ceased to be a place for mutual love and sharing. On the other hand, it is not the case that the actual conflicts between management and labour, and the actual business arrangements in any country (including the United States), are necessarily the best for dealing with the fundamental conflict between consumers and producers. The truth is rather that we have not discovered any perfect 'system' for dealing with the situation but that there is a rich range of possibilities open to us in the experience of different forms of business in different countries.

What I want to do is to illustrate in more detail the nature of this conflict of producers with consumers and thus to illuminate the role of the business-man, who, incidentally, is neither necessarily an individual person nor necessarily working in a system anything like 'the American business system'. There is a function to be performed in any complex modern economic society of linking production with consumption, and it is this that I mean by the role of the business-man. In its esential nature it is a two-facing role.

On the one hand, the business-man organizes production. He has to combine the heterogeneous factors of production, raw materials, machinery, buildings, power, labour, managerial staff, money capital, etc., so as to make the best use of them and to produce his product most efficiently. It is in this, more or less managerial, role that the business-man comes into conflict, at least potentially, with the interests of the workers and of all his employees. On the other hand, the product has to be sold; however much producers may like to make things of a certain kind, or to make things in this way rather than that, their desires are irrelevant if consumers do not want these goods. In the last resort, production, unlike certain sorts of artistic creation, is not something that occurs for its own sake; and even artists have to eat. Goods and services are produced for someone to buy and enjoy. The consumer has to be satisfied. And so the second face of the business-man is turned to the consumer; he appears here as salesman. As salesman, he may find himself in conflict with his desires as manager. The ultimate conflict comes when a business-man has to close down his plant because it does not pay. This is not something he likes to do, and, even if it hurts the workers far more than it hurts him, it still hurts him to some extent. But, if the goods cannot be sold, it is no good producing them.

In a capitalistic free-enterprise system of any kind the link between producer and consumer is made by means of profits. *If* incomes are fairly distributed, and *if* consumers act rationally in buying what they want, then everybody will be best satisfied if prices reflect costs. If prices do not reflect costs, then production could be reorganized to satisfy everybody better. The importance of costs is that they reflect the alternative uses to which resources could be put; the importance of prices in a free market is that they measure people's choices. If prices reflect costs, then resources flow to those forms of production that people want to buy; if not, a delicate form of democratic elective process is disturbed. There are thus three conditions to be fulfilled: (*a*) a 'fair' distribution of income (to give people an 'appropriate' voting power to start with; and there is no mechanism that insures this in a modern economic system, unless one believes that what tends to happen is automatically 'fair'); (*b*) rationality of consumers in the market (which is not only unrealistic to assume in a post-Freudian world but doubly unrealistic in a world where business-men deliberately try to make us act more irrationally than we naturally would); and (*c*) prices reflecting costs. I deliberately ignore the problems arising out of the first two assumptions, not because they are unimportant, but because they lie outside the field here under discussion. Special action could be taken to deal with them, at least partially.

Clearly, prices do not reflect costs in the real world, and they are even farther removed from the special sort of reflection of costs that economists require in their models. But, broadly speaking, it can be said that a competitive business system produces a rough-and-ready correspondence between prices and costs. It is here that profits come in. Production that does not cover costs will cease. The danger is that prices will be too much above costs; in other words, that profits will be much too high. And here competition comes in to level profits to some not too unreasonable norm. Hence the importance of anti-monopoly action to prevent positions of strength being built up, where profits can be excessively high and competition precluded in advance. In the actual world of oligopolies, large firms, and monopolistic actions of all kinds, the way in which the economic system reflects costs and responds to consumers' wishes is very imperfect. I am not concerned here to defend the present position, as it happens to be in America, Britain, or any other country. Whether the system reflects consumers' wishes as perfectly as they could be reflected in any society, or distorts them so badly that almost any possible alternative would be better than the actual situation in America, Britain, Germany, etc., does not matter to my main point. This is, that there is a function that, more or less clearly, or more or less dimly, is performed in the system by profits. Somehow or other this function must be performed in any complex modern industrial society.

To talk in terms of prices reflecting costs as we have done is much too simple in a world where probably the major decisions are not so much whether too many cigarettes are produced and too little tomato juice as whether capital resources are to be devoted (on a large scale, as they must be) to expansion of steel, aircraft, shipping, or atomic energy and, linked with this, whether new products of one kind or another are to be floated on the market. In the medium term and in the long run equally, decisions about capital investment and new products are more decisive in the economy than day-to-day decisions about detailed quantities of products of particular kinds. Prices could reflect costs very exactly and the major decisions be all wrong, and, vice versa, the major decisions could be more or less right without prices very accurately reflecting costs. But here again, whether well or badly, profits provide a signal to the economic system as to the direction in which it is to move. There has to be some signal, or some 'plan', as we make arrangements for tomorrow; and the future being what it is—unforeseeable—all signals and all plans will be more or less unsuccessful. But again there is a function that has to be performed, and again it is a link between consumers (of tomorrow) and producers (of today). (Again, as an aside, where the business-man, as provider of new products, selling to us a new pattern of life, in fact moulds us to his own reflection, he is a most dangerous character, as dangerous as any other purveyor of ideologies, such as priests, psychiatrists, politicians, publicists, and poets, and perhaps the more dangerous as not being an open professor of the arts of persuasion.)

The business-man thus faces two ways—toward consumers and toward producers. He has to make decisions, and he commits himself to his decisions in the sense that, once large schemes have been set in train, the possibilities of retreat are limited. The commitment is tested through the sieve of profitability. And what this test measures is the pressure of costs, on the one hand (the producers' incomes), and of prices, on the other (the consumers' preferences). The ultimate conflict is between the producer, who wants to produce as little as possible for the highest price, and the consumer, who wants the maximum quantity of goods at the lowest price. (Of course, any complete analysis would show that people are neither so selfish nor so pleasure-loving as this simple statement implies. But all that is required for our purposes is that it roughly corresponds to some important traits in human behaviour.) If this conflict is a real one, it is reflected in the strain that the business-man feels when he has to try to keep prices up as against consumer pressure for reducing them (as reflected in the market) and to keep costs down as against producers trying to extract higher incomes from him (as most clearly exemplified in trade-union pressure). There is an inherent strain here in the business position, whether one man or a collectivity have to bear it. Nor has this strain anything to do with any adverse climate in which the business-man may have to live due to popular denunciations of profits or to any unreal image of his role that may be foisted upon him by his or other people's ideologies about the business system.

If we are right in arguing that there is a natural conflict here which manifests itself in a particular form in a business system, such as the American, and is, in that system, reflected in the two-facing role that some persons and some organizations have to perform, which is most clearly reflected in the dubious nature of profits, then we should also be right in deducing that there can be no perfect method of meeting the conflict. Sometimes producers will do too well at the expense of consumers; sometimes consumers will 'exploit' producers. Sometimes, at the expense of wages and prices, profits will be too high. Sometimes profits will be too low to enable consumers to benefit from adequate research and long-term investment. Sometimes prices will be too low (or profits too high) to enable producers to avoid exploitation and inhuman conditions of work. Sometimes profits and wages will be too high to enable consumers to benefit to the full from the productivity that is inherent in the system. This will apply not only to the system as a whole but to all the varied sectors in the economy. The push and pull will go on as long as we have a complex economy, where producers and consumers (though the same individuals) do not perform the roles of production and consumption concurrently. It is clear that many different judgments could be made as to the success of different systems or different parts of one system. It is not my purpose here to pass such judgment, much less to assume that all systems are equally bad (or equally good).

It may help to make these points clearer if we look at the way the fundamental two-facing role is met in systems of economic organization which are remote from the American business system, which we have largely had in mind hitherto. I refer to systems of socialization or nationalization and take most of my examples from the British nationalized industries, with which I am most familiar. But the problem exists in Russia also. The immediate post-revolutionary situation, when trade unions organized factories, broke down because of its failure to meet the needs of consumers and was replaced by a system of autocratic management. There has to be an autocratic manager in Russia, because there is a plan to fulfil, and the plan represents the interests of the 'consumers'. (It is irrelevant to the principle that the plan may only partially provide for what the planners conceive to be the needs of the consumers and be more concerned with the needs of the state; the state is then the 'consumer' and, as consumer, is concerned to see that workers do not, by too high wages or slack work, fail to produce the goods that are planned.) But even autocratic managers in Russia cannot entirely ignore the interests of their workers. No doubt, in Yugoslavia the problem is to reconcile the needs of the economy as a whole (the consumer) with a measure of independent plant control; the logic of this requires greater dependence on a market to reflect consumer preferences.

The British nationalized industries face the conflict within a framework much more like the American business system. Because they are statutorily bound to cover their costs, taking one year with another (i.e. over a reasonable period), and because they have by and large chosen not to make profits (which, legally, they could), they are not thereby freed from the pressures of a 'profit system', as some had blithely hoped. Though largely monopolies, they are still subject to consumer pressure to keep prices down, and there is additional political pressure in so far as some of these prices are important constituents of the cost of living. The result has been a continuous pushing from Ministers to restrain well-justified price increases, and by 'gentleman's agreement' the nationalized industries have agreed on several occasions to keep prices down when no commercial firm would have done the same. This has inevitably meant pressure on their boards to keep wages from rising, however much they might have liked to come to an agreement with the trade unions, as has often been the case. Political pressure has been exercised on this side too, as governments have several times taken evading action to avoid railway strikes. It is not clear, in the event, on which side the pressure has been the stronger; but it is very clear that the problem of producers versus consumers has not been solved by the mere act of nationalization.

It has thus been shown that the trade unions in Britain were, from their own point of view, most wise to reject any suggestions at the end of the war that they should be officially represented on the boards of these industries. They realized clearly enough that they would need to defend their own members' interests even against a management which put the 'public interest' first. The few outright syndicalists in the trade-union movement have been disillusioned by the results. In the one case in Britain in which trade-union representatives share managerial responsibility, the National Dock Labour Board (which is responsible for providing continuous employment for all dockworkers whether there is work to be done or not, and for allocating workers to the particular firms on the wharf), the result has not been happy. There has been continuous friction between management and men and between workers and trade-union officials, which has been, at least partly, due to this shared responsibility. The problem cannot be supposed to be an unreal one.

However the role of the business-man is met, and under whatever framework businesses are organized, there is this continuous pressure from both consumer and worker that the business-man has to meet. That is the price of the responsibility he undertakes, and the strain is inherent in the creative possibilities that open before him. No doubt, there are systems in which these inevitable strains are magnified by unnecessarily inefficient arrangements. As has been implied, much depends on the whole market framework within which business operates; this is rarely perfect. Much more could be done about proper consultation with trade unions. Businesses could give more accurate information about their affairs and cut down the sales talk. They could take steps, or be forced to take steps, to pay more attention to real consumer preferences and not spend so much effort on 'adjusting' consumers to their own preferences. There is no space to discuss all this. The essential point is that, however perfect the organization and environment of business, the inherent strain will remain. It is not something unnatural, and it cannot be avoided. Whether it is greater or less than the equivalent strains of other responsible jobs (such as a civil servant responsible both to 'his department' and to the political Minister, or a university professor torn between his students and their needs and the 'research' that is necessary to keep him ahead in the academic rat-race), I do not know. But it is certainly not inevitably different in kind.

Sources of Quotations

Chapter 1. Geoffrey Faber, *Jowett* (1957), p. 359.
S. T. Coleridge, *The Friend* (1844 ed.), Vol. ii, pp. 175, 209.
Julian of Norwich, *Revelations of Divine Love* (ed. by Dom R. Hudleston, 1935), pp. 32, 81.

Chapter 2. T. L. Peacock, *The Novels* (ed. David Garnett, 1948), pp. 48, 51.
S. T. Coleridge, op. cit., Vol. i, p. 124.
Lesslie Newbigin, 'The Perils of Co-operation' (*Frontier*, Winter 1959), p. 267.

Chapter 3. Edmund Burke, *Thoughts and Details on Scarcity* (1795) (*Works*, 1823 ed., Vol. 7, p. 330.)
Geoffrey Faber, op. cit., p. 336.
William of St. Thierry, *The Meditations* (translated from the Latin by a Religious of C.S.M.V., 1954), p. 37.

Chapter 4. Dean Hicks. Quoted in *The National Church and the Social Order* (Church Information Board, 1956), p. 53.
J. K. Galbraith, *American Capitalism* (1952), p. 87.

Chapter 5. Bishop Latimer, *Sermons* (Parker Society, 1844), pp. 125-6.
J. Carcopino, *Daily Life in Ancient Rome* (Penguin, 1956), p. 10.

Chapter 6. G. F. Fisher, Archbishop of Canterbury, quoted in *The Times*, 16 October, 1957.
Lesslie Newbigin, ibid.

Chapter 7. George Eliot, *Middlemarch* (Everyman ed.), Vol. i, p. 95.
T. L. Peacock, *Poems* (ed. Brimley Johnson, 1906), pp. 292-3.

Chapter 8. G. F. Fisher, Archbishop of Canterbury, the *Observer*, 15 March, 1959.
A. M. Ramsey, Archbishop of York, *Listener*, 25 February, 1954 (from address to British Association in 1953.).

INDEX OF NAMES

PRINTED IN GREAT BRITAIN BY THE WHITEFRIARS PRESS LTD.
LONDON AND TONBRIDGE